American Generosity

American Generosity

Who Gives and Why

PATRICIA SNELL HERZOG

and

HEATHER E. PRICE

OXFORD
UNIVERSITY PRESS

OXFORD
UNIVERSITY PRESS

Oxford University Press is a department of the University of
Oxford. It furthers the University's objective of excellence in research,
scholarship, and education by publishing worldwide.

Oxford is a registered trademark of Oxford University Press
in the UK and certain other countries.

Published in the United States of America by
Oxford University Press
198 Madison Avenue, New York, NY 10016

© Oxford University Press 2016

Library of Congress Cataloging-in-Publication Data
Names: Herzog, Patricia Snell, author.
Title: American generosity: who gives and why / Patricia Snell Herzog and
Heather E. Price.
Description: New York: Oxford University Press, 2016. | Includes
bibliographical references and index.
Identifiers: LCCN 2015020895 | ISBN 978-0-19-045649-8 (cloth : alk. paper)
Subjects: LCSH: Social ethics—United States. | Humanitarianism—United
States. | Charities—United States. | Voluntarism—United States. | Social
action—United States.
Classification: LCC HN90.M6 H478 2016 | DDC 302/.14—dc23
LC record available at http://lccn.loc.gov/2015020895

1 3 5 7 9 8 6 4 2
Printed by Sheridan

To our mothers-in-law, both of whom passed away during
our writing of this book and in whose loving memory
we searched for deeper understanding of a spirit of generosity.—
PSH & HP

To my children, who I hope will learn to be givers in their own
ways.—PSH

Contents

Foreword

AMERICAN GENEROSITY: WHO *Gives and Why* is the flagship volume of the Science of Generosity Initiative, a major social science research endeavor seeking to better understand the sources, manifestations, and consequences of human generosity. Its authors, Patricia Snell Herzog and Heather E. Price, give us perhaps the most comprehensive and in-depth book about American generosity written to date. This volume presents a multidimensional picture of generosity that is firmly grounded in solid quantitative and qualitative empirical evidence, vast in its breadth, theoretically insightful, and highly accessible in its presentation. It takes an interdisciplinary approach to define and analyze multiple forms of generosity involving different kinds of giving, focusing especially on donating money, volunteering time, and taking political action, but also exploring giving blood, bodily organs, material possessions, and relational attention, and environmental sustainability.

Herzog and Price's analysis takes some refreshingly different approaches to probing its evidence, stretching our imaginations about how empirical data can be investigated to reveal new insights. Its qualitative case studies also help to flesh out the ways that more abstract causal processes and mechanisms work to foster and restrain generosity. Not only does this book rigorously analyze American generosity and contribute significantly to our social scientific understanding of generosity's dynamics; it also offers practical suggestions for different kinds of readers interested in increasing their giving or encouraging generosity in others and suggests fundraising ideas for nonprofit, foundation, and religious leaders. Readers interested in better understanding the what, how much, who, where, and why questions of generous practices and their analytical and practical implications need look no further than this book. I recommend it enthusiastically.

Christian Smith
University of Notre Dame

Acknowledgments

BEFORE WE BEGIN our analysis of American generosity, we first owe a debt of gratitude to the very many people who have been incredibly generous to us over the years, without whom this book would not be possible. First, we are enormously grateful to our husbands for putting up with our obsessions with studying generosity, late nights of work, and numerous outpourings of ideas in progress along the writing path. Also thanks to our parents for being true teachers of generosity and for modeling unconditional compassion for others.

Thank you to the thousands of survey and interview participants who generously opening their lives to deepen our understanding of their perspectives. This project would not have been possible were it not for their gracious gift of time.

Heartfelt thanks to the many teachers and mentors who have been generous with their time, talents, and patience along the way. Most notably Christian Smith, for being a guide, critic, friend, and role model of a generous spirit. Also thanks to Omar Lizardo, Jessica Collett, Kraig Beyerlein, Richard Williams, Rory McVeigh, Dan Myers, Atalia Omer, Jason Springs, Michael Emerson, Elaine Howard Ecklund, Steven Kleinberg, Michael Lindsay, and Jean East for their numerous forms of input, challenges, support, and learning.

This project is also the result of many collective endeavors by students and staff, including Rae Hoffman, Katie Spencer, Nick Bloom, Peter Mundey, Brandon Vaidynathan, Hilary Davidson, Meredith Whitnah, Justin Farrell, Brad Vermurlen, Dan Escher, and Christina Williams.

We are deeply indebted to a number of conversation partners along the path to this book who contributed indirectly to its insights, especially Jared Peifer, Casey Harris, Shauna Morimoto, Anna Zajicek, Kevin Fitzpatrick, Song Yang, and other colleagues.

The project was made possible with the generous support of the John Templeton Foundation—especially Kimon Sargent—and the institutional and collegial support of the University of Notre Dame, Rice University, the University of Arkansas, and Basis Policy Research. We are also grateful for the input of the Indiana University–Purdue University Indianapolis School of Philanthropy and Lake Institute of Faith and Giving.

Many scholars gave their time and feedback to the broader Science of Generosity initiative, including J. P. Shortall, Keith Meador, Stephen Vaisey, Mark Wilhelm, Carolyn Warner, Pamela Paxton, Nicholas Christakis, James Andreoni, Ariel Knafo, Omri Gilath, Abigail Payne, Paul Zak, Rohini Pande, Bradford Wilcox, Stephanie Brown, Sonya Lyubomrisky, Felix Warneken, Yaojun Li, David Campbell, Lisa Keister, Roy Baumeister, William Damon, Glen Elder, William Enright, William Galston, Jonathan Haidt, Paulette Maehara, Theodore Malloch, Michael McCullough, Cathy Pharoah, Stephen Post, Miroslav Volf, René Bekkers, Pamala Wiepking, Christopher Morrissey, and Ryan Lincoln.

We are grateful to the numerous readers, attendees, and fellow panelists at conference presentations to the American Sociological Association, the Society for the Scientific Study of Religion, Urban Affairs Association, and the University of Arkansas Department of Sociology & Criminal Justice and Community and Family Institute.

The wording and accessibility of the book were enormously enhanced by the insightful contributions of Adam Pope and the careful eyes of Anna Sutherland.

Oxford University Press editors and reviewers contributed in important ways to the clarity of analyses, and we are indebted to the book reviewers for their contributions to the entire manuscript and particularly for their insights on the generosity inequalities discussed in the conclusion.

We are also thankful to each other for the many emails, discussions, metaphors, and inspirations that produced this book.

For all these, and so many more generous efforts, we are grateful.

American Generosity

Introduction

Who Gives and Why?

AMERICAN GENEROSITY IN PERSPECTIVE

THIS IS A book about American generosity. In it we study what exactly generosity is. First, we offer a bit of background about ourselves as authors: We are both sociologists by training and share a love for interdisciplinary thinking. While we focus on how social context shapes behaviors, we also give credit to the ways personal orientations influence behaviors. We are among a growing body of scholars who find the most interesting insights to be at the intersections between fields, and thus we intentionally study generosity from an interdisciplinary perspective. Together we have professional training and experience in sociology, psychology, social work, education, youth and emerging adults, American ethnic studies, social psychology, social stratification, social networks, sociology of religion, and community-urban sociology. Sociology of course forms the core of this work. We supplement that core, however, with a range of methodological approaches in order to investigate generosity from multiple angles and to engage a wide view of American giving.

In the pages to follow we present a picture of generosity that is unique in its breadth, theoretical in its background, refined in its methods, and intentionally accessible in its presentation. We expect that readers join us from a variety of backgrounds and viewpoints, and therefore we seek to explain concepts and ideas in ways that speak to a range of starting points. We hope those who have never read anything before on the topic of generosity will leave with a clear picture of how generosity looks and acts in America. At the same time, we hope readers who are deeply engaged in the practice of or scholarship on generosity will leave with a broader and more nuanced understanding of the subject. We begin by defining generosity.

Defining Generosity

We will review a variety of generosity-related studies, but first we describe exactly what we mean when we refer to generosity:

- Generosity *is giving good things to others freely and abundantly.*
- Generous behaviors are *intended to enhance the well-being of others.*
- However, *the giver can benefit,* which distinguishes generosity from "pure" altruism.
- Generosity *can be actualized through various forms of giving.*

We do not think we could state that last point any better than one of our case study participants did during an interview. As the participant said, "Giving comes in different forms. It's not always in money."

Theoretical Underpinnings

We think that motivations can be manifold, and we see our definition of generosity as analytically "between" rational choice theories and theories of altruism. In our view these theories share in common an overly reductionist view of social behaviors. They seem to us to be polar opposites of the same idealistic reasoning, sharing in common assumptions about human nature that are rarely, if ever, met in actual life. Rational choice theories assume actors act first out of self-interest. A pure act of giving therefore presents a puzzle for rational choice theorists to resolve within their theoretical underpinnings. The resolution comes from reasoning that the benefit of giving for the giver, rather than the recipient, is the foremost motivator of the act to give, even if the benefit is indirect or unknown. Theories of altruism, at the other end, assume that giving must be fully other-interested, with no benefit to the giver. An altruistic giving act must be shown to be free of intention for self-benefit, including ulterior motives to gain social standing or without other giver kickbacks. Otherwise such results would undermine the non-beneficial requirement for generous acts to be considered purely altruistic.

We subscribe to neither of these theories. We understand that reality is more complex than these ideals allow. Who is to say where the line is between a purely other-oriented and truly self-beneficial intended act of generosity? We would argue that there is a fine line between a gift without benefit and one with obvious gain, and there is an even finer line between an intention to give for self-sacrificial reasons and an indirect, perhaps unintentional gain. Consider a person who volunteers in a soup kitchen because she is concerned about the growing number of homeless in her city but happens to serve on the food line next to someone who is the CEO of a major corporation in the area, and the following week that person hires her for a job others believed she was unqualified to receive. Is this an altruistic motive or a rational choice? If it is the former, it is necessary to show that the volunteer had no prior conception that a job, or any other sort of social benefit, could be gained through her volunteering effort. Impossible: anyone walking around half awake in America is aware that relationships can be created through such experiences. If it is the latter, it is necessary to show that the volunteer had a prior evaluation of the potential benefit of getting a job or other social good from the exchange, was able to weigh that against the potential cost of expending free labor, and evaluate the difference. Also impossible, in our view. Unless one is clairvoyant, these kinds of intangibles are impossible to predict, let alone evaluate the costs and benefits of. To us it seems inapposite for researchers to attempt to deconstruct this series of events in order to prove something that can never be truly known; the attempt would simply bolster idealistic notions of human motivations and would not enhance our understanding of how to foster or support generous activities.

We are not suggesting that nothing can be done to assess the extent to which giving behaviors are other-oriented versus self-oriented (one of us even has an analysis on this exact concept in progress). Our point is rather that we see both theoretical perspectives as problematic in their assumptions of human motivations. While they may be analytically "clean," they can never be realized in the messiness of real life. We situate our definition of generosity as lived in reality between these two extremes because the constraints of rational choice and altruism theories artificially simplify our assumptions regarding human motivations. We hold the assumption that behaviors that are generally intended to benefit someone else (singularly or as the collective good) contribute toward social good. This means that a direct, an indirect, or an absent benefit to the giver does not change the existence of a giving act.

Granted there is most definitely a range of self-benefit between the person who gives a $500,000 check to have his name engraved on the building constructed in his honor and the person who drops off a $500,000 check every year at Christmas to the church pastor and swears the pastor to complete anonymity as to the source of the donation. But who are we to say that the giver of the building check did not see a social benefit and self-cost in acknowledging his generosity? Or that the anonymous (or mostly so) church donor did not receive some self-benefit in knowing the pastor held him in high regard, or in believing in a gift in the afterlife in return for the exchange? To us it seems inconsequential to attempt to dissect the true motive for such actions in this way. Instead we promote the science of generosity as the study of all behaviors intended to contribute to social goods.

Generosity-Related Studies

In this study we have opted to use *giving good things freely to enhance the well-being of others* as our operating definition of generosity. Using this definition, we began our initial investigations in 2006–2008. Those early investigations resulted in an extensive set of literature reviews from numerous disciplines via an exploratory project funded by the John Templeton Foundation. This project then led to an ongoing initiative called the Science of Generosity (SciGen), under way since 2009. These projects culminated in this book, in addition to other publications and presentations from the SciGen Initiative, and they set the background for the broader project that we summarize here.

The SciGen project intentionally does not narrow to a single topic of generosity; instead the SciGen scholars study a range of generosity-related topics that seek to broaden our understanding of the many ways that generosity can be understood. Among the topics investigated in the initiative are the following:

- Charitable giving
- Philanthropy
- Volunteering
- Civic engagement
- Religious giving
- Organizational citizenship
- Blood and organ donation
- Altruism
- Gift giving
- Prosocial behaviors (e.g., reciprocity, helping, hospitality, sharing)
- Philosophical orientations
- Virtue ethics

This work by SciGen scholars builds upon decades, in some cases centuries, of scholarship on these topics. Yet it also contributes to the remaining unknowns, especially through its comprehensive and interdisciplinary approach.

Despite the considerable body of scholarship that already exists, research from the SciGen Initiative shows that there is still much we do not know. René Bekkers and Pamala Wiepking, both experts in the field of philanthropic studies and the authors of an extensive literature review for the initiative, highlight the plethora and variety of existing studies on generosity.[1] They explain:

> An overwhelming body of knowledge is available on philanthropy in the social sciences. Research on philanthropy appears in journals of very different disciplines, including marketing, economics, social psychology, biological psychology, neurology and brain sciences, sociology, political science, anthropology, biology, and evolutionary psychology.[2]

However, after reviewing hundreds of generosity-related studies they conclude, "While the preceding review shows that there is a vast amount of knowledge on determinants of philanthropy, there are also considerable gaps in our knowledge."[3] There is still much for us to learn.

Bekkers and Wiepking are not alone in this assessment, as a quick look at other research shows. For example, two social psychologists, Jessica Collet and Christopher Morrissey, concluded their own extensive literature review of hundreds of generosity-related studies by stating, "We find that while there is a wealth of information out there about individuals helping others, the research and literature lacks the integration and conceptualization necessary for theoretical growth in the field."[4] Likewise, Ryan Lincoln, Christopher Morrissey, and Peter Mundey—after comprehensively reviewing the religious giving literature for the initiative—concluded, "The future of research into religious giving is open and ready for further development."[5] We can expand our knowledge even further.

Needed Investigations in Generosity

Vast literatures exist on generosity-related studies, but still missing is a thorough integration of these highly specialized findings into a broader conceptualization of generosity that retains and combines nuances into a more unified field. We need studies that explore generosity by drawing on the strengths of various disciplinary approaches to fill gaps in our knowledge. The authors of the literature reviews described above point to the following gaps in understanding generosity:

- Integration of knowledge across discipline-specific topics
- Theoretically rich conceptualizations of generosity
- Definitions of generosity as occurring in a variety of forms
- Investigations into who tends to participate in which forms of generosity
- Better understandings of why people are more or less generous

In this book we begin to address these gaps. While we do not answer every question that was raised in the generosity literature reviews, we offer a robust and interdisciplinary understanding of generosity in many forms.

Forms of Generosity

In this book we focus on nine specific forms of generosity, all of which were done freely to enhance the well-being of others. Of these nine forms, our research has found that three are most prominent:

- Giving money: donating to charitable causes
- Giving time: volunteering for charitable causes
- Giving action: taking political action for charitable causes

We call these the "Big 3," and they represent the primary focus of the charitable activities we discuss. In addition to the Big 3 we also provide some investigations of six other forms:

- Giving blood: donating blood to aid in the medical welfare of others
- Giving organs: donating bodily organs to aid in the medical welfare of others
- Giving property: willing estates to charitable causes
- Lending possessions: lending possessions to friends, family, and neighbors
- Giving sustainability: contributing efforts to care for environmental resources
- Giving attention: engaging with friends, family, and neighbors

While these additional six forms are less prominent than the Big 3, we consider them a part of the generosity picture.

Looking at all nine forms of generosity in one book is unique to the SciGen Initiative. With these various forms side by side, we can comprehensively account for the giving behaviors of Americans. We can identify who gives nothing, who gives some, who gives much, and who gives what to others.

Overview of the Science of Generosity Initiative

Before diving into our findings on the nine forms of generosity, we would like to take a moment to explain the methods and methodologies that produced the data we analyze. Almost all of our research draws on the products of the Science of Generosity Initiative, a multimethod, collaborative study of American generosity. As we describe below in more detail, the initiative includes a nationally representative survey, geocoded residence research, personal interviews, ethnographic observations, and photographs to create a complex and multimodal vision of generosity in America.

Nationally Representative Survey

As mentioned, the SciGen Initiative at its core is a nationally representative, cross-sectional Internet survey conducted with adult Americans (age 23 and over) in 2010.[6] The panel had a final sample size of 1,997 survey respondents with a 65.2 percent response rate.[7] Figure I.1 depicts the minute discrepancies between our panel and the broader US public. Suffice it to say that both random sampling[8] and statistical weighting[9] (which accounts for national disparities in gender, age, race/ethnicity, education, Internet access, region, metropolitan area, volunteering levels, and nonresponse status) were used in order to allow confident reporting on the surveys as nationally representing American generosity (see Appendix Table A.I.1 for full descriptive statistics).

Geocoded Residences

Because one aspect of this book is to assess generosity in relation to place of residence, we geocoded respondent addresses, mapped coordinates, and linked to tract-level data from the U.S. Decennial Census.[10] Map I.1 shows the location of our survey respondents, which further evidences

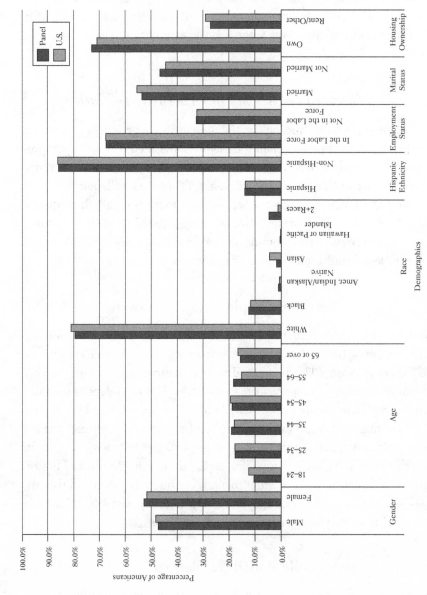

FIGURE 1.1 Survey respondents compared to US population demographics.

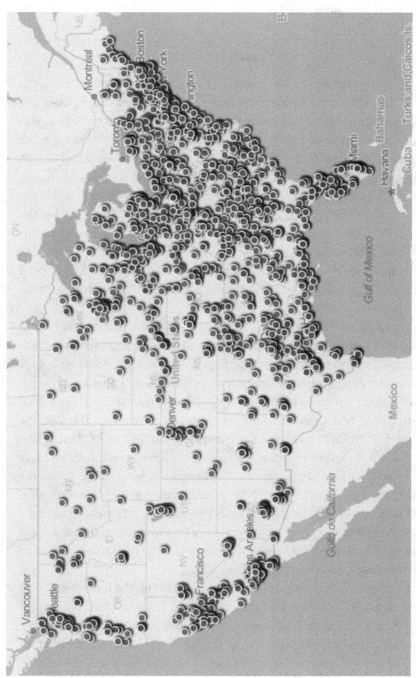

MAP 1.1 Geocoded residences for Science of Generosity survey respondents. While some Science of Generosity respondents are located in Alaska and Hawaii, due to their small respective sample sizes, these states are not depicted in the maps.
Science of Generosity 2010, Esri map in GeoCommons. Used by permission. Copyright © 2015 Esri, DeLorme, NAVTEQ. All rights reserved.

representativeness by shown location densities that generally reflect American population density.

In-Person Interviews

To enhance our survey work, we also conducted qualitative research. From the nearly 2,000 survey respondents, we selected a stratified-quota sample of 40 respondents for in-person interviews. If the survey respondent was married or had a live-in romantic partner, we also included the spouse/partner in the interviews and observations. For 22 of the 40 respondents, spouses/partners were interviewed and observed in person, for a total of 62 interviewees. We called this portion of the study the "40-Families Study,"[11] since the unit was the family and household of the respondent who participated in the survey. Figures I.2 and I.3 highlight some of the key demographic characteristics for the 40 families, evidencing the diverse representation among our participants of core social statuses. Appendix Table A.I.2 includes more extensive demographic details.

These interviews included three data collection efforts: traditional interviews, ethnographic observations, and extensive photographic evidence. Interviewers from the project spent four to eight hours with each household, during which we interviewed, observed, and photographed the people, their households, and their neighborhoods. Interviewers visited participating households on a number of occasions in order to reduce the length of each visit and to avoid observing a household on its "best behavior," as can sometimes happen with a single interview visit. In most cases the interview of each respondent took place in two parts, so we visited the household twice for the primary respondent interview and, if applicable, two more times for the spouse or live-in partner interview. Traditional question-and-answer interviews accounted for about half of the time spent with the families. All interviews were recorded and transcribed, resulting in more than 1,000 pages of interview data.

Ethnographic observations were also collected on the household. Field notes detailed the households and the neighborhood in which the respondent lived. In addition interviewers spent some unstructured, unrecorded time with families, joining them for dinner or observing other aspects of their daily routine and lifestyles via unstructured and nonverbal methods. Combined this averaged to six hours spent per family, and the field notes total more than 500 single-spaced pages of observations on the families,

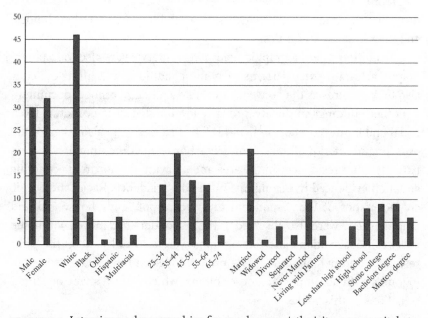

FIGURE I.2 Interviewee demographics for gender, race/ethnicity, age, marital status, education level.

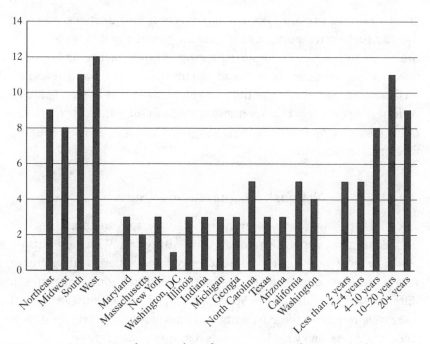

FIGURE I.3 Interviewee demographics for region, state, homeownership status, housing type, tenure.

including the interview participants, their children (if any), their homes, and their local communities.[12]

In addition to ethnographic field notes, interviewers also took photographs to capture visual forms of home conditions and lifestyles. They also took pictures as they traveled around each neighborhood, documenting other buildings in the area, relative level of disrepair, economic level, racial and ethnic composition, and safety. Pictures were also taken of the exterior and interior of the respondent's house, documenting how it compared to other residences in the area and showing the apparent economic situation evidenced in belongings inside the residence. Racial and ethnic characteristics of the respondent and the respondent's household and neighborhood were also observed. If the respondent had moved within the past year, observations and photographs were also collected on the prior residence and neighborhood. The project collected more than 1,000 photographs with accompanying descriptions, which helped shape our interpretations in this book.

Presenting Multimodal Data

Together these five modes of data collection and analyses provided the comprehensive portrait of American generosity that we share in the pages to follow. We employed a range of quantitative and qualitative analyses to attain both broad, quantitative trends and in-depth, qualitative understanding of the way generosity exists in real, complex American lives. Every chapter draws upon both the nationally representative survey data and the American giver case studies in presenting these multimodal data.

Nationally Representative Survey

In each chapter we first present the national averages and trends that we gleaned from the nationally representative survey data. With these data we also show how the averages and trends vary across different subgroups of Americans. For example, we show how the trends differ for Americans in different regions of the United States and different educational attainment levels. We reflect on these patterns and draw upon the interview data to understand how and why these trends happen the way they do.

Case Studies of American Givers

We selected from the 62 interviewees several exemplary case studies that typify the many findings about generosity. We selected these cases based on their capacity to qualitatively explain the quantitative findings and provide the context and meaning of generosity in real lives. Given the sampling method for the interviewees and their representation of key demographic characteristics, we are confident that these cases represent typical American lives and are not exceptional. It is important for readers to know that our statements about the case studies that we highlight in this book are recorded observations (either audio or visual recordings); they are not snap judgments or assumptions, but collected data. We do not claim that they represent everyone, but we think readers will see connections between these cases and people that they know personally, or at least those they know about more generally.

The Approach of This Book

In this book we make use of a few key systematic approaches and themes. Throughout our various analyses we consistently explain two primary generous behaviors:

1. Whether or not someone gives, that is, givers versus nongivers
2. How much is given, that is, amount of money or time

Each analysis assesses how these two measures vary with a range of factors. The results show the contrast between givers and nongivers as well as between those who give more and those who give less. We do this in two parts because we want to investigate whether the processes that relate to giving (at all) also relate to amounts given. We can imagine that the factors that influence a person to participate in giving may be different, or at least have a different magnitude of influence, from those influencing the amount someone gives. This nuance refines our understanding of generosity in America.

An important caveat to underscore our assessments is that we use only cross-sectional data in our analysis, as this dataset does not have survey data on changes that occur over time. We do, however, have interviewee accounts of changes over times. Thus we cannot fully conclude that our findings represent cause and effect in a certain direction. Rather we know that the reality of social lives is complex and that cause-effect relationships can occur in multiple directions or be spurious to unstudied changes.[13] Thus, finding that people are more likely to be givers, or that they are more likely to give greater amounts, if they have certain characteristics does not necessarily mean that the latter caused the former. It could certainly be the reverse. What we can conclusively state is that there are associations between factors that indicate potential causal relationships. It is those associations we investigate here.

The Organization of the Book

In the pages to follow we present quantitative and qualitative analyses on American generosity that begin to fill gaps in our understanding of American generosity. In these chapters we explain the following:

- The "what" of American generosity: identification of nine forms of generous behavior
- The "how much" of American generosity: participation rates in generosity forms
- The "who" of American generosity: social status variations in giving behaviors
- The "where" of American generosity: regional variations in giving behaviors
- The "why" of American generosity: through intra- and interpersonal approaches
  - Social psychological explanations for giving behaviors
  - Sociorelational explanations for giving behaviors.

We focus on giving behaviors—the reported actions of respondents—as the outcome. We do not focus on intentions of generosity, nor do we focus on the effects of generosity. Others do that quite well.[14] For us it is important to focus on the outcomes of generosity—the actual giving action—because it is from these combined actions that the well-being of others can be enhanced.

The book begins with an introduction to our 12 case studies. We summarize each case in a shorthand label and provide a brief description of their social statuses, household characteristics, and neighborhood contexts. Each summary also includes information about their standing for the key statistical patterns described in the remainder of the book chapters.

Chapter 1 illustrates American generosity by describing participation rates in nine forms of generous behaviors. Drawing on a wealth of social science literature, ranging from Alexis de Tocqueville to Robert Putnam,[15] we find somewhat low levels of voluntary participation in the United States today. Snapshots of American generosity are taken across nine forms of giving behaviors and reveal a fairly dim picture when we look at any one form at a time. To begin to explain these findings, we examine how access to resources may further develop the snapshots of generosity.

While we confirm that resources do further develop the picture of American generosity, a large part of that picture as a whole remains unexplained because resources do not consistently predict giving behavior. Among those with access to the most resources, we find nongivers, and among those with the fewest resources, we find givers. As most sociologists do, we find that the *Homo sociologicus* approach is at least as important as a *Homo economicus* approach.[16] In other words, people are not purely economically conditioned in the world; expendable resources do not fully explain our behaviors. To understand generosity we will need more complex representations of the myriad social factors involved in generous behaviors.

We conclude chapter 1 by presenting an in-depth, qualitative analysis regarding how resources and giving behaviors operate in the lives of our 12 case studies. These illustrate the quantitative trends in real lives. In summary, chapter 1 provides answers to the "what" and "how much" questions of American generosity and demonstrates that focusing on any one particular giving form promotes a "glass half-empty" perspective, while evidencing that availability of resources only partially explains giving differences.

Chapter 2 zooms out from the individual snapshots of each generosity form to take a wide-angle view of American generosity. From this view the "glass half-full" perspective is revealed in the landscape of participation in giving. That is, when we look at all nine forms of generosity as a whole, American generosity appear to be greater than when we assess giving of any single form. We especially focus on the Big 3 of American generosity: donating money, volunteering time, and taking political action for charitable causes.

In chapter 2 we begin to explore which factors beyond resources help to explain variation in giving. Based on the research of scholars from Peter Blau onward,[17] as well as that of conflict theorists showing the importance of race, class, and gender in social behaviors,[18] chapter 2 focuses on demographic and regional patterns in generous behaviors. We investigate patterns by gender, age, socioeconomic status, race and ethnicity, political party affiliation, and religious service attendance, among other demographics. We also draw on normative culture theory regarding the role of regional US cultures in social life and how regions relate to generosity.[19] We present our 12 case studies to show how these demographic and regional trends operate in the lives of real men and women from different backgrounds, locations, and socioeconomic resources.

Viewing giving with a wide-angle view, chapter 2 shows higher participation and answers the "who" and "where" questions of American generosity. This approach finds the landscape of generosity to be flourishing, and we examine a number of regional and social status patterns to help us understand who participates in which expressions of generosity.

We further explore variations in American generosity in chapter 3 by investigating different approaches to giving. We draw on a wealth of theory and evidence in psychoanalytic and cognitive psychology regarding processes for actualizing behaviors,[20] combined with a Bourdieuian approach to the habitus of social behaviors,[21] and employing a Weberian ideal-type methodology.[22] Using this theoretical orientation, we find that the approaches people take to giving range from more to less conscious, sporadic, and systematic. The resulting typology of American giving identifies four primary types of givers: Planned, Habitual, Selective, and Impulsive. Each giver type relates to differences in social status, demographics, form of generosity, and amount donated.

Our case studies in chapter 3 bring to life each of the giver types we identified. Through in-depth explorations, we see how the giver typology works to explain the distinct approaches of American givers. Examining the broader context of individuals' lives helps flesh out the statistical patterns in American giving approaches by showing variation in the social, psychological, and relational experiences of these 12 Americans.

Chapter 4 begins to answer *why* Americans vary in their participation in generosity. In this "Why 1.0" we analyze the intrapersonal social orientations of Americans that relate to giving. This social psychological approach draws on the theories of Mead, Cooley, Durkheim, Marx, and Weber in examining a number of central factors that explain intrapersonal social aspects of Americans' giving, including having a generous self-identity.[23] We find variation in giving behaviors and types of givers by these key social psychological factors. In doing so this chapter reveals how the personal, social psychological orientations of Americans explain why there are differences in approaches to giving and the actualization of generosity.

To further explain our findings, we return to our cases and provide a thorough analysis of how these social psychological orientations operate in daily life. We see how personality, upbringing, and social interactions color the picture of generosity. These cases shed light on how different combinations of factors that we could consider incompatible can be held in tandem in these lives. By gaining this understanding of social psychological orientations, we can better analyze the role of these factors in generous activities.

Chapter 5 shifts to a sociorelational approach to understanding why Americans participate in giving differently, allowing us to advance our explanations for giving to a "Why 2.0." Though the *intra*personal orientations of chapter 4 which are clearly important; we also look at the importance of *inter*personal affiliations, focusing on the support for giving that Americans have in their social groups. Based on a Simmelian explanation of the differentiation of social relationships in modern times,[24] we explore how social webs of affiliations may help to explain generous behaviors. In so doing, we investigate the role of social groups in the actualization of generosity.

Chapter 5 considers spousal relationships, parental influence, friends, religious calls, and local community and national giving contexts. The sociorelational contexts of American lives can grease the wheels of actualizing a generous personal inclination—or provide friction that inhibits it. We find that varying configurations of affiliations do play a role in explaining giving behaviors and types of approaches, and they relate to personal orientations and a generous self-identity. Key web configurations of givers are identified, including which relational configurations associate with being a giver and giving greater amounts.

In the conclusion we sketch implications for specific generosity-related activities. One implication is a proposed theory of "circles of generosity," which groups giving targets, reasons for giving, and giving identities into logically coherent circles of generosity that ripple outward in their reach. We see each circle as extending its reach through greater access to social and economic resources and sketch implications for different kinds of readers. We propose some specific implications for ourselves as givers, parents, spouses, friends, and community members, including some practical tips. We also discuss implications for nonprofit, foundation, and religious leaders, as well as the key contributions for interdisciplinary scholars.

Understanding American Generosity

In summary, we provide in this book an investigation of generosity, philanthropic expressions, and different forms of participation in civil society within their broader social context. Understanding the social context of giving helps explain why some Americans give more than others and how social contexts can bolster or inhibit personal desires to give. Through thorough quantitative and qualitative analyses we show the complex interplay of social factors at work in the lives of real Americans and how it affects their generosity. What results is a theory—incorporating resources, social status, region, identity, and relationships—about how and why Americans become involved in different kinds of generosity.

There are numerous implications from these analyses. We especially highlight implications for nonprofit, philanthropic, religious, and civil leaders in their requests for generosity. The results of this book can aid such practitioners in gearing engagement efforts to particular kinds of Americans and their preferred giving approaches. Individual donors can gain a better sense of their own generosity, especially in considering possible changes to their current giving, as well as knowledge of how to support friends and family in their giving efforts. Numerous implications also exist for scholars interested in improving interdisciplinary efforts to study generosity, as well as broader theories of social action, to which we turn in the conclusion.

We invite you to walk through these pages with us to find a bit of yourselves, loved ones, and those whom you serve. We each have our own journey with generosity. In the pages to follow we hope you will see that we also share much in common, as even differences among people reveal collective patterns. The stories and findings of this book are included to inspire and challenge you, and all of us. Through the moments of disdain, sorrow, surprise, joy, empathy, and compassion, we offer you a dynamic understanding of lived American generosity.

Case Study Introductions

An In-depth Look at 12 Americans and Their Giving

TO PUT GENEROSITY within the context of real social lives, we begin by introducing 12 Americans in our study. Out of the nearly 2,000 Americans who participated in our national survey, we selected 40 families to participate in extensive ethnographic and in-person interviews. In 22 households, our primary survey respondent had a spouse or live-in romantic partner whom we also interviewed, resulting in a total of 62 interview cases. For the 22 nonsurvey respondents whom we interviewed, we infer their partners' survey answers to their situation, such as how hard the recession hit them, their household income, and housing status.

After becoming deeply acquainted with these 62 interviewees, their lives, families, households, neighborhoods, and giving patterns, we chose 12 to best demonstrate the patterns we describe in this book. These qualitative cases help explain the real-life thoughts and processes behind the behaviors and guide our understanding of the broader quantitative patterns presented here. We share these cases throughout the book to enliven the statistics and numbers and to give real-life context and meaning to the generous actions in Americans' lives. The inclusion of these cases is intended to encapsulate the many patterns and findings presented here and helps to put a real face on American generosity.

In our grappling with these interviewees and all their beauty, idiosyncrasies, and enjoyable life-messiness, we came to admire them for the way they breathed life and meaning into the numbers and trends that we present. Just as in life, we found some of these interviewees easier to like than others, but all of them revealed themselves to us and explained how their complex life stories shaped them. Our goal in sharing their stories is for readers to find their words as insightful as we did and that peering into their lives will build a greater understanding of others. We hope these 12 people resonate with you, remind you of people in your life, and familiarize you with people otherwise unfamiliar to you. We hope too that their lives illustrate the generosity within each of us that rings in the human heart with all of its beauties, sad realities, and funny inconsistencies.

In each of the snapshots in this introduction, we provide each interviewee's story, listing their social status characteristics, demographics, and neighborhood composition data. This provides a brief introduction of the range in qualities that each of these case studies represents, showing that they typify very different kinds of Americans: upper-middle-class and impoverished, high givers and low, men and women, parents and not, married or cohabitating or single, a range of races and ethnicities, and so on.

Susan Baker: Upper-Middle-Class "One and Done" Los Angeleno

Susan Baker is a short and slim, physically fit woman in her mid-40s with short brown hair and small dark eyes.[1] In terms of demographics, she is a white (non-Hispanic) Democrat who has a master's degree and is employed. She owns her home, is married, and has a 12-year-old daughter. As a hobby, Susan likes to cycle. As is typical of upper-middle-class Americans, Susan lives with her family in a wealthy, urban, mostly white (89 percent), well-educated (7 percent have less than a high school degree), high-income suburb of Los Angeles, surrounded by new "McMansions." She has lived in the neighborhood for 16 years. The neighborhood itself is fairly stable: 61 percent homeowners, 12 percent mobility rate, and 39 percent with work commutes of longer than 30 minutes.

As a parent Susan is very pro-education and takes a concerted cultivation emphasis on child rearing. She is an independent contractor who uses complicated mathematical modeling to project feasibility of products for various industries. This job allows her a flexible schedule to accommodate her family life, which she describes as very stable. During the interview Susan speaks quickly with a very animated face. She describes herself as committed, dedicated, conscientious, smart, and friendly ("but not overly so," she says, "as in [not so friendly as to seem] fake").

In our survey Susan reported that she and her husband gave about $2,310 to charitable causes in the past 12 months. She also reports volunteering about 67 hours and spending two hours taking political action during the past month. Susan also is an organ donor, lends possessions, works on environmental sustainability issues, and is relationally generous. As we will explain in chapter 3, Susan is a Planned giver who says she and her husband "sat down" and "broke things into causes" in order to "figure out what our total giving should be . . . and how to divide it up."

Ryan Dewey: High-Achieving, Religious Midwesterner

Ryan Dewey is a tall and skinny, unmarried man in his 20s who attends graduate school in the Midwest. He is pursuing his doctoral degree in a reputable program. He is white and has no children; he has a master's degree and is a full-time student who rents in Michigan. His apartment is in the middle of an area with a high student population near the university campus that has qualities of a college neighborhood: high mobility (78 percent), low homeownership (6 percent), and relatively short work commutes (30 percent commuting more than a half hour to work).

Ryan keeps his apartment minimally decorated; in fact he possesses few belongings. The interviewer noticed he was in the process of moving and asked him how much he had moved out already, thinking that could explain the sparseness. Ryan replied that all he had moved so far was a large bookshelf, some books, and an armchair. In short, he appears to live simply. Ryan is very methodical and follows a well-worn path between his apartment and his graduate laboratory. He was impressed by the timeliness of our interviewer and gave prompt and fairly unexpressive responses throughout the interview. His keywords for himself were introvert, quiet, hard-working, diligent, patient, "overthinks" things, "nature lover," likes to read, good listener, generous with time, gives his honest opinion, and friendly to be around.

In terms of Ryan's giving, he reported an annual household income from his graduate stipend between $20,000 and $25,000. He reported giving about $1,850 in the past year to charitable causes. Ryan also reports volunteering about 11 hours in the past month and taking no political action (in chapter 1, he explains why). In terms of other forms of generosity, Ryan listed only lending possessions. In chapter 2 we discuss the important role that Ryan's religious convictions play in his financial giving and volunteering; in chapter 3 we describe his social status and explain that Ryan is a Planned giver who exemplifies how this approach helps him use his modest resources to be a giver.

Jackie Sawyer: Thrifty, Type-A, Religious, Midwestern Mom

Jackie Sawyer is a middle-class, suburban mother in her mid-30s. She is white, Republican, and married; has two children (9-year-old son and 8-year-old daughter); earned her bachelor's degree; is employed; and owns her house. Their neighborhood is an average Michigan suburb: low density, mostly white (more than 90 percent), highly educated (2 percent have less than a high school degree), and high income (median household income of $74,817). Ninety-three percent of Jackie's neighbors own their home, and there is high stability (only 6 percent mobility rate). Only 24 percent of households commute more than 30 minutes to work.

Jackie is an immunization nurse for the health department and describes her job by saying, "I poke babies and teenagers and adults all day long. It's a great job." She says that she likes the job because it is "black and white" and fits her highly organized personality. Jackie is well-educated and during the interview often critiqued the wording of our questions, seemingly wanting to edit them for more technical grammar. She describes herself as a "conservative Christian" and sees being a disciple as her highest calling. She described herself as a mother, nurse, wife, helper, busy, overwhelmed, Type-A, financially stable, coupon cutter, and bargain shopper.

Jackie is one of our spousal interviewees, meaning her husband was our original respondent who completed the survey. As such we do not have all the same survey data on her as we do other respondents, though we are able to fill in many estimates for her based on her interview. In terms of Jackie's giving, her husband (our primary respondent) reported that their annual household income is between $75,000 and $80,000 and that in the previous year they gave about $11,850 to charitable causes. He reported volunteering about 25 hours in the past month and took no political action. In terms of other forms of generosity, Jackie mentioned only relational generosity in the interview. As we explain in chapter 3, Jackie is a prototypical Habitual giver who describes her approach to giving in this way: "How much do I pay attention to it? Not a whole lot. It's probably something that is just automate[d] and assumed." We will discuss how

Jackie exemplifies the typical trends of high-income, frequently attending religious Habitual givers.

George Nettleson: Comfortable, Religious Southerner Takes Time

George Nettleson is a family man living in a suburban neighborhood in the South. He has two daughters, one in college and the other in high school. His household is moderately resourced and middle class. In terms of his demographics, George is white and a moderate Republican with a master's degree who is employed, owns his home in North Carolina, and attends an Evangelical Protestant church more than once a week.

His home is modest and a little outdated, likely in part because this aging couple is on the brink of retirement and in part because the neighborhood itself is about 20 years old. This family is used to a schedule and wanted to quickly get to the business of the interview. George works in IT, and his wife works for a management company. George is a methodical and deliberate thinker who evidenced some low self-esteem in repeatedly seeking validation for the correctness of his interview responses. Over the course of the interviewing visits, he grew more comfortable and began to joke around from time to time. He used the following keywords to describe himself: "child of God," "faith plays a big role," employee, laid back, gentle, and a bit "neurotic."

George is another of our spousal interviewees, which means his wife was our survey respondent. As such we do not have all the same survey data on him that we do other respondents, though we are able to complete many estimates for his generosity, personal orientation, and social affiliations based on his interview. In terms of George's giving, his wife (our primary respondent) reported that their annual household income is between $100,000 and $125,000. They gave $14,100 last year to charitable causes. George's wife also reported volunteering about 11 hours in the past month and taking no political action. In terms of other forms of generosity, we think that George would claim his donating and volunteering. As we explain in chapter 3, George is a Habitual giver who describes his approach to giving as being fairly dependent upon his wife, who is a Planned giver. He says in the past he was more of an Impulsive or Selective giver but has deferred to her more planning-oriented approach, becoming

Habitual in his own giving as a result. George exemplifies the relationship between being a Habitual giver and being a college graduate who regularly attends religious services.

Michael Johnson: Hard-Working, Politicking, D.C. Widower Takes Action

Michael Johnson is a white, upper-middle-class man in his late 60s; he is a Democrat, has a professional degree, is employed, and is a home-owner. He lives in a cul de sac near Washington, D.C., in a secluded, scenic, and affluent suburb around neighbors who are mostly white (more than 90 percent), highly educated (fewer than 2 percent have less than a high school degree), and wealthy (median income $190,801). The neighborhood has high homeownership (93 percent), low mobility (6 percent), and long work commutes (64 percent spend a half hour or more commuting to work). Michael lives in a modest house with few belongings and outdated décor, but he does enjoy the finer things in life. He has an extravagant pool, a sports car, and nice clothes. In fact he took our interviewer shopping with him and spent $3,000 within the span of only a few hours. He is very health conscious and prides himself on eating well and exercising regularly.

Michael has an adult daughter. He was happily married until recently, when he lost his wife to a relatively quick-paced terminal illness. He now lives only with his live-in housekeeper who helped care for his dying wife. Michael gave us the impression that he continues to employ her mostly as a way to maintain the connection they shared with his wife and their caring for her in her illness. He describes his life as a whole this way:

> I mean there's obviously a big hole in the fact that I'm widowed. And I certainly would prefer to maybe have some kind of a relationship, but the fact that I do not have that relationship does not mean that, my life is a disappointment at this stage. I've learned to adapt, and I've learned to live as a single person. I think people make adjustments.

While Michael is of retirement age and financially secure, he continues his fast-paced, intensive career due to his political convictions and desire to continue regular use of his intellect. Though he no longer needs to work for the money, he enjoys working hard and still considers his career as central to his identity. When we asked him how similar to or different from his friends he was, Michael said, "Well, I'd say the primary difference is I work much more than most of my friends and, you know, most people that I know. I mean there'd be very few people who could physically do what I do during the tax season. I'm going seven days a week, 18 to maybe 20 hours for maybe 11 weeks or 12 weeks. It's very strenuous and very demanding." Despite being so career-driven, Michael also professes his desire to enjoy his life and take some time to travel. He says, "I've got a book, *A Thousand Places You Should See before You Die.* Of course I will never live long enough to achieve that number, but there are certainly maybe about 10 or 15 that I think I would like to visit before I do, before I die."

When we asked, "What would you say are your highest life priorities?," he answered:

> Well, my highest life priorities. Certainly, family. My career, to do well in my career. To have, you know, good friends that I enjoy and can count on. And then, to be satisfied with certain things that I consider intellectually important, like politics, or things that I enjoy reading.

Michael also clearly enjoys being a part of the "in" crowd and throughout the interview periodically dropped names of important people that he knows and lives near.

Michael is one of the few interviewees who is very politically involved. He reports spending 27 hours in the past month on unpaid political action in addition to serving as a paid political consultant. He also donates money and volunteers time to charitable causes. His reported annual household income was more than $175,000. He reported giving about $16,100 in the past year to charitable causes. Michael also volunteered about two hours in the past month and reported no participation in any other generosity. Michael is a Selective giver who exemplifies a style of "picking and choosing" causes and opportunities to give. While he occasionally attends Catholic religious services, he selectively adheres to the Church's beliefs. In chapter 2 we examine these beliefs and their role in his giving.

Linda Chesterfield: Midwestern
Soccer Mom Puts Family First

Linda Chesterfield is in her mid-40s, an upper-middle-class stay-at-home mom to eight children from 9 months to 17 years. She and her husband have been married for 17 years. Linda is white, a homeowner, earned a bachelor's degree, and leans Republican. She is an "EAC" Catholic, meaning she seldom attends mass but does attend on Easter, Ash Wednesday, and Christmas. For 16 years the family has lived in a typical middle-class Illinois suburb with a high homeowner rate (89 percent), low mobility (13 percent), high income ($120,893 median household income), some diversity (20 percent nonwhite), and long commutes to work (62 percent commute 30 minutes or more).

Being a mother is an enormous part of Linda's identity. She puts it succinctly: "If I had to put a label on myself, probably 'the mom.'" Attending to family needs takes up the vast majority of her waking hours and leaves her little time to herself. In telling us how her friends would describe her, she said, "I'd say they'd probably just say, 'she's too busy,' or they'd tease me and say I'm crazy because I have so many children." She describes her busy lifestyle this way:

> As you can see, we have a lot of children. And their lifestyles take us all over the place as far as picking up, dropping off for practice, that sort of thing. We never have just our family around, it doesn't seem. They all have multiple friends going in and out too. So it's kind of a busy place to be. But it's fun, and I really wouldn't have it any other way. I feel like, outside of family and what we do around here, we really don't have time for much other stuff, so we sacrifice other things. Well, I don't know if I would call it sacrifice or not. Sometimes I would consider it sacrifice.

Linda is an only child who was often lonely and bored while growing up, so she decided at a young age that she wanted to have a large family. Her life is pretty stable, and nearly everything she discussed had to do with her children's many activities. When asked what things keep her busy, Linda said:

> Just housework. The kids' schedules, I mean the kids' schedules probably keep us the most busy. And a lot of that is just dropping

off, picking up, really having to, you drop one off, you come home, pick up the other one, drop. I mean some of them you can do all at the same times, but sometimes they're overlapping, or they're going in different directions. And it's just like, that's busy. I don't know what else to call it. I don't have much down time, because if I'm not doing that, then I'm cleaning something, or doing laundry, or trying to catch up with things that need to be done around here. . . . There's not much free time.

When we asked Linda what she was most proud of in life, she said, "Probably just my kids. I'm so incredibly proud of my children." She goes on to say she is proud "that I'm with their father. They all have the same dad." Linda explains, "I'm proud of that because you don't see a lot of that in this day and age. I have friends who've got a bunch of kids that they're from a bunch of different fathers. There's no stability there. So I figure, I feel like I offer my kids some stability." Keeping her family intact is of high priority for Linda, and she sees it as part of the gift she gives her children. However, she does confess that the childrearing wears on her from time to time and chalks this up to be one of her greatest weaknesses:

Sometimes I feel like I don't have the patience that I would like to have. I mean I used to consider myself a very patient person, but as I get older my patience is getting shorter. And sometimes I feel like I wish I had more patience. I wish there was just more time. But some of those things you just can't change.

Linda's keywords to describe herself: "the mom," wife, friend, nonattending Catholic, busy, "woman in the shoe," serious but also fun.

Linda's husband (our primary respondent) reported their annual household income between $100,000 and $125,000. On the survey, Linda's husband reported that they gave about $25 in the past year to charitable causes. He also reports volunteering about 14 hours in the past month. As with so many Americans, neither reported taking political action. Because Linda is a spousal respondent, we do not have all the survey data on her that we have for other respondents, though we are able to estimate her responses based on her disclosures during her interview. Linda claimed no other generosity except relational generosity, where she counted her children as recipients of her giving. As we explain in chapter 3, Linda is a prototypical Selective giver who is married to a Planned giver. If it was up to her, they would give less than they do, though she tries to support her husband's giving decisions.

Cindy Phelps: Young, Professional Texan Tutor in New York City

Cindy Phelps earns a high income ($60,000–$75,000 annually) as a young professional. She is white, in her late 20s, has never married, has no children, is a Libertarian, was raised as a Mainline Protestant but never attends church, and she rents her apartment in Manhattan. Cindy has a professional degree and comes from a well-educated family. Asked what she is most proud of, she replies, "What I've been able to accomplish in my life. Going to [college]. Moving to New York. Being able to do that." Despite her high income for her age, she says, "I'm always trying to become more secure financially."

Cindy is originally from Texas and told us she always felt like an outsider there. She likes living in New York because everyone is an outsider, and she can be anonymous without the responsibility of having to know her neighbors or let them into her life. She has lived in New York for three years and says, "I love it. I've always wanted to live here." She has moved four times in her short three years there, but she is now happier with her living situation, even though she has to walk up and down three flights of stairs daily. Cindy has less admiration for her job, saying, "There are ups and downs. I wish I had done something a little more creative with my life. I sit behind a desk for most of my days. And I have really long hours. And I'm doing what someone else is telling me to do, so it's not what I expected. But I do have good days too, so I think it's like any job." In addition she feels very "busy" and "stressed out" about work.

She lives in a studio apartment in a residential area surrounded by businesses. The neighborhood is a typical affluent, high-density urban area. The median income of her neighbors is $102,391, one of the highest of all of our cases. The education level in the neighborhood is also high (only 3 percent have less than a high school degree). The mobility rate is among the highest of our cases, at 28 percent. Cindy herself has been in the neighborhood for only about a year. Almost all her neighbors are white. They too mostly rent, with only 20 percent owning their homes. As expected in Manhattan, the neighborhood commute rate is fairly high, with 42 percent spending 30 minutes or more getting to work.

Cindy's apartment is small but feels roomy because it has two large windows and is decorated sparsely. She is a naturally reflective person and seems to be at ease in the interview. While she makes good money in her professional career, she says she does not enjoy being in a cutthroat industry that does not support her creative side. When she was younger she had a bit of a wild side and was arrested, a blemish she credits for her not getting into a better college. She decided after the arrest to turn her life around and transform into a giving, kind, good person. Her keywords to describe herself were these: lawyer, particular, detail-oriented, eccentric, neat, strong beliefs, judgmental, snobby, artistic, creative, friendly, reserved, responsible, and frugal.

Cindy reported giving nothing financially in the past year to charitable causes, but she volunteered about nine hours in the past month. During the interview she explained that her volunteering consists of spending one to two hours a week tutoring in an after-school program for Section 8 housing recipients. She admits that sometimes she misses tutoring when she has to work late. She reported taking no political action and reported no other forms of generosity.

As we explain in chapter 3, Cindy is an Impulsive giver who described her approach to giving as "whenever I have the ability, or whenever I have some extra cash." She has a bit of a "hodge-podge" of religious influence: she does not attend church but adopts a "Golden Rule" version of diffuse Mainline Protestantism. We discuss this further in chapter 2.

Tanika Sandaval: Single Los Angeles Mom Fights for Her Children's Future

Tanika Sandaval is a mid-30s woman of color who is a single mother to three elementary school–age boys. Her income level is among the lowest of our case studies, between $10,000 and $13,000 annually. As we explain in chapter 1, Tanika receives disability income and uses this as a way to maintain being a stay-at-home mother without spousal support. She is a Democrat, identifies as multiracial but describes herself as African American, and completed a high school degree. She values education highly mainly because she views it as her children's way to a better life.

Tanika and her boys live in an apartment in a densely populated Los Angeles neighborhood that has a high level of violent crime; famous murder cases occurred just around the corner from her apartment. Her place, like many in the low-income (median income $28,701), mostly renter (15 percent homeowner) neighborhood, has bars over the doorway. Despite the crime rate and bad reputation of the area, it has a low mobility rate (only 5 percent), coupled with a very high commuter rate (75 percent spend more than 30 minutes per day commuting). Like her, many of Tanika's neighbors also have a modest education, with 34 percent having less than a high school degree. Her neighborhood is the most diverse of our cases: 67 percent Latino, 18 percent black, and a mixture of Korean and other racial and ethnic groups.

The only major possession of note in Tanika's apartment is a mini-shrine with a painting of a muscular Jesus. Life has not been easy for Tanika. She talked a number of times during her interview about fairy tales. She seems to be a bit taken by imagining a different life. Previously she had worked as a cosmetologist and created glamour shots, giving people a touch of class in otherwise tough life situations. She told us that after the birth of one of her sons, she needed a spinal tap that led to loss of mobility in her hand and neck. She decided not to have surgery on it and is "hoping everything be all right that way." She tries to get by with physical therapy alone. Tanika chooses to collect only her disability check but struggles to make ends meet. At first we found ourselves wondering why she would choose to stick with this tenuous financial situation when she has so many capabilities, but over the course of the interview it became clear to us that Tanika values caring for her children more than earning more income.

Most important to Tanika are her children and "how you treat people." She described her life's highest priority this way: "Hope that I'm being a good mom." This appears to be a major motivator for her volunteering, as she donates time to serve as a community liaison for her children's school. Tanika says, "I'm very, very proud. So that's my whole thing, it's me and my children, my children and I, yeah, that's what that would be." Tanika's keywords for herself were inviting, friendly, conservative, fun, dreams of going to Africa, active, former athlete, loves cooking, honest, values respect, blunt, "crazy but cool," down to earth, independent, grounded, has "good roots," "only take what you need," stable, inspirational, and strongly identifies with her African American heritage.

Tanika reported on the survey that she gave nothing in the past year to charitable causes, although during her interviews it sounded as though she may occasionally give money to causes without keeping track of the amounts. She reported on the survey that she volunteered about 11 hours in the past month; however, during the interview she told us she spends about 10 hours per week volunteering at her children's school. The discrepancy in hours appears to be because some of her hours as a school liaison are paid, the number of hours fluctuates monthly depending on the number of meetings she attends, and she counted the parent involvement meetings as volunteering. Tanika reported taking no political action for charitable causes and reported lending possessions as another form of generosity. During our interview Tanika described herself as very relationally generous, and this is mostly directed toward her children.

Regina Buckner: Southern, Rural, Stay-at-Home Mom Takes It Day by Day

Regina Buckner is a 30-year-old stay-at-home mom in North Carolina who is married to a blue-collar worker and has two girls and a boy, ranging in age from 1 to 8 years. Regina is currently pregnant with their fourth child. She is white and a Republican who went to college but did not earn a degree. Her family earns a poverty-level income: $20,000 to $25,000 with five, going on six, family members. She was raised as a Catholic and attends a few times a year (EAC Catholic).

The family rents their home in a rural, fairly impoverished part of the South. Their neighborhood is on a small street that abuts a trailer park. This is the most rural of our twelve cases. The neighborhood is low density, with modest household income ($42,654 median household income), high homeowner rate (74 percent), low mobility (12 percent), and low education level (20 percent have less than a high school degree). It is a prototypical southern rural neighborhood that is one-third black and two-thirds white. Commuting times in the area are long; half the neighborhood spends 30 minutes or more getting to work. Regina and her husband share a car, so the children come along when Regina drives him back and forth to work every day. Regina is most proud of her family; she says her greatest challenge in life has been being a mom and that it has been more challenging than she expected. She wishes she could change their "money situation." Despite a "couple of bumps," she believes her family is content and says, "Everybody seems pretty happy with where we are. The kids are doing good; finally giving them the help that they need. My oldest has ADD, so we're finally getting that taken care of. My youngest has a speech delay, and we've had problems with the school districts and had to move because of that." Given all of this, Regina takes life day by day and paycheck to paycheck.

During the interviews we got the feeling that Regina was eager to have an adult conversation and be able to spend some time focused on herself. Throughout the interviews she was patient and kind to her children and husband. On the second day she seemed a bit more guarded, perhaps being somewhat defensive about having had to talk about her low giving levels during the previous interview. She was open but was one of our most curt interviewees. Regina used the following keywords to describe herself: a "farm girl," honest, hard-working, quick learner, dependable, mom, wife, farmer's daughter, country girl, fun, loyal, and "content."

Regina reported that she and her husband gave nothing in the past year to charitable causes. On the survey she reported volunteering about 40 hours in the past month; however, during the interview she described no regular volunteering behaviors. We suspect that, when answering the survey question, she was counting her unpaid labor taking care of her children. Regina reported taking no political action and reported lending possessions as her only other form of generosity. Regina is an Impulsive giver who gives when she can afford to do so. She evidences a pattern of Impulsive giving typical of those with low income and no college degree.

Deon Williams: Retiree Living It Up in Detroit with Residual Poverty

Deon Williams is a retired, middle-aged, single black man who rents a flat in a Detroit neighborhood that is 96 percent black. He voiced concern for the interviewer's safety in his neighborhood, as he would be the only "white man" around, and so he asked that they meet instead at a local university campus. Deon is in his mid-50s; he retired from a blue-collar industry and is a Democrat. He attends a Black Protestant church once or twice a year when he visits his mother. His neighborhood is lower-middle-class: 13 percent of the adults have less than a high school degree; the median income is $32,123; the homeowner rate is 50 percent; the mobility rate is 12 percent; and 26 percent of workers have a half-hour or longer commute.

Deon seemed comfortable in the interview and appeared to enjoy having the exchange even though there was no laughing or smiling. He was matter-of-fact in his answers. Afterward our interviewer asked him how he liked being interviewed and he replied, "It's cool." Deon describes himself as never having married, although he has "been close to it, but just didn't happen." He has one grown child who lives in Alabama near his maternal family. Deon spends a fair amount of time alone, expressing enjoyment in the company of our interviewer during their meal. He describes himself as a "free-wheeling" retiree who does what he wants with his time. Though he leads a modestly comfortable life with an annual income between $40,000 and $50,000, he has "residual poverty" that lingers from his childhood. He grew up in a family that received welfare assistance and he still feels the need to hoard resources, "just in case." He used these keywords to describe himself: arrogant, intelligent, hard worker, a person, a man, no-nonsense, "don't like drama," likes his own space ("I love my space"), taking one day at a time, and trying to do the right thing.

Deon says that in a typical day he will

Go get something to eat if I don't have anything to eat at the crib. I normally like to go out and get something to eat, cause it's fresh and it's hot. Have a few drinks, beer, shot of booze, and basically that's my day. Come back home, maybe get back on the computer, watch TV, watch some of the reality shows, and chill. Every once in a while, I might get with one of the girls in the neighborhood, or whatever, do the do, or whatever. That's basically my life.

He has been retired for "about three and a half years" from a blue-collar company where he worked for 30 years. He says he was "kinda forced out" by the company "bringing in the younger guys and paying them less money. And they're getting rid of all the old dinosaurs."

Reflecting on his current lifestyle, Deon says:

I'm enjoying my retired life, but it's a little boring, you know. When you're used to going, getting up and going to work for 30 years. But it's okay, though, it's okay. I'm not gonna complain. Get a good little pension and stuff, I'm all right. As you can see, I haven't missed any meals [laughs].

Though Deon lives alone, his mother and sister live in a two-family apartment next door to him. He likes this arrangement: "It helps to live around family, and stuff, you know, mom, have good old home cooking and stuff. A lot of times I don't have to spend money on food, I can just go next door to Mom's house and grab a plate."

Deon has not married by choice because "marriage brings a lot of drama." He explains:

I'm a guy who likes my own space. I love my space. I'm just taking it one day at a time and just trying to do the right thing. Though I've never been hurt, or anything, I've never been beat up or fired or, I've never really been under—or locked up. I just try to live life in a good way, and contribute to life at the same time, and just stay out of trouble.

Overall Deon describes his satisfaction with his life by saying, "It's okay. I mean, it's just okay. It's not like I'm doing great, but I'm not doing bad either. It's somewhere in the middle. Thanks to a good pension, I'm okay. I'm all right."

In terms of Deon's giving, there is little to speak of other than some occasional financial giving, which he reported on the survey as $20 in the previous year. As we explain further in chapter 3, Deon's giving approach is what we label an Atypical giver. Throughout the interview it became clear that he leads a fairly unreflective life, not being entirely sure why it is that he leads his life the way he does. At the end of the interview he told us he had never thought about the vast majority of the questions we asked. This helps explain why his responses were fairly inconsistent, often claiming behaviors and attitudes that were inconsistent with others he claimed. While nearly ever interviewee displays some level of inconsistency, Deon's level was above average.

Rosa Perez: Pregnant and Unemployed in Brooklyn

Rosa Perez is a Latina in her late 20s who is pregnant and becoming a foster mom. She is cohabitating with her African American fiancé, who is a security guard. She is recently unemployed. Rosa went to college but never earned her degree. She grew up Catholic and is an EAC Catholic who attends once or twice a year.

Rosa and her fiancé live in a Brooklyn housing project. It is bustling with people sitting on stairs or playing basketball and children on the playground. Her fiancé describes the area as one of the worst parts of Brooklyn, with shootouts just around the corner. They have even developed a plan for what to do if Rosa is out on the street during a shootout. Their neighborhood is among the densest and most diverse of our case studies: 33 percent black, 40 percent Latino, and the remainder a mix of white, Asian, and other. Homeownership is moderate (31 percent), median income is modest ($36,624), and low education is not uncommon (17 percent have less than a high school degree). Despite this, mobility is low (9 percent), providing some stability in the area. Rosa has lived in the area for more than 20 years. Work commutes are long, with 67 percent traveling 30 minutes or longer.

The area where they live is fairly infamous, in part from the hip-hop scene and movies documenting it and in part because Robert Kennedy targeted the area for improvement in the early 1970s (largely a failed project). Our interviewer did not feel safe using a camera to take pictures in the neighborhood. In terms of their apartment, Rosa and her fiancé have very few possessions; for example, their mattresses lay on the floor without bed frames. The TV was on throughout the interview. Her keywords to describe herself were these: friendly, loveable, funny, likes to be with family, and "I'm more just cool, calm."

Rosa opened the interview by describing her overall situation:

> I moved in here. This is my first apartment [, at age] 28. I'm recently expecting.... Right now I'm unemployed. Not planning on looking for a job, I guess, cause I'm expecting. I'm recently gonna be foster mother to my nephew, gonna take care of him and take care of my kid until I don't know when.... Planning on getting married, but financially, its not too good.... I want to. I really do. But cause I don't have a job and stuff like that, his income is just covering the bills and stuff, so I'd have to get a job to make some kind of extra money to put aside for the wedding.

Rosa explained that she was recently fired after working for about a year as a teacher's assistant. She had been taking up a holiday collection, and when some of her Jewish coworkers said something about Christmas that Rosa did not like, she decided to write a note that said "Hum-bug fuckers" with a heart around it. She left the note for her classroom teacher to find. The teacher showed it to all the people Rosa had been referring to in the note. Things escalated, and at some point Rosa told some of her coworkers, "Ooh, if she keeps it up, I'm gonna let the ghetto out of me." She says this scared them, and they started acting as though she were dangerous. Rosa was confused by that. She recounts, "That's all I did. I didn't throw no chairs. This other teacher made it seem like I was gonna be some big, evil ghetto person." They called a meeting and fired her.

Rosa recounts her conversation with the director after the firing:

> I was like, "Verbally saying something and physically doing something is two different things." I said, "Do you know what *ghetto* means?" There's two different ghettos. There's ghetto where you walk into a job and your pants is off your butt, and you're like, "Ohh what's up? How you doin? Dadada." And then the other ghetto is like, "I'm gonna curse you out. Put you in your place." That's the ghetto I was talking about. She was like, "[Rosa], I know what ghetto you was talking about." "So then why are you gonna fire me?" But whatever. I said—I was just pissed.... Right now, I'm lost. I don't know what to do. I want to have a job, but then I don't want to risk anything. Because I was pregnant before, with triplets, and I miscarried because I was working at a day care. And went into denial because I'm still doing all things that a teacher's assistant is supposed to do. And my teacher's like, "Sit down Rosa!" And I just felt helpless, and I don't feel like feeling helpless. I'm the type of person that likes to work. So I think [I am] in denial.

Rosa dreams of opening her own child care facility: "I would like to do my own day care. Like one of my dreams is to do my own day care, but the day cares out here, especially the family-based ones. . . . I have the little certificate. I have the certificate for teacher's assistant/child care provider, so I could do it." She says she feels her greatest sense of belonging at work when she is with the kids.

Rosa and her fiancé reported a combined income between $35,000 and $40,000, likely including the pay from Rosa's previous job. This is not considered a high income for a couple living in New York City and expecting twins. Rosa reported that she gave no money, time, or action in the past year to charitable causes, but she ranked as one of our highest cases of effort in heavy relational giving. Rosa explained in the interview that she counted the free babysitting for neighbors and relatives as part of her relational giving. Though we do not know how long ago this ended, it is clear that she is not currently babysitting.

Anthony Ross: In Between, Regrouping, and Poor in D.C.

Anthony Ross is Latino, in his mid-20s, and lives in a dense, predominantly black (69 percent black and 11 percent Latino) urban neighborhood in Washington, D.C. The neighborhood is fairly run-down and congested with heavy traffic and long commutes (50 percent commute 30 minutes or more to work). Despite these qualities, the median income in the area is $63,958, with a 63 percent homeowner rate and only a 9 percent mobility rate. Anthony is single, does not attend religious services, is a Democrat, and has lived in this neighborhood for 14 years.

Anthony lives in two different homes and interviewed at both. His mother's house is his secondary residence. His primary residence, about 10 to 15 minutes away, is where his mother used to live until it became overcrowded with extended family members. Anthony's life struck us as somewhat chaotic, transient, and lacking stability at home and at work. Things are not easy for him. His keywords to describe himself were "guy who's got to throw a lot of stuff in the past away," lost weight, and makes his own rules.

The interview began with Anthony describing his life by saying, "Currently, now, I would say I am in between, probably, three places, in terms of actually living. . . . The house is right now in the moving stage, people are moving, coming in coming out. So it's pretty messy, boxes everywhere, so I don't necessarily, can't stay there. A lot of distractions." In addition to his home life, Anthony's work life also entails a great deal of fluctuation, as he works on commission:

> It has its good highs and its lows. Because it's a commission job. So when you make money, it's really good. I mean for something you, how do you say, it's like a craft. I mean you build it up, you know how to do it, you know how to pitch, sell, it's selling. But there's also low seasons where there's just not enough people coming in or enough people buying that particular thing, or you're just not having a good day, you're having a bad day. Sales has its highs and lows. . . . But it's basically a migraine sometimes.

In many respects Anthony is a typical emerging adult who lives in a fairly low socioeconomic context with limited opportunities.

Understandably it is hard for Anthony to see where his life is heading. He wants his life to improve, but his aspirations are unclear. He wants to learn more languages as a way to enhance his prospects, but he is unsure what career this would lead to. It seems that Anthony is in a period of transition, as are many emerging adults, with an unclear career perspective and not yet settled down. He told us that he had gone through a period of unemployment that made him reevaluate his life circumstances:

> May to November gave me a lot of perspective on things. Basically the main motivator there was I didn't have money. Money had run out. So I couldn't live the way I was living. It's like, after you lose your first job that you've been at for three or four years, you have to actually look at things a different way. I used to take that stuff for granted before, and now I actually have to make money. Or I actually have to scrape money. Live more wisely. . . .
>
> It made me realize things. If I had still been in that job, I would have still probably been doing the things I was doing before. Not taking responsibility for a lot of things in my life. Just living day by day, as if I had kind of a moderate salary that I could kind of waste away without thinking about it. But now I'm buying my own food, now I'm doing a lot of stuff in terms of my own expense. I keep a checkbook. I'm more independent, basically. When I lost my job, okay sure, I may borrow a few bucks here and there. But other than that, I don't think nearly anywhere like I was doing before. I mean I was borrowing a few bucks while I was unemployed.

Anthony describes working to get his life back on track:

> I think slowly, gradually, very slowly I'm making my life work better for me. Back then [a year ago], I would say, nothing's really been a major change, I would say, until really last year. Because back before that I was still probably, had old bad habits of just buying stuff, not thinking about it. Not having money, overdrafting, going on credit, still owing money, not really learning anything new. It really, in the period, like the dark ages, I would say. So I would say I didn't like where my life was headed until probably like last year. I just accepted where my life was headed before that. Or accepted it, I lived day by day, not really thinking of the future.

Now he is trying to be more future-oriented, to work, and to get his life in order. Though he is not sure how to do that, things are already looking better than they did in the past.

Of Anthony's giving there is nothing to report. He gave nothing in terms of money, volunteering, or action to any charitable cause, and no other forms of giving except relational, of the noneffort heavy kind. As we explain further in chapter 2, Anthony is just trying to get by at this point and figure out what is next. He has no giving method because he does not give in any traditional sense.

Looking Ahead

We revisit these twelve case studies in every chapter as a way to bring life to our quantitative findings. They represent the main characters of the book, and their ranges of characteristics, regions, social statuses, giving levels, approaches to giving, personal and social orientations, and affiliations typify the findings that we examine in the remainder of this book.

A Picture of American Generosity

PARTICIPATION IN GIVING BEHAVIORS

WE BEGIN BY asking: How generous are Americans? To answer this question, we must first define *generosity*. Generosity is an inclination to give good things to others, freely and abundantly, in a way that is intended to enhance their well-being.[1] We think generosity can be actualized or expressed through various behaviors. These are sometimes referred to as "philanthropic expressions" because giving is directed at others' unmet needs, which has the effect of contributing to the collective good. In this book we concentrate on generosity to others by analyzing giving behaviors. We answer the question "How much do Americans give to others?" by presenting snapshots of participation in *nine forms of giving* that together provide a comprehensive picture of American generosity.

Of these nine forms of generosity, three are most common forms:

1. Financial giving: donating money or possessions to charitable causes
2. Volunteering: donating time or services to charitable causes.
3. Political activity: donating time to take political action or be civically involved on behalf of charitable causes.[2]

These three forms of generosity, which we call the Big 3, are the core focus of this chapter and the majority of this book, though we also undertake an analysis of six other forms of generosity:

4. Blood donation
5. Organ donation

6. Estate giving
7. Environmentally sustainable consumption
8. Possession lending
9. "Relational" giving to friends and family

These nine forms of generosity paint a more complete picture of American generosity than most other studies because we treat a generous inclination as something that may be expressed through any of these forms of giving (see Appendix Table A.1.1 for participation rates in all nine forms of generosity).

We surveyed Americans about a wide variety of charitable causes. (See Appendix Table A.1.2.a for further details.)[3] For each charitable cause, we asked respondents whether they gave money, volunteered time, or took political action. For each "yes" answer, we followed up by asking about their participation level, meaning the amount of money they donated during the past year[4] or the number of hours they spent volunteering or taking political action for that cause in the past month.[5] We then combined responses across the causes to generate measures of overall participation in financial giving, volunteering, and political activity.[6] This results in a comprehensive view of participation in the Big 3 forms of generosity. For each of the Big 3, we will report on:

- *Rate of giving:* rates of giving versus not giving.
- *Amount of giving:* total amount of (a) money, (b) volunteer hours, or (c) political action hours donated by those who gave.

Our picture is therefore two-dimensional, showing both the prevalence and the amount of giving. After presenting this quantitative picture of American generosity, we take an excursus through our case studies, which qualitatively represent the range of giving trends.

Snapshot of American Financial Giving

In this section we look at the overall levels of donations among all Americans. We follow that up with a more detailed analysis that looks at donations by poverty status among nonpoor and poor Americans. The resulting picture both conforms to and breaks expectations.

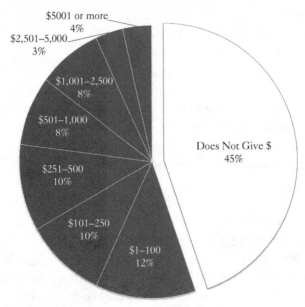

FIGURE 1.1 Financial giving in past year, combined.

Our initial snapshot of American giving presents a dismal view of the landscape, with nearly half of Americans giving nothing in the previous year to any cause, whether through a formal organization or not. Figure 1.1 displays the reported donation amounts in the previous year.[7] Of those who did give money to any of the 31 causes our survey listed, more than 30 percent donated less than $500. Only around 20 percent contributed $500 or more. In short, the picture looks quite gloomy on the face of things. But among the majority who did donate to charity, 50 percent donated substantial sums of money.

What explains this gap between the majority of Americans with little to no participation in financial giving and the minority with high participation? People commonly assume that resources limit people's ability to donate money and that those who give a great deal of money are wealthy and well-resourced. Certainly resources are a part of the explanation, but we present evidence showing that resources do not entirely explain the differences. We break down the financial resources snapshot into raw numbers and proportion of income in order to more closely examine giving patterns and the influence of financial resources.

We start by examining donation rates and amounts by poverty status (seen in Figure 1.2).[8] On the surface these results fit existing

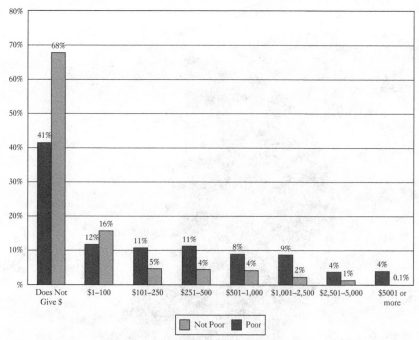

FIGURE 1.2 Annual financial giving total by poverty level.

assumptions: people in poverty represent a greater proportion of those who give nothing and are 1.5 times more likely to not donate money than others, and givers who are not impoverished donate larger amounts, on average. However, digging deeper we find that appearances can be deceiving.

When we look at the percentage of income that is donated, we see that giving does not increase proportionally with wealth and resources. Figure 1.3 displays annual financial donations as a percentage of household income for Americans not in poverty.[9] Forty percent of nonpoor Americans donated none of their income in the previous year; an additional 50 percent gave only a small amount, 3 percent or less of their income. More than 25 percent of nonpoor Americans gave less than *half of 1 percent* of their annual income. A small minority, only 3 percent of nonpoor Americans, reported contributing 10 percent or more.

When we examine financial giving as a percentage of income by poverty status (Figure 1.4), we see that poor Americans are more likely to give zero dollars. However, the combination of 0–1 percent givers reveals that nonpoor Americans are more than twice as likely to give less than 1 percent of their annual household income to charitable causes. When the

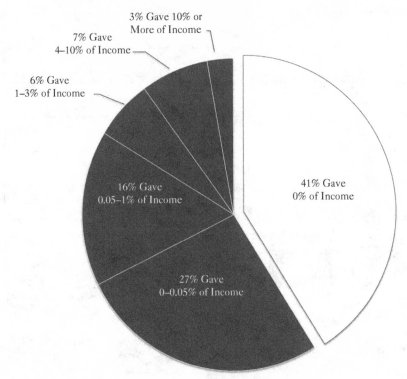

FIGURE 1.3 Percentage of annual household income given to any cause.

categories above 1 percent are combined, there are no differences by poverty status for those who give 1 percent or more of their income. In fact
giving 1 to 3 percent and more than 10 percent is slightly more likely for
poor Americans. Given the many fixed costs of living, the sacrifice related
to donating 1 percent or more of their income is higher for people in poverty than others giving at this level. Looking at the snapshot in this light
demonstrates the tremendous generosity that can be found among those
with the least financial resources and the overall thinness of generosity
among many with more financial resources.

To summarize, we find that many Americans gave nothing, some gave
a little, and a few gave generously. Nearly 50 percent of all Americans gave
nothing to charitable causes of any kind in the past year, and 25 percent
of all Americans gave more than $500. While giving is tied to income,
we find giving among Americans in poverty that may be considered quite
generous relative to giving by Americans not in poverty. About 30 percent
of Americans who are struggling to meet their own basic needs gave to
charitable causes. Conversely many nonpoor Americans give at low levels,

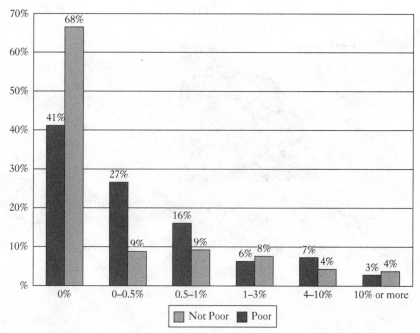

FIGURE 1.4 Annual financial giving as a percentage of household income by poverty level.

with less than 50 percent donating 1 percent or more of their income to charitable causes.

Snapshot of American Volunteering

Perhaps the somewhat dim picture of American generosity is brightened when we account for Americans' giving of time instead of money. To examine this we divide the analysis into volunteering time to charitable causes and taking political action on behalf of causes.

When we examine rates of giving time or services to charitable causes,[10] we find an even more dismal snapshot for volunteering than for financial giving: 75 percent of Americans reported no volunteering in the past month (Figure 1.5).[11] About 10 percent volunteered one to 10 hours in the past month. To put this into perspective, the typical American with eight hours of sleep per night is awake 480 hours in a month; therefore 10 hours a month of volunteering constitutes less than 2 percent of waking hours. Only about 5 percent of Americans generously volunteered 10 percent or more of their waking hours to charitable causes (greater than 40 hours in

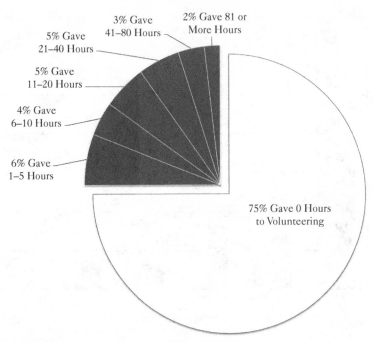

FIGURE 1.5 Volunteering in past month, combined.

a month). The vast majority of Americans do not volunteer, and only a few volunteer a great deal of their time.

What explains the overall low rates of volunteering? Does income influence ability to volunteer? The answer is yes, but volunteering and resources do not correlate linearly. The lowest income earners (those earning less than $5,000 per year) do have the lowest volunteering participation rate, with about 10 percent of people giving any of their time. Figure 1.6 shows household income level relative to the amount of hours volunteered in the past month. However, nearly 25 percent of people who earn just $10,000 to $13,000 per year still manage to volunteer. And yes, there is a general upward trend, with people at higher income levels volunteering more, but the highest earners are not those who give the greatest amount of time. Those who give the greatest time are the upper-middle-class households, with incomes of $100,000 to $150,000. Nearly 50 percent of these Americans regularly volunteer, and many volunteer a substantial number of hours. Thus while in general those with more resources volunteer larger amounts of time per month to charitable causes, there is a good deal of variation in the upper echelon of income earners.

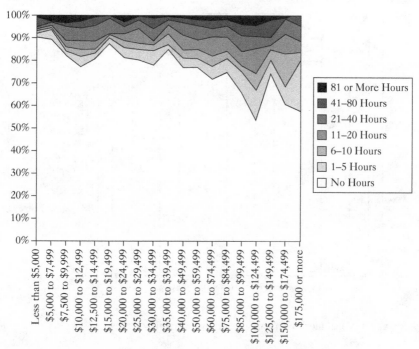

FIGURE 1.6 Volunteering in past month by household income.

Perhaps volunteering is related to availability of time. Yet the data also resist supporting this common sense notion. A lack of free time does not appear to explain lower levels of volunteering (see Figure 1.7). While time availability appears to play a role, it is not the case that busy Americans gave no time. Hours spent volunteering are quite evenly distributed among the groups; most volunteer a few hours a month. In fact about 25 percent of full-time workers or full-time students and 33 percent of part-time workers or students spent time volunteering in the past month. Moreover 20 percent of nonelderly, retired Americans donated time, only slightly more than do disabled or elderly Americans. Although we may think of these two groups as having a similar number of available hours, we would presume that the disabled and elderly status would make them less available to volunteer than the more able-bodied retirees. Stay-at-home parents are the most active volunteers, with nearly half volunteering regularly. Stay-at-home parents and part-time workers and students are exceptions, with most offering more time per month than others and stay-at-home parents being the most active (nearly half volunteer).

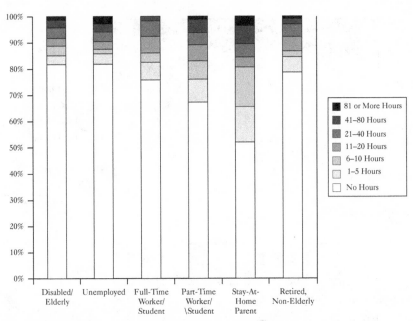

FIGURE 1.7 Volunteering in past month by availability status.

An interesting caveat is that when we interview Americans who do not currently volunteer, they often say that they intend to do so when they have more time later in their life (i.e., after they retire). However, if the current generation of retirees is representative of future generations, we would expect only 5 percent of today's nonvolunteering, full-time workers to begin volunteering when they retire. That leaves the bulk of volunteering to the busiest Americans, namely workers, students, and parents.

Perhaps Americans are busy with other responsibilities besides their jobs that limit their amount of spare time.[12] To investigate the notion of available time in another way, we compare discretionary time to volunteering time. Our measure of discretionary time sums the hours that our respondents reported watching TV, surfing the Internet (not for work-related tasks), and shopping for nonessential goods (goods besides, say, groceries).[13] We refer to the total of time spent on these three activities as "leisuring" hours and compare these to the hours respondents spent volunteering per month. When we look at the patterns between leisuring and volunteering, we find nearly an inverse relationship, with more volunteering time related to less leisuring time.

Figure 1.8 compares the percentage of estimated waking, nonworking hours spent volunteering in the past month (left) to the percentage of

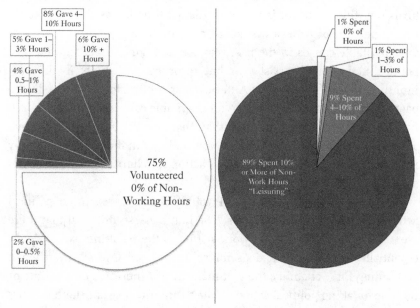

FIGURE 1.8 Volunteering in past month (left) and time spent on "leisuring" as a percentage of estimated nonworking hours (right).

estimated waking, nonworking hours spent on leisure in the past month (right).[14] Here we also can observe a related pattern, namely that Americans contribute significantly greater proportions of their discretionary time to leisuring than they do to volunteering for charitable causes. Specifically 75 percent of Americans spent zero hours in the past month volunteering, while fewer than 1 percent spent zero hours on leisure. Conversely 6 percent of Americans spent 10 percent or more of their discretionary hours volunteering, while 89 percent spent 10 percent or more of their discretionary hours on leisuring.

In summary, we see little evidence that Americans compensate for their low level of financial donation by giving time to charitable causes. Quite the opposite appears to be the case. Americans spend far more hours on personal leisure activities than on volunteering. Those with the greatest financial resources and those who theoretically have the most free time to give do not volunteer the most.

Snapshot of American Political Action

Perhaps Americans contribute some of their time to another form of generosity, namely taking political action for charitable causes. As it turns out, this snapshot is the most dismal thus far, as the vast majority, 80 percent of Americans, spent no time taking political action for any charitable causes in the past year. An additional 6 percent did take political action in the past year but recorded no activity in the past month.[15] In fact 8 percent of Americans spent one to five hours in the past month taking political action for charitable causes, and only a handful of Americans gave more time than that (see Figure 1.9). Thus while 21 percent of Americans spent time volunteering in the past month, only 13 percent spent time taking political action for charitable causes, a considerable drop in participation.

Mirroring our investigation in volunteering, we examine political action hours by availability status. The hours are so minimal that there are hardly any differences by work status, so the resulting pattern looks essentially the same as it does for volunteering.[16] Overall, even when accounting for availability, the vast majority of Americans devote little or no time to taking political action, while a minority give substantial hours of time.

When we compare political action time to potential discretionary time, we again see a pattern similar to that of volunteering: 95 percent of Americans spend twice as much or more time on leisure as on political action each month. Only 4 percent spend about the same amount of time on both activities, and a mere 1 percent spend twice as much

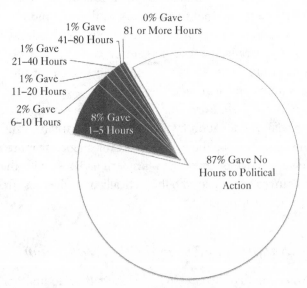

FIGURE 1.9 Political action in past month, combined.

or more time taking political action for charitable causes as they do on leisure.

In summary, the political action snapshot is even more dimmer than the volunteering snapshot, with 90 percent of Americans spending no time on political action in the past month. Financial resources again play a role but do not fully explain this dearth of action. Nor is this dearth entirely attributable to availability; as for volunteering, time spent on political action is severely outweighed by personal leisure time, with 95 percent of Americans spending at least twice as much time watching TV, surfing the Internet, or shopping as taking political action.

Picture of Time Given

In a final analysis we take a brief look at the combined time to volunteer and take political action in order to assess if by viewing the two under the same lens we can brighten our image of American giving. Figure 1.10 illustrates how nonwork time is distributed toward answering: What proportion of time do Americans spend on volunteering and political action compared to leisure and other activities? We have used estimates of waking and work hours to generate this chart, so it is not meant to be analyzed with any specificity; rather it provides a visual summary of our respondents' approximate use of time. The respondents are sorted according to the proportion of time they spent leisuring (bottom), and the chart illustrates how the combination of leisure and other activities fills Americans' nonwork, discretionary hours. The lines representing volunteering and political action time are short and often barely discernible. There are a few exceptions in which political action or volunteering consumes more of a respondent's free time than leisure and other activities. However, in the vast majority of occurrences, volunteering and political action are mere blips on the radar of how Americans use their time.

When we compare volunteering and political action to other uses of Americans' spare time, the picture grows dimmer yet. The vast majority of Americans spend more than twice as much of their discretionary time on shopping as on volunteering or taking political action. Even for people with the most available time (e.g., nonelderly retirees, the unemployed, and part-time workers/students), shopping still consumes as much time as volunteering and taking political action combined. Thus

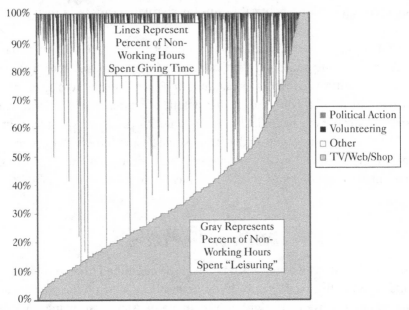

FIGURE I.IO Percentage of nonwork time spent on leisure, volunteering, political action, and other activities.

even when we exclude watching TV and surfing the Internet, which may occur during night hours when people cannot easily donate their time, we still see an incredibly low amount of spare time donated to any charitable cause.

So while simply combining the numbers of volunteering and political action does allow for a slight improvement in our picture of American giving, the snapshot is still quite dim. Volunteering and especially political action are rare activities for all but a handful of Americans whose donated time exceeds the time they devote to other discretionary activities. Even for Americans who have relatively large amounts of discretionary time, volunteering and political action take up few hours compared to the hours spent watching TV, surfing the Internet, or shopping. Able-bodied and nonelderly Americans and those who work less than full time donate slightly more hours, but still just a small proportion of their overall discretionary time.

Based on this analysis of the Big 3 forms of giving, it appears that Americans are not terribly generous with their money or their time, at least not on a regular basis. There are a number of other ways that people can give, however, and we will examine these other forms of generosity before we dive deeper into analyses of why Americans differ in their giving.

Snapshot of the "Little 6" American Generosity Forms

While giving money, volunteering, and taking political action are three major ways that people give of themselves for the collective good, there are six other possible forms of giving that constitute what we term the "Little 6."

Donating Blood and Organs. Blood and organ donations are unique categories in that they both rely on truly giving of oneself. *Giving blood* refers to the unpaid donation of blood among those who are physically able to donate.

Estate Giving and Possession Lending. Estate giving and possession lending each look at how individuals make use of their possessions, either during their life as a loan or at their death as an inheritance. *Estate giving* refers to provisions in a will or trust to donate wealth or property to charitable causes. Two standards were used to measure lending possessions: whether a valuable personal possession, such as a tool, book, appliance, or other item, was loaned to a friend or acquaintance who needed it or might benefit from it ("lending"), and whether the lender expected the item to be returned ("lending to give").

Environmental Sustainability Giving. We refer to Americans' participation in consuming environmentally friendly, organic, or fair-trade products—even if these items cost more—as "sustainability giving." While most of the forms of generosity we discuss in this book have to do with giving away a resource, sustainable consumption is a form of giving that contributes to the collective good in a different way, often through spending (as a form of giving). For example, people who pay more money for resources that cause less harm to others or that make less of an impact on the environment than other resources incur a personal cost that contributes to a good. These people may end up having less money available to give to charitable causes as a result of this form of giving. Also we can imagine that the need for charitable causes redressing the damages caused by harmful consumption habits could decrease if this form of generosity were practiced more widely.

Relational Giving. What we call "relational giving"[17] refers to the frequency with which people (a) visit with family relatives in person or have them visit, (b) have friends over to their home, (c) take care of other people's children, (d) watch over the house or property of friends who are away, or (e) help a friend or neighbor with a job at their house or property.[18] We all know people who sacrifice their own needs to give attention to their friends, relatives, and acquaintances. Like sustainability giving, this kind of generosity has the potential to benefit the collective good. It also may make these givers less able to contribute time to volunteering or other forms of giving.

Next we analyze participation in each of these generous activities. As with the Big 3 forms of giving, levels of participation remain low across the Little 6. While there are some forms that trend higher than others, the picture of American generosity is not fantastically brightened by the addition of these six forms. Figure 1.11 depicts Americans' participation in the Little 6 forms of generosity.

Organ and blood donation varied significantly in their levels of practice. We find that 88 percent of those physically able to give blood did not do so in the past year, leaving only slightly more than 10 percent of able-bodied Americans donating their blood for others. Organ donation had one of the highest participation rates of any generosity type we examined, with 40 percent of Americans claiming to be organ donors. More surprising,

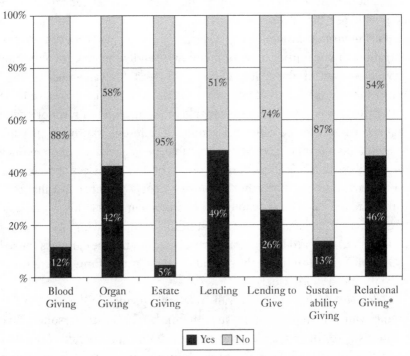

FIGURE 1.11 Participation in other forms of generosity.

however, is that becoming an organ donor is as easy as checking a box when getting a driver's license or ID card, and yet nearly 60 percent of Americans did not offer to donate their organs after they die. While some Americans have religious or other belief-based reasons for declining to participate in this type of generosity, they are unlikely to account for this low overall rate.

Estate giving had the lowest participation rate of any form of generosity we examined; only 5 percent of Americans are leaving some property or possessions to charitable causes through their will. The process of donating via a will is much more complicated than becoming an organ donor. In fact 70 percent of Americans do not have a will in place. However, of the 30 percent of Americans who do have a will, only 15 percent donate their estate resources to charitable causes.

Lending possessions seems on the surface our best bet for brightening the picture of American generosity, but any positives associated come with a significant caveat. Lending possessions to friends or acquaintances had the highest participation rate of all the forms of generosity, with nearly 50 percent of Americans loaning something valuable to help someone else in the past year. However, when we asked respondents if they would lend to someone if there were a chance the possession would not be returned, participation was cut in half.

The rate of sustainability giving—sometimes referred to as socially and environmentally conscious consumption—was also low. Only 14 percent of Americans ever bought sustainable products if they cost more than less-sustainable options. We might expect this form to be among the highest levels of participation since it does not necessarily require extra effort or availability on the part of the giver and may not require expending more resources. However, it likely does entail spending time to investigate available options. Some Americans may unknowingly pick sustainable options, but describing themselves this way on the survey would require that they invested effort in investigating available product options, thereby potentially explaining its low rate.

Relational giving, the final factor, had one of the highest participation rates of any form of generosity, with nearly 50 percent of Americans giving through their interpersonal relationships. However, this also meant that slightly more than 50 percent do *not* visit with, care for, or help their family and friends more than a handful of times per year.

The broad definition and high rates of relational giving make this form of giving worth analyzing a bit further. In examining the relational generosity of those who participated in each type of relational giving activity semiregularly (i.e., more than three times a year), we found that visiting with family in person was the most common activity, with 95 percent of relationally generous Americans at least somewhat regularly visiting with family. While relational giving has one of the highest levels of participation, closer examination reveals that most of this activity may be more about hanging out than providing intensive support to others.

To explore this further we look at relational givers' participation in "effort-heavy" forms of relational giving, such as child care, house-sitting, and helping with jobs (see Figure 1.12). We find that only 50 percent of relational givers perform these effort-heavy activities. About 33 percent do so at least a few times a year, and 20 percent do so regularly. We refer to this last group as "high-frequency, effort-heavy relational givers." Relational givers often incur costs for supplies, utilities, and transportation as well as their lost earning potential.

When we examine the role of resources in relational giving, we see that relational giving is correlated with financial resources, but not in the way one might expect. Americans in poverty are significantly *more* likely than nonpoor Americans to be high-frequency, effort-heavy relational givers

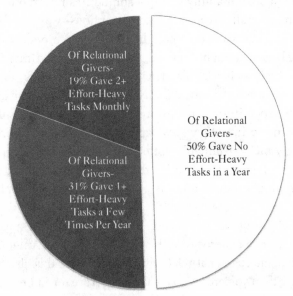

FIGURE 1.12 Effort-heavy relational giving (child care, house-sitting, job helping).

(not displayed). This is despite the fact that poor Americans likely must expend more resources than nonpoor Americans to help others in their interpersonal network.

To review: We find participation rates in alternative forms of generosity to be generally low. No form of generosity is performed by the majority of Americans. Some forms of generosity have particularly low participation rates, namely giving blood, estate giving, and sustainability giving. The highest participation rates are in activities that require the least amount of effort: organ donation (requiring only checking a box on a form), lending possessions (which is less prevalent when there is a chance the item will not be returned), and relational giving (which is most widespread in its least effort-intensive forms).

Summary of the American Generosity Picture

Having pieced together the snapshots of various forms of giving, we are left with a fairly dim picture of American generosity. While few people do not participate in giving at all, the vast majority are not regularly generous. Forty percent of Americans do not give away money, more than 70 percent do not volunteer their time, and 90 percent do not regularly take political action for charitable causes. Only 50 percent of Americans regularly relationally give, and only 20 percent participate in effort-heavy relational giving that is akin to informal volunteering. American generosity is unevenly distributed: many give little, and a few give tremendously.

As we zoom out from the specific snapshots we have described here, it is important to note that each of these is a single frame of a highly dynamic and nuanced scene. We have captured a good bit of data, but these data do not amount yet to a definitive take. For example, many people may be generous in one way or another at different points in their lives, yet—for whatever reason—they were not able to participate in certain giving behaviors within the past month or year in which we took the survey, leaving their giving activities invisible to our investigation. These snapshots are good at providing us a look at the distribution of generosity at any one moment among Americans, but that is their limit: a moment in time. Without a doubt, generosity exists in many forms, in all places, and across all levels of the socioeconomic spectrum, in a dynamic way. This dynamic give and take is why we include our twelve case studies. They offer a more complex exploration of the ways these generosity patterns fit together for real people.

Case Study Excursus

We breathe life into our static quantitative snapshots by investigating participation (or a lack of participation) in these various forms of generosity for each of our qualitative case studies. This begins by looking at participants who exemplify Big 3 giving practices, then cases that better exemplify the Little 6 forms, and then cases with low participation in any giving.

Case Studies of the Big 3

To explore the Big 3 further through qualitative data, we will look at Susan Baker, Ryan Dewey, Jackie Sawyer, Cindy Phelps, and Michael Johnson.

Susan Baker: Upper-Middle-Class "One and Done" Los Angeleno

Susan Baker gives large amounts of money, volunteers many hours, and even takes some political action. Her case shows how being a highly resourced, upper-middle-class woman helps enable her generosity. She also engages in nearly all other forms of giving, including effort-heavy relational giving. As a very generous giver, Susan exemplifies the ways a high giver thinks about her activities and makes giving a priority in the midst of a busy life.

Susan's general motto is "I think it's more important to care for people than to give away money," yet she still gives over $2,000 a year to charitable causes. When we asked her, "How much do you tend to think about or pay attention to the issue of volunteering—of giving time to charity, religion, or other good or needy causes or people?," she replied:

> Oh I, well I think about it a lot cause it's pretty much a part of my day, every day. . . . I think everyone should volunteer. . . . I think everybody needs to give back. I think that volunteering time, everybody can afford some. And I think it's critical for our community that everybody does some because it's a way to actually touch and feel other people and have a stronger community.

Later in the interview we asked Susan, "About how much time do you spend volunteering for each of the groups that you volunteer for?" She replied, "A million hours [laughs] ... about 40 hours a month." Thus Susan is personally and highly committed to giving to others, especially through volunteer work and effort-heavy relational giving.

We asked, "What do you think gives you that desire to volunteer? Where do you think that comes from?" She replied, "I don't know. Part of it is just academic knowledge that 'thou shalt give back.' Part of it is seeing something that needs to get done and doing it. And realizing someone's gotta do it or it's not gonna get done, so. And since nobody's gonna pay me or somebody else to do it, I'll just do it." Even in discussing whether she would like to volunteer more than she does now, she gave evidence of her high commitment to volunteering as a regular part of her life:

> If there were more hours in the day, then I would certainly volunteer more. I mean there are so many projects that I would love to do. And there isn't a meeting I go to that goes by without me coming away from it and saying "I could do that!" And then thinking "Okay stop, no you can't." So it's not so much that necessarily I want to do it, but there's a need out there and I think I might be able to do a good job at it. Which is not to say I could do a good job at everything, like I never, ever, ever sign up to be on a phone bank. I never, ever, ever volunteer to solicit money. Those are things I just don't do. But like organizing events, I'm really good at that. So, if something needs to be organized, I love to jump in and do that, because I can.

This last statement hints at the themes that we will return to in chapter 4 regarding the importance of self-efficacy in believing that one's efforts can make a difference.

Another element comes through in Susan's words that she reflected on further into the interview: that sometimes it is possible to give too much. Susan described her level of interest in volunteering as almost a problem: "I've watched this pattern repeat itself over and over and over again with me. I will fill up my day with volunteer work, helping [do] whatever at the school, or whatever anyone else wants me to do, rather than spend

the time doing, cleaning my house, exercising. I don't know what it is."
Susan brings to life the issue that generosity delicately balances tending to
one's own needs and to the needs of others. Generous people, especially
those who give large amounts, express the need to be careful not to lose
themselves in too much giving to others. Susan continued by explaining
that heavy volunteering can lead to a "martyr" complex:

> Yeah, here's the problem. I don't know whether I've somehow
> inherited my mother's martyr complex. I hope not, cause hers has
> led her astray. But objectively, when I sit there and look at my time,
> I mean everyone's got the same 24 hours in a day and it sucks,
> cause we could use some more. But I do my fair share of goofing
> off too. I watch more TV than I should. So certainly that hour or
> two I spend every day watching TV, I could certainly be doing some-
> thing else with that time. But on the other hand, I'm not doing a
> very good job of taking care of myself. I mean I don't put that high
> enough on my priority list. And so a lot of people I know who "don't
> have the time to volunteer." It's because they're spending an hour a
> day at the gym taking care of themselves. And another two hours a
> week at their book club, and two hours a week knitting in their knit-
> ting club. So the internal clock I might have— that internal warning
> signal I might have — [never] goes off to say, "Oh now you can't
> volunteer."

Susan gives so heavily of her time and attention that she has created
a personal problem, not always remembering to attend to her own
well-being. If this problem lasts long, she may end up not being helpful
to others.

On top of all her volunteering, Susan and her husband have also been
regular participants in a program in which they host exchange students
in their home. But Susan is juggling so many forms of generosity that
she had trouble remembering the exchange hosting as something to discuss. To prompt her to summarize her relational giving, we asked her,
"Thinking about your personal relationships with other people, would
you say you are a giving person?" She replied, "See the, when I think of
that word, I think of that word as an emotional word. Emotionally giving. So I guess I would say I'm not. But if it's in the sense of giving your
time, then that's an obvious one [yes]." We followed up, "Do you spend
a lot of time taking care of other people?" Susan replied, "Taking care of

other people? . . . I wouldn't use those words. My daughter self-raises, so I don't feel like I really take care of her. [My husband is] a grown man, I don't take care of him." We then asked, "Has there ever been someone other than your immediate family who lives in your home?" Susan then recounted, "Oh yeah, we've had exchange students up the wazoo. We've had more than, sadly, I can count or remember." Susan summarized all the foreign-exchange hosting they have done over the years by saying, "I tend to put other people's wants and needs above my own. I guess I don't really think of it as a sacrifice. Yeah."

In summary, Susan and her husband give away large sums of money, and Susan regularly volunteers and relationally gives, including effort-heavy forms such as hosting foreign-exchange students. Giving appears to be part of the fabric of her life, wrapped up with her very identity. Though she is a busy, middle-class woman, she finds a way to make time—perhaps even to a fault—to give of her resources to help others.

Ryan Dewey: High-Achieving, Religious Midwesterner

Ryan also exemplifies the life of a high giver, especially relative to his current standing as a graduate student. He gives a high percentage of his income and volunteers a large proportion of his discretionary time, which is limited. When we looked at financial giving as a percentage of income, he was one of the most generous financial givers among our interviewees. He lives on a modest graduate stipend (which some students consider too meager to live on without a student loan supplement), and yet he gives away a significant portion of this salary.

Ryan describes the targets and amounts of his giving by saying, "To the local church, I give 10 percent of my income, which is probably, over the course of the year, about $2,000. World Vision I pay two installments over the year, and I think it's about $40 a month per child, so that is probably about $1,000 a year."

He also volunteers a good deal of his available time, explaining that he volunteers time for charitable and religious causes because he sees it as part of an overall equation to give on behalf of others through either money or time, or some combination:

I'd say because there sorta is a time-money equation involved there, so I think your giving could be in terms of time, but it could also be in terms of money. I think there is a moral obligation to give, but

exactly how that is broken down between time and money is probably pretty flexible.

Considering Ryan is a graduate student in a reputable program, in which
some students find they barely have time to eat, let alone sleep, it is impres-
sive that he finds the time to give an average of about 11 hours a month to
help out with Campus Crusade for Christ. This is an especially intensive
program that reaches out to international students to help build a community and practice speaking English with other students.

Though Ryan is very generous financially and with his time, he is not
interested in taking political action. He said:

> I just feel like it is not something I could really see myself doing,
> and hence I am not very political. I think I am fairly well-informed
> about a lot of political issues, and I think I have opinions about
> these issues, and I definitely want the best for my community, but
> I don't think I would ever be one of those people who would be
> out in the streets running a rally or that sort of thing, so I don't
> know. "Politically interested, but not politically active" would be how
> I would describe myself.

Ryan's response represents a prototypical perspective among the vast
majority of our interviewees regarding participation in political activities
for charitable causes.

In summary, Ryan is a high giver who manages to donate time and
money out of his more modest resources. He explains his strong commitments to giving as stemming from his religious beliefs, and he has no
interest in political action activities.

Jackie Sawyer: Thrifty, Type-A, Religious, Midwestern Mom

Jackie is another high giver who takes a tithing approach to her monetary
donations and who also volunteers and gives relationally. Jackie and her
husband give a very large amount of money, especially relative to their
income level. They consider a 10 percent tithe to their church the baseline
of their giving. Additionally they give money to various causes:

> Church gets the top 10 percent; that goes to our organized congre-
> gation. Then there's another, probably 5 percent that, like I said,

that gets shuffled off and then it goes here, there, and everywhere. The kids' school gets a decent amount. If they need something, they—we find a way. . . . And then, there's other random [stuff, e.g., a mission trip, supporting an international child]. . . . There's things that come up at church, a memorial fund for a young mom with two little kids. I have a friend who couldn't pay tuition for school, and we paid her tuition. So there's just kind of random, assorted things that cover the rest of it.

Thus the Sawyers give away approximately 20 percent of their after-tax income to their church and various other charitable causes.

Jackie also devotes a lot of time to volunteering for charitable causes. She said that she volunteers "through church. I teach a class to the two- and three-year-olds once a month." She also volunteers at her children's school "to serve hot lunch twice a month," "volunteering to drive for field trips," "volunteering to schedule all the fair workers," and "painting for several eight-hour days already this summer." She continued, "It's just a lot of hours for school stuff . . . and then there's all the other assorted things that just crop up, and you find [out] about where they need a hand." She also appears to be generous in her relationships:

> I'd say probably helping someone in need is more important than the giving of the money. The being able to be of assistance for a human being is huge. . . . Because, I guess, if someone's physical needs aren't met, someone's emotional needs, the need to be able to function, then it doesn't really matter if you give money because money doesn't fix it. They have to be emotionally stable or—you have to meet those needs before you can meet financial needs.

Jackie finds a way to give of her time and attention relationally and still maintain volunteering and financial giving.

In summary, Jackie represents a tither who, with her husband, gives large donations to their church and other charitable causes. She also exemplifies how a busy stay-at-home mother finds time to volunteer and be interpersonally generous through her relationships. Her approach to giving seems to start in her immediate circle and radiate outward, and she focuses her giving attention primarily on her family, close friends, and religious congregation.

Cindy Phelps: Young, Professional Texan Tutors in New York City

Cindy exemplifies someone who volunteers her time, albeit modestly, in the midst of a busy work schedule. She is also representative of Americans who do not give anything financially, despite available economic resources. In her case this appears to be due primarily to her persistent sense of financial insecurity, which seems to be a result of her mother having to file for bankruptcy during Cindy's teenage years: "When I was younger, my family was pretty well off.... But when I turned 13, my parents got divorced. So there was some financial difficulties. My mom filed for bankruptcy. So that was very, things were very bad at that time." She goes on to say, "But things are better now." Yet financial instability remains a worry for Cindy. When we asked her, "How much do you tend to think about or pay attention to the issue of financial giving—of giving money to charity, religion, or other good or needy causes or people?," she said:

> I don't think about it very much. But I have given money.... I mean I'll get like a mailer, like a St. Jude, the children's network. I guess I've given them money before, so I get mailers all the time. And so I'm like "Oh I should probably give to them again," because I use all those little address stickers that they send in the mail. So I think about that sometimes, but it's nothing that, it's not really on my radar.

We followed up by asking, "Do you have any idea why it's not a big thing in your life?" And Cindy replied, "Probably because I don't have, other than just giving $50 here and there maybe. It's not something I really have the wherewithal to do, to make huge gifts to anyone or like set up my own kind of foundation. Just financially limited."

Despite giving very little of her relatively high income, Cindy does volunteer regularly. We asked her how much she thinks about volunteering, and she said, "I think about it quite often because during the school year I volunteer through the Junior League with programs for after-school children and programs for Section 8 housing residents." She does this once a week for a couple hours. It seems mostly to be a work-networking opportunity, however, though it is still a way that she gives to the community.

Like so many Americans we talked to, Cindy specifically chooses not to be involved in taking any kind of political action:

> I try not to get involved in politics. I really, I just try not to get involved. I mean I'm aware of politics and people's positions on

things. I mean, I plan on voting. I just think that the state legislature is so messed up. I mean politics here, politicians here are on a scale the worst schmucks you've ever come across. It's ridiculous.

In summary, Cindy is a modest volunteer of her time despite being among those with the least discretionary time available. She does not give financially, despite having economic means, apparently due to a residual financial insecurity from her childhood that colors her perception of her economic resource availability. And she exemplifies someone who gives possessions as a form of generosity.

Michael Johnson: Hard-Working, Politicking, D.C. Widower Takes Action

Among our more unusual Big 3 givers, Michael is prototypical of the few Americans who put most of their "giving eggs" into the basket of political action. Being politically active is so central to his identity that when we asked him if he thought life had a purpose, he responded, "I think life has a, certainly has purpose. And I think it's more than just what you're doing for yourself, and also for your family, but also what you do for others." He then recounted a number of things he had helped accomplish through taking political action and described them as "an achievement, in my judgment, and something that I could point to and was very satisfied in terms of achieving." When we followed up by asking if he could put his life purpose into one or two sentences, he said:

> I would say that it is to be helpful for others as well as working for your own interests and your family's interests. One simple sentence, I guess, compound[ed]. I mean the fact that you can do more than one thing, and these things are not mutually exclusive. I mean you can work to benefit your family but also work to benefit others too.

In this way Michael explicated how taking political action on behalf of the collective good was a core part of his identity and life purpose. One reason he is so politically involved may be that in his career he has met many people who are also well-educated and generally active in their community. He describes this by saying, "One of the things that benefits me in terms of my work is that I come in contact with so many different kinds of people. And you try to draw upon what you think are the good aspects, their personalities and their lives."

Michael does not think other Americans have the same degree of political consciousness:

> At times, I mean from a political standpoint, I become sort of dis-
> enchanted with the way that I think Americans react, but this is not
> going to make me a manic-depressive or something like that. I love
> my country very much, but I think that Americans have a tendency
> to be very lazy from a political standpoint. What are examples? More
> than half the people in the country cannot identify their U.S. rep-
> resentative. I think more than half the people in the country could
> not even identify one single Supreme Court justice. Americans are
> not all that well-informed as they should be, in my view.

Perhaps his motivation to give so much of his time to political causes is the
thought that no one else will do it.

While Michael also participates in giving monetarily and in other types
of volunteering, these also have political angles. His main financial giving is to support political causes: "I contribute to political campaigns.
I would say the past election, for 2008, I'm estimating maybe like $2,500
to $3,000 I contributed." In addition to contributing financially, he also
spends time taking other forms of political action. For example:

> I write statements on a wide range of issues, on economic issues
> and aging issues, and then I've given those to certain groups. I was
> asked at one time to run for office and was very seriously consider-
> ing [it]. This was very long ago. I was much younger. And my wife
> was a little reticent about privacy, and we decided, well, she pre-
> ferred to have our privacy, and I thought this was a joint decision,
> and so I went along with what she said, and I did not, you know,
> run for office.

In summary, Michael exemplifies the kind of American giver who contributes toward the betterment of others through taking political action.
Even his financial and other volunteer activities are politically directed.

Big 3 Summary

Susan, Jackie, and Michael show that one's resources do aid in creating
a more abundant and robust giving portfolio. And yet Ryan and Cindy
demonstrate that having financial means is not a key that automatically

unlocks generosity in people. Ryan is able to practice high levels of giving despite his currently limited financial resources, and Cindy is able to practice moderate levels of volunteering despite her busy work schedule. Thus these case studies illustrate our quantitative findings that resources clearly play a role in people's generosity, but they do not entirely determine it.

Case Studies of the Little 6

We now move to our cases of people who are less invested in giving through the Big 3 forms of generosity but who still find ways to give to others, primarily through more relational means: George Nettleson, Linda Chesterfield, and Tanika Sandaval.

George Nettleson: Comfortable, Religious Southerner Takes Time

George makes time to be relationally generous and caring to his network of friends and family. While he does not talk a great deal about relational giving efforts, he did say:

> Your circles of caring diminish in importance as they go out from you. So it's more important to tell your spouse, and your children, and then your family and close friends, to let them know how much you care about them and love them and actually care for them. If everybody did that, there wouldn't be as much need to care beyond that, I guess. So I think it's very important.

George is someone who spends a good deal of time being relationally available and participating in some volunteer activities.

Linda Chesterfield: Midwestern Soccer Mom Puts Family First

Linda participates in Big 3 giving only because of the financial giving of her husband. She used to volunteer but does not currently, exemplifying the dynamic nature of giving participation over time. The primary means through which Linda herself, a stay-at-home mom of eight, gives is being relationally available to her children. She thinks she may be relationally generous to a fault, allowing herself to be taken advantage of by others.

Linda explained that the money that their household gives to charitable causes is really due to her husband's preference, not hers. When asked about specific people, organizations, or causes to which she gives, Linda said:

> Our church, both of [my husband's] colleges. What I actually do like to do [is] for the kids, their school, they'll have these different read-a-thons or math-a-thons that part of the proceeds go to St. Jude, which was my mom's favorite charity. So I like to do that. But it's, because I don't work, it's not my money to give away!

When asked to enumerate her financial giving, she said, "I really have no idea. I don't even know what we currently give to the church every week or what he gives to his colleges." We asked why they donate money, to which she replied, "Cause my husband wants to. And it's, if somebody asks us to, and we can, and we're in this situation. And as far as his colleges go, I think it's important to give back to your school, if you can."

It is worth noting that the amount of money her household gives seems to have dramatically increased between the time of the survey and the time of the interview. On the survey Linda's husband recounted that they gave about $25 per year to charitable causes. However, during his interview he enumerated about $5,000 in annual giving. We think that the recent conflict regarding his giving to his alma maters may indicate relatively recent large donations. Though we do not know this for sure, it is possible that his actions were a result of his participation in our survey. A number of our interviewees recounted at the end of their interviews that participating in the survey and interviewing process made them reflect on their giving more than they ever had, and so perhaps even asking these questions resulted in a more conscious reflection to give. The disgruntle-ment expressed by Linda may be due to her husband's change in giving amounts. In any case, Linda clearly did not share her husband's desire to give financially, and instead views her attention to her children as her giving.

Asked whether she volunteers, Linda said, "Not currently. Like I said, I did teach religion, which was all voluntary for years, but I haven't done that [recently], so no, currently nothing." Despite having an intense family life that demands a great deal of her attention, she described herself as a highly relationally generous person: "I'm a giving person. I love to help out others when I can. I'm a good listener. I'm always there to give peo-ple advice." Like other interviewees who practiced high relational giving,

Linda is concerned that her kindness puts her in a vulnerable position, especially toward her children:

> There are some times that I think they [the children], they take advantage of my kindness and my willingness to let them do things. Like "Oh Mom will say yes. Let's not ask Dad because he'll probably be too practical, and Mom just wants us to have a good time. So we'll ask Mom." So I wish I were more consistent, and I wish I could get across the message that "I'm still your mother. You still have to respect me, and treat me the way you treat your dad."

Linda, like Susan, can see her relational giving as a problem, describing the personal and emotional toll it takes, in addition to the resources of time and effort.

In summary, Linda is a very relationally generous person who worries she may be *too* giving to her children and be getting taken advantage of by them. She volunteered in the past but does not currently, and her household is among the financial donors due to her husband's interest in giving money, which conflicts with her desire not to give financially, or at least not as much as they do now.

Tanika Sandaval: Single Los Angeles Mom Fights for Her Children's Future

Tanika exemplifies a very active, effort-heavy relational giver. Technically her giving counts as volunteering, but her explanation for why she spends so much time participating at her children's school is all about her relational generosity to better their lives.

Recall that Tanika gives very little financially but regularly volunteers. When we asked if she currently donates money to charitable causes, she said:

> Not right at this moment, but like I said, if Joel Osteen[19] is in town, something like that, definitely. Or sometimes I went to the museum, [but] it's been a couple years ago. It was the African American museum, and so we went, and there's nothing to [pay to] get in. But you can donate, so definitely I put $20 in.

Tanika goes on to explain that she has a broader conception of giving than only financially:

> When people say *giving*, it's not always with their money, and that's through church. Giving can be you helping somebody, just calling someone, saying, "Hi." Giving comes in different forms; it's not always in money.

Tanika volunteers as a community representative for her children's school and described: "I've been volunteering there for the last four years." She continues, "Like 10 hours a week, but it kinda varies within that, though, cause then you have meetings. And so that kinda [varies it]. Sometimes I don't even think about it when I'm actually doing it." By this we understood Tanika to be saying that she may undercount the hours she spends volunteering, since she does not always consider it to be volunteer effort that she clocks and tracks. When we asked her how she decided the school was a worthy target of her giving, she said:

> My children go there. Definitely cause of my children. Cause after I was community rep, I felt like I'm the leader, in a sense. You're not someone like the principal, but the leader of the school morale and the spirit of it. That's what the community rep does; you see what's going on within the communities. So I try to [steer it] right. I'm not perfect; don't get me wrong, I'm not perfect, but I try to – if you see me, nine times out of 10, I'm gonna smile and gonna say "Hi" to you. That's just the type of person that I am.

There were periods when Tanika was paid for her positions with the school, but mostly the work has been on a volunteer basis. She recounted:

> So for the last past few years with them, I've been working more or less within the schools, on committees. And from there now, last year, I was offered the community rep position, so I did that for this past year. But you know how it is with the budget, we don't know how it's gonna be coming this fall. So [I am] now currently not working, but you know . . . It's volunteer, was volunteer and then, then there was some pay. There was some pay with the position of the community rep, there was. But before then, those [other

experiences] don't pay. It is just the experience being there and helping all the children.

Being involved in her children's school is very important to Tanika and
something she discussed passionately throughout the interview. For
example, when we asked her, "What things in the past couple of years have
made you the most happy or excited?," she paused and then said, "I guess
being involved [with] my kids, within the school, learning more within the
school system, how things work in that arena, and then meeting the different parents and people—that's been the most exciting lately."

Tanika describes her commitment to volunteering by saying, "I feel like
you [should] give something. It's not the same not to give." She continued,
"I do it. Just do it. I mean it's like, sometimes you feel like you don't have a
choice in a sense, cause if you want something done, you want something
[done] right. Yeah it comes down to volunteering—being there."

Tanika's primary reasons for volunteering are to support her children's
education and be a part of a support community with the other parents:

Definitely because of my children and [to] know what's going on
with their education. Then again to give, it's like for me with other
parents to come together, support with the other parents. And [you]
see what's going on. I call it the triangle. Where the child's on top.
That's the priority with everything, the child or the children. Second
is the teachers, [next] the parents. So you put that, next that [indi-
cating the top point of the triangle and then the two bottom points
connecting to it]. I call it my little angel triangle.

Volunteering in this sense is an extension of Tanika's parenting.

While Tanika does not give through any of the other generosity forms,
she said she would do so, if it came down to a relational need involving
her children. For example, when we asked if she was a registered organ
donor, she said, "No, no, no," but then continued, "I would [register], if
something was [to] happen to any of my children and that's what they
needed, in a heartbeat. My immediate family, in a heartbeat . . . if I had to
give, I would do it." She went on to describe the ways in which she is relationally generous:

When I'm helping someone, making someone just smile. Knowing
that I'm able [to] just be able to help somebody in any kind of way.

Sometimes persons needs a little encouragement or just a little push, "You did good." You know, [to] be that team player.

In summary, Tanika exemplifies someone who volunteers regularly out of a desire to relationally give her children a better life. She is also an example of how giving can be significantly dampened by a lack of economic resources, as she seems to be someone who would give more financially if she could. However, her case also complicates a resource-only storyline, since her limited resources actually fuel her relational investment into her children's school.

Case Studies of Limited Giving

The final four cases studies represent more limited forms of participation in any kind of generous activities. Some help to exemplify how someone with means equivalent to our more engaged givers winds up not giving as much, and others help to shed light on what appear to be baseline economic and social resources needed to be able to give beyond taking care of oneself. The four case studies representing more limited giving are Regina Buckner, Deon Williams, Rosa Perez, and Anthony Ross.

Regina Buckner: Southern, Rural, Stay-at-Home Mom Takes It Day by Day

In Regina's case, having the same availability and resources as a more engaged giver does not translate into giving. Like Tanika, Regina is a busy stay-at-home mom, but she is not involved in volunteering on behalf of her children to the same extent as Tanika. Perhaps this is because all her children are not yet in school, or perhaps it reflects the differences in rural and urban environments. In any case, Regina is among our low-giving cases. She described the amount of money she gives to charitable causes by saying, "It's usually between $10 and $15. It's usually because they ask for outlandish amounts, and I'm like, 'Yeah, I don't think so. Sorry' [laughs]."

In the interview Regina reported giving very little time to volunteering. However, on the survey she reported giving 40 hours a month to charitable causes. We suspect that she may have counted the hours she spends caring for her children and visiting them at school when reporting on the survey the amount of unpaid time that she gives away. In talking about her lack of volunteering, Regina said, "I would love to be able to volunteer, especially with the school, a lot more. Because I feel that volunteering is a better way, being that I don't have financial means to help support them, that I could give them my time. But unfortunately, I don't have much of that either [laughs]."

Regina points to something we explore further in chapter 2: the extent to which certain demographic factors—particularly living in poverty, in the southern United States, and in rural locations—limit what people can and do give away.

Deon Williams: Retiree Living It Up in Detroit in Residual Poverty

Deon is an example of the retired, nonelderly low-giving participation quantitative trends earlier in this chapter. Because chapter 3 finds him to be an Atypical giver who is not regularly involved in giving activities, it is difficult to describe his approach to giving. He also exemplifies a concept we discuss in chapter 2 regarding the role that early childhood experiences play in later life.

Recall that Deon gives virtually nothing through any form of generosity, with the exception of donating about $20 per year spontaneously when asked and some relational giving that is not effort-heavy. His lack of financial giving appears to be a residual effect of his impoverished youth. He explained:

> Growing up poor, you don't have a whole lot to give. I mean, that's no excuse for today, but, I don't know, maybe I'm stingy. I'm trying to hold onto what I got, because you never know, you never know what tomorrow brings. You might want that money back, depending on the situation, circumstance, tomorrow. Car break down, or house get vandalized, or you might [want] an important item, or something. You might be done wishing you had that money back. I'm just speculating, but, I'm just not a giving person. Like I said, I never had nothing to give.

Deon's fear of becoming broke is an effect of residual poverty since his financial standing is not, and has not been for years, one of poverty. The habits and outlook he formed growing up in an impoverished household clearly have stuck with him through his entire adult life and now into retirement.

Deon is able-bodied, not elderly, and in generally good health. Theoretically he is the type of retiree with a great deal of discretionary time to give. He even described himself as bored and not having much to do. He could donate some of his free time to charitable causes, but when we asked him what he does with his free time, he reported, "Surf the Web on my computer. Watch reality TV. That's about it. Have a cold beer, drink cold beer. Watch TV. And get online. Download porn [laughs]." In fact, even though he worked in a place that provided many opportunities for volunteering, Deon reported that he did none, saying: "You know, I worked for 30 years and they had all kinds of [charitable] baseball teams, softball teams, and little golf outings and everything." But he never had an interest in being involved in those activities: "I never volunteered for none of that stuff. I didn't want to be bothered."

As with volunteering, Deon had no interest in taking political action for charitable causes. When describing his similar lack of involvement with political action, he said:

> Politics is a joke. But, since I [was] raised up a Democrat, I still pull for the Democrats and all that, but I think it's a joke. The Democrats, Republicans, the way they fight and put down each other, and can't wait till one of them "I gotcha" moments, and stuff. It's a joke. And I voted yesterday too, in case you wanna ask that.

In this statement Deon hints at the role that social trust plays in giving, a topic of chapter 4.

In summary, Deon exemplifies a low giver who has financial resources available to give but does not donate and a nonvolunteer who is retired, able-bodied, and willingly admits he has lots of free time to the point of regularly being bored.

Rosa Perez: Pregnant and Unemployed in Brooklyn

Rosa has limited economic and social resources, perhaps explaining her low giving, especially after her recent loss of employment. She provides an example of the dynamic nature of giving, for in the past she was more relationally generous, and she points to a time in the near future when this may be the case again. For now, however, it seems to be all she can do to concentrate on her own circumstances and that of her growing family.

Like Deon, Rosa exhibited some residual effects of poverty in conjunction with being recently fired from her job. At the moment she gives nothing. When asked whether she thinks giving money to charitable causes is a good thing, she said, "I don't think it should be a 'have to' thing. If you want to give and you got it, give it. If you don't, then you don't." Questioned about her volunteering involvement, she said, "As of right now, nothing. I don't give. I don't think about it." When we asked how she feels about politics in general, she said simply, "I don't care." Thus Rosa does not participate at all in any of the Big 3 forms of giving. When we asked if there are any specific feelings that keep her from giving, she said:

> I would say yeah, because of not knowing the outcome of the situation. Like if you volunteer something physically, and it's being done right there and then. That's frowned upon, cause, you know, you did it. It's done; you have no worries. But when you do something, like money-wise and stuff like that, like I said, you don't know where that's going. You don't know if it's actually gonna help feed a human being, or if it's actually gonna be in someone's pocket.

When the transcriber asked our interviewer to clarify that statement, she wrote, "This is what she actually said, although it sounds contradictory." It is hard to make heads or tails of what Rosa's meaning is here: she wants money to go directly to people in need and yet not wind up in their pocket. In fact this part of the interview seems to be a jumble of various words and phrases that do not fit together into a coherent thought. Perhaps we were simply misunderstanding her, but it does exemplify the attitude of a typical nongiver: it is so disconnected from the entire experience of traditional forms of giving that when put into words, it makes little sense.

Despite Rosa's low level of involvement in the Big 3 forms of generosity, she has been very active in relational giving, even of the effort-heavy variety. One of the key activities was providing child care for her neighbors as she was growing up: "I babysat a lot of kids in the neighborhood . . . for free. They didn't pay me. They're not paying me. And that's where I got most of my skills for being a teacher's assistant." For this reason Rosa is one of the few interviewees who have been involved in a kind of effort-heavy relational giving that goes beyond minimal social support. As did many of the women who are high relational givers, Rosa viewed the extent to which she helps others as a fault:

> Yeah, I guess that I'm sweet. I'm friendly. I'm caring. My mother always says I have an open heart. Like I'm always the type to give,

give, give, give, give, and never receive. So it gets to the point where people just step all over me. They just take advantage. And I'm trying to teach myself not to be that way, and it's hard. And I try to [give] people the cold shoulder, but their sad stories always get to me, and I always give in.

Rosa illustrates the fine line in generosity between giving away abundantly to help others and not tending to oneself enough. The boundaries in relational giving seem blurrier than those in the other forms of giving. In some cases it appears that people with low personal orientation may be prone to a problem in which high relational giving can lead to neglecting themselves, a topic we return to in chapter 4. Rosa also exemplifies how a certain baseline of economic and social resources appears to be needed in order to participate in generous activities beyond being self-reliant.

Anthony Ross: In Between, Regrouping, and Poor in D.C.

Anthony does not practice generosity in any form. His economic and social resources are even more limited than Rosa's, and he is trying to subsist in a way that is not a drain on his family. Rosa and Anthony are both young, but in contrast to Cindy, they have not yet clearly established sustainable adult trajectories.

When we asked him about his current giving, Anthony told us of a time 10 years earlier, when he was still regularly attending mass with his grandmother and putting money in the collection plate: "This could be like $5 every time I was there. That was the highest probably, at one time." When resuming a focus on his current giving, he said, "Other than that, no, I usually don't give money." About volunteering he said:

Now probably none through actually volunteering. Like, being someone volunteering. I'm not sure if it's a busy, a thing I can't maintain with my schedule. I know other people probably do it for other reasons, because they want to, or they were raised that way, or because that's how they meet people, contacts. But I would say I don't spend any time doing that.

In fact Anthony can see himself volunteering only if he were angry:

I can do it out of spite. I could probably volunteer out of spite for something. Or if a situation is affecting us, or people around, like me, who I know, then I could see myself doing that. But I don't really, just out of wanting to do something, it's like I don't think it really works that way.

Anthony helps shed light on nongiver trends, as he cannot even begin to think about giving to others when his basic economic and social needs are a daily struggle.

Summarizing the Case Studies

Having revisited all of our case studies, we now have an expanded and more nuanced picture of American giving. Anthony, Rosa, Deon, and Regina help us understand how lower levels of giving can be connected to resource-depleted contexts, where one of the best choices people can make is to focus on taking care of themselves and their families. On the other hand, Tanika demonstrates how people in a similar life situation can take care of their own family in a way that also supports the broader good of the community of parents and teachers. Linda and George exemplify relational giving, among other forms. At the other end of the giving spectrum, Susan, Ryan, Jackie, Cindy, and Michael all show what it looks like when giving takes a more central priority in the lives of Big 3 givers.

Conclusion: The "What" and "How Much" of American Generosity

We set out in this chapter to provide a series of snapshots of American generosity. Having done so, we can piece together the general picture of generosity among the majority of Americans—a picture we find to be rather dismal, at least on this first take. Though 90 percent of Americans we surveyed practice at least one of nine forms of generosity, participation in any one form was low. Nearly 50 percent of Americans did not give any money to charitable causes in the past year. Nearly 75 percent did not volunteer their time. Hardly any took political action. Only 50 percent give relational attention, but only 20 percent of those do so through interpersonal services. Why do so few Americans participate in any one generosity form? The common-sense response is that they cannot afford to give money or time. However, we showed that is not entirely the case. Though resources partially explain variations in levels of generosity, 40 percent of nonpoor

Americans still donated zero dollars in the past year. The vast majority of nonpoor American givers donated 3 percent or less of their annual income, and almost 50 percent gave less than a half percent of their annual income. Perhaps, we thought, the answer lies with limited time resources instead. And yet that does not appear to be the full story either.

A lack of monetary and time resources does not fully explain low levels of giving. The participation rate for volunteering is higher among full- and part-time workers and students than for nonelderly, retired Americans, that is those who should, theoretically, have the most free time to contribute. Almost all Americans spend far more of their free time on leisure—watching television, surfing the Web for non-work-related reasons, and shopping for nonessential goods—than on volunteering or political action. We found, for example, that 75 percent of Americans spent zero hours volunteering in the past month, while 89 percent spent more than 10 percent of their waking hours on leisure. Money and time are not the solution to the American giving puzzle.

We found as well that American generosity is unevenly distributed. Many give little, even when they have abundant resources, while a few give tremendously, even when they have relatively little, or less than some of those who give nothing. Thus the vast majority of Americans are not *regularly* generous, and yet there are many generous activities occurring in the United States.[20] Thus, the glass may seem half-empty to those concerned about the health of charitable causes and interpersonal service relationships.

From a more optimistic perspective, our findings reveal tremendous untapped potential to raise levels of generosity and enhance the collective good. Many have yet to enter the generosity picture, and nearly all who give can up their giving amount. If we all did a little more, together we could do much to contribute to the common good. Our case studies show that people with fewer financial resources find ways to give toward the benefit of others, providing inspiration for more resourced Americans.

Besides levels of personal resources, there are a number of other social status and regional characteristics that may affect giving. In particular the factors of marital status, race and ethnicity, religious attendance, regional location, and education deserve further attention. In the next chapter we will dive deeper into understanding differences in giving levels by asking: Who are American givers? What are their characteristics? Are people in different parts of the country generous in different ways?

The Landscape of American Generosity

SOCIAL STATUS AND REGIONAL PATTERNS

THE PREVIOUS CHAPTER presented a somewhat dismal picture of American generosity, with relatively few Americans participating in each form of generosity. Of those Americans who do give, we found that many are lightly involved in giving their resources to others and only a few are heavily involved. This chapter focuses on who gives. To do this, we zoom out from the frame-by-frame snapshots and survey the overall landscape of American generosity with a wide-angle lens. This view lends itself toward the "glass half-full" perspective because when we consider the landscape of generosity, we see that Americans are generally quite active in working to help others, expressed through one form of giving or another. To assess who gives we consider the role of social status and pay particular attention to regional variation.

Big 3 Giving

The vast majority of Americans, 90 percent, have recently participated in at least some form of generosity, and the majority have given via at least one of the Big 3 forms: giving money, volunteering, or taking political action for charitable causes. To illustrate this, Figure 2.1 shows combined participation in those three ways of giving:

- Sixty-six percent of Americans participate in Big 3 generosity (and, in many cases, also participate in other forms of generosity).
- Twenty-four percent of Americans practice forms of generosity besides the Big 3.

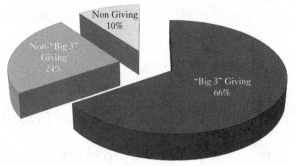

The Big 3 of American generosity.

- Only 10 percent of Americans report not participating in any of these nine forms.[1]

Thus while the picture of any one form of generosity is somewhat dim, the overall landscape of generosity is relatively bright. Given the dominance of the Big 3 forms of giving among Americans, we focus primarily on these forms for the remainder of the book.

Our findings highlight the prominent place of monetary giving over other forms (see Figure 2.2). Of the 66 percent of Americans who participate in Big 3 giving:

- Seventy-four percent practice a combination of forms that involves financial donations (i.e. money only, money and volunteering, money and political action, or all three).
- Sixteen percent participate only in nonmonetary ways (e.g. volunteering only, political action only, or both).

For the vast majority of Big 3 givers, then, donating money holds some place in their portfolio of giving. It may not be the highest or the most important form of generosity to the giver, but it is commonly done and often combined with some other giving expression. We focus on financial giving since it is the most widely practiced form of giving, though we will situate it within the broader context Americans' giving portfolios.

The "Who" of American Generosity

Who are givers? Are some individual characteristics more likely to predict Americans' giving in one form over another? Are these characteristics

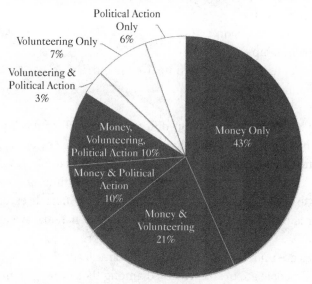

FIGURE 2.2 Important role of donations in Big 3 giving.

mutable or fixed? To find answers we consider the role of social statuses in giving differences. We look at demographics among Big 3 givers, the role of discretionary time and ability to give, and how these characteristics work together to predict Big 3 giving and donation amounts. In considering the national-level landscape of American generosity, we examine how social demographics associate with giving, specifically in the forms of donating money, volunteering, and taking political action.

Big 3 Participation by Social Characteristics

In this section we focus on participation in Big 3 giving based on the following social status characteristics:

- Age
- Gender
- Marital status
- Households with youth (children under 18 years of age in the home)
- Race/ethnicity
- Frequency of attending religious services
- Political affiliation
- Educational attainment
- Employment status

- Household income
- Impact of the recession
- Homeownership status
- Residential tenure (length of time lived in current home)
- Metropolitan residence

Figure 2.3 shows participation differences in each of the Big 3 forms of giving based on these social characteristics.[2] In most cases participation rates are relatively close to the national average. For example, 80 percent of Americans who live in metropolitan areas give money, time, or action, which is similar to the national average. However, there are notable exceptions, in which participation rates are notably different from national averages:

- Females are underrepresented among political activists.
- Married people are overrepresented among those who give money and volunteer.

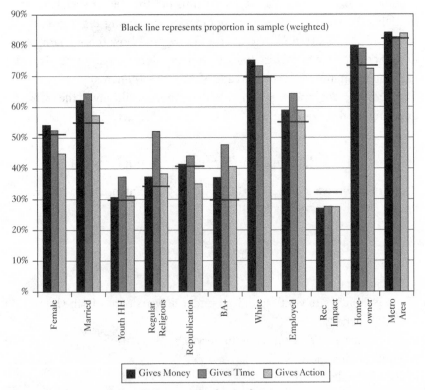

FIGURE 2.3 Demographic differences by form of giving.

- Americans with youth in their household are overrepresented among volunteers.
- Regular religious attendees are overrepresented among volunteers, with 50 percent of volunteers being regular religious attendees, versus 33 percent in the general public.[3]
- Republicans are underrepresented among political activists, relative to those who do not identify as Republican (e.g., people who identify as Democrat, Independent, or other, or who have no political party affiliation).
- College graduates are greatly overrepresented among all Big 3 givers.
- Employed Americans are overrepresented among all Big 3 givers, most dramatically in the case of volunteering time.
- Americans hit hardest by the recession are underrepresented among all Big 3 givers.
- Homeowners are overrepresented among those who give money and volunteer.

In addition the following findings are not shown in the figure:

- The average age of adult Americans is 49, whereas monetary givers' average age is 50 and volunteers' is 48. There is no difference between the average age of adult Americans and political activists.
- The average household income of our adult Americans is $40,000 to $49,999, versus $50,000 to $59,999 for all Big 3 givers.
- There is no difference in residential tenure between the general population and Americans who participate in any of the Big 3 giving forms.

Looking at individual forms of giving, married couples, college graduates, and homeowners are overrepresented in giving money. Married couples, households with youth, regular religious attendees, college graduates, and employed Americans are overrepresented in volunteering. College graduates are overrepresented, while women and households affected by the recession are underrepresented, in political action.

Ability and Discretionary Time

When we compare group characteristics of Americans by ability and available time (Figure 2.4), we again see that most groups are close to the national average. Yet there are these small differences:

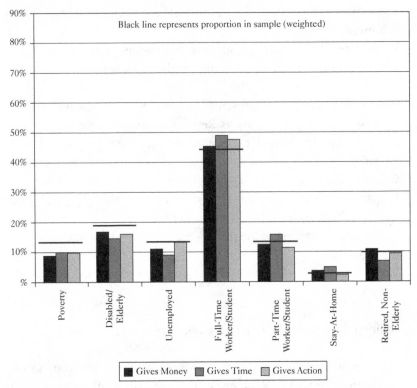

FIGURE 2.4 Participation differences by form of giving.

- Americans in poverty are slightly underrepresented among Big 3 givers, though, as discussed in chapter 1, not to the extent that one might expect.
- Disabled and elderly Americans are slightly underrepresented among Big 3 givers.
- Unemployed Americans are slightly underrepresented among financial givers and volunteers.
- Full-time workers and students are slightly overrepresented among volunteers and political activists.
- Part-time workers and students are slightly overrepresented among volunteers.
- Nonelderly retired Americans are slightly underrepresented among volunteers.

These initial descriptive statistics reveal some emerging patterns about who is likely to engage in generosity by giving money, time, or action. Those with physical disabilities participate at slightly lower rates, while those with more ability participate at slightly higher rates; however, these differences are not as large as we might have expected.

Assessing the Patterns of Differences

Before emphasizing too heavily the differences in giving that emerge, we first need to filter out relationships between characteristics that may be creating false impressions. For example, the trends on homeownership may be inadvertently picking up marital status, since people who own homes are more likely to be married. To tease apart these possible spurious relationships, we statistically model the social status characteristics simultaneously in order to assess the independent relationship between Big 3 giving and each characteristic net of all the other characteristics.[4]

Tracking Money, Time, and Action. To further assess these characteristics, we look in Figure 2.5 at three models that track whether or not individuals give money, time, or action.[5] We find that monetary givers are older and higher-income than average and are more likely to be female, married, white, not Republican, college graduates, and not greatly impacted by the recession. Those who volunteer time are more likely than the average American to be married, have children in their household, attend religious services regularly, and hold a four-year college degree. Characteristics of volunteers are largely distinct from Americans who take political action. Those who take political action are more likely to be male, not Republican, college graduates, high-income, and renting their home.

Another way of understanding the results in Figure 2.5 is to explain them in terms of social status characteristics (rather than by form of giving). We find that, on average:

- Older Americans are more likely to donate money than younger Americans.
- American women are more likely to donate money and less likely to take political action than men.
- Married Americans are more likely to donate money or volunteer than unmarried.
- Americans with youth living in their household are more likely to volunteer than Americans without youth in their household.

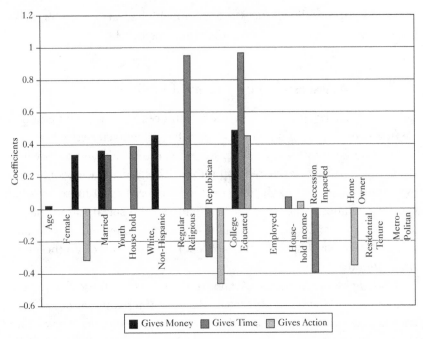

FIGURE 2.5 Demographics of whether individuals give (money, time, action).

- White, non-Hispanic Americans are more likely to donate money than people of other races and ethnicities.
- Americans who regularly attend religious services—once a month or more—are more likely to volunteer than those who attend religious services less often or never.
- Republicans are less likely to give money and take political action than Democrats, Independents, and those who do not identify with a political party.
- Graduates of four-year colleges are more likely to donate money, volunteer, and take political action than Americans without a college degree.
- Americans with higher incomes are more likely to donate money or take political action than those with lower incomes.[6]
- Americans who were impacted by the recession are less likely to donate money than those who were less impacted.
- American homeowners are less likely to take political action than are renters.
- Employment status, how long someone has lived in his or her home, and whether he or she lives in a metropolitan area are factors that are

not significantly related to whether or not someone gives money, time, or political action.

These statistical models confirm that—even after other social status characteristics are accounted for—marital status, educational attainment, and gender remain significant in Big 3 giving.

Tracking the Amount Given. The same three models of social status characteristics in Figure 2.6 predict *how much* different Americans participate in each of the Big 3.[7] These models focus on factors related to the amount of dollars or hours given. Donating larger amounts of money in a year is associated with older age, regular religious service attendance, Republican affiliation, having graduated college, higher income, being less impacted by the recession, and shorter residential duration.[8] Spending more hours per month volunteering is associated with older age, being male, regularly attending religious services, and not living in metropolitan areas. Spending more time on political action is associated with being nonwhite and infrequently or never attending religious services. We see from the comparison of Figure 2.6 to Figure 2.5 that the characteristics related

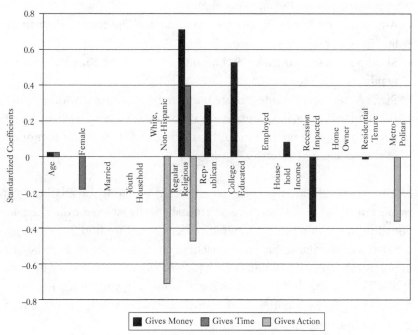

FIGURE 2.6 Demographics of greater giving (money, time, action).

to whether someone is a giver are quite distinct from the characteristics related to giving greater amounts (among those who give).

Another way to understand the results in Figure 2.6 is to focus on the generosity findings in terms of each social status characteristic. In so doing we find that on average:

- Older Americans donate larger amounts of money and more volunteer hours than do younger Americans.[9]
- Men volunteer more hours than women.
- Nonwhite Americans spend more hours taking political action than white, non-Hispanic Americans.
- Those who regularly attend religious services donate more money and more volunteer hours than those who never or infrequently attend, while less regular or nonattending individuals spend more hours taking political action.
- Republicans donate larger financial sums than Democrats, Independents, and people not identifying with a political party.
- Americans with four-year college degrees give more money than those with less than a four-year college degree.
- Americans with higher household incomes donate greater amounts of money than lower-income households.[10]
- Americans hit harder by the recession donate less money than those less impacted by the recession.
- Short-term residents make larger monetary donations than longer-term residents.
- Rural Americans volunteer more hours than urban Americans.
- Being married, having youth living at home, being employed, or being a homeowner are not significantly associated with giving more money or time to charitable causes.

All of these results are net of the other factors, meaning the relationships we described for each characteristic are statistically isolated from the relationships of the other 12 characteristics. As a result we find that the characteristics of marital status and household characteristics seem to be less important for donation amounts than for whether or not someone donates at all. We also see that across the Big 3 forms of giving, religious attendance, college, and income are the most consistent predictors of being a giver and in giving greater amounts.

Putting It All Together

Table 2.1 provides a summary and a side-by-side comparison of givers and giving amounts for the Big 3 giving forms: donating money, volunteering, and taking political action. Focusing first on giving money, we can see that Americans who are older, college graduates, higher-income, and less impacted by the recession are more likely to give money *and* to give greater amounts of money than Americans who are younger, not regularly attending religious services, not college graduates, lower-income, and more impacted by the recession. Female, married, white, and non-Republican Americans are more likely to donate money than male, unmarried, non-white, and Republican Americans, but these characteristics do not relate to amounts donated. Being a Republican, attending religious services

Table 2.1 Who gives, summary

Financial Giving		Volunteering		Political Action	
$ At All:	$ Amount:	Vol. At All:	Vol. Hours:	Pol. At All:	Pol. Hours:
✓ Older	✓ Older	✓ Older			
✓ Female		✓ Male		✓ Male	
✓ Married		✓ Married			
		✓ Youth HH			
✓ White					✓ Non-white
	✓ Reg. Relig.	✓ Reg. Relig.	✓ Reg. Relig.		✓ Non-Reg. Relig.
✓ non-Repub.	✓ Republican			✓ non-Repub.	
✓ 4yr col. degree	✓ 4yr col. degree	✓ 4yr col. degree		✓ 4yr col. degree	
✓ Higher income	✓ Higher income			✓ Higher income	
✓ Less recessed	✓ Less recessed				
	✓ Less tenure				
				✓ Renters	
			✓ Non-metro		

regularly, and living in a residence for fewer years do not relate to being a giver, but they are associated with giving greater amounts. We see from this that there are related numbers of social patterns to being a giver and to giving greater amounts.

While social patterns also exist for volunteering, they are less consistent. Married Americans, those in households with youth, and college graduates are more likely to volunteer than others, but these characteristics do not associate with the number of hours volunteered. Volunteering more hours is related to older age, being male, and living in rural areas. Americans who regularly attend religious services are more likely to be volunteers *and* to give more hours than Americans who attend infrequently or never.

Turning to political action, no single social status characteristic that we examined associates with both the likelihood of taking political action *and* the amount of time spent on it. We do find that males, non-Republicans, college graduates, and renters are more likely to take political action than others, but these characteristics do not relate to the number of action hours. While nonwhite Americans and those who seldom or never attend religious services are no more likely to take political action, when they do, they average more monthly hours. This means that the qualities that distinguish who is a political activist are not the same as those that decipher who among activist gives more time.

As Table 2.1 shows, there is no single group of Americans who are more likely to be Big 3 givers and give in greater amounts. A multitude of characteristics relate to giving outcomes. This reveals differences between who is likely to give at all and, among givers, who is likely to give more. There is not a sole predictor that distinguishes who gives in what form or how much. Instead understanding the "who" of American generosity means assessing a wider array of social statuses. At the same time, the three most consistent predictors of generous outcome, across all of these models, are having a college degree, earning greater income, and regularly attending religious services.

The "Where" of American Generosity

Thus far we have focused on American generosity at the national level. Now we turn to examine within-nation patterns: the regional landscape of giving.[11] We here map giving trends by the four primary US Census regions: Northeast, Midwest, West, and South.[12] As Map I.1 showed in the introduction, the general clustering pattern of respondents mirrors the clustering of the US population (i.e., the Northeast and West have higher density of population than do the Midwest and South, respectively).[13] With this in mind, we proceed with a representative regional analysis of American generosity that explores the landscape of Big 3 giving by regional location.

Landscape of Financial Giving

For monetary giving the regional differences are statistically small, but they nevertheless represent important substantive differences, especially considering a couple of regional-level percentage points represents thousands of Americans in absolute numbers.[14] With this in mind, we find that the West has the most residents giving money: 59 percent donate to charitable causes. With 57 percent of residents giving money, the Midwest has the second highest participation rate.[15] The Northeast and South rank third and fourth, with 53 percent of residents giving money. However, the difference between the Midwest and the Northeast is not a statistically significant difference, nor is the difference significant between the Northeast and the South. The difference between the Midwest and the South is statistically significant, substantially more financial giving occurs in the West than in all other regions, and the South noticeably lags behind the financial giving of other regions.

Whereas rates of giving are relatively similar across regions, the average amount of money donated varies widely. Americans in the West give the most money, with a median amount of $121 given annually, which means that half of all western residents gave $121 or more in the past year and half gave less. Midwesterners rank a distant second in the median amount of money donated, at $40. The median donation amounts in the Northeast and South are $25 in a year. This means that half of the residents of the Northeast and South reported giving less than $25. It would take almost five average northeastern or southern donors or three average midwestern donors to match the giving of one western financial donor.

However, these general results are skewed by the fact that nearly half of Americans do not donate money at all. After removing from the median donation estimates those who do not give, we find that the median dollar amount donated by givers in the West is $501 annually. In the Northeast

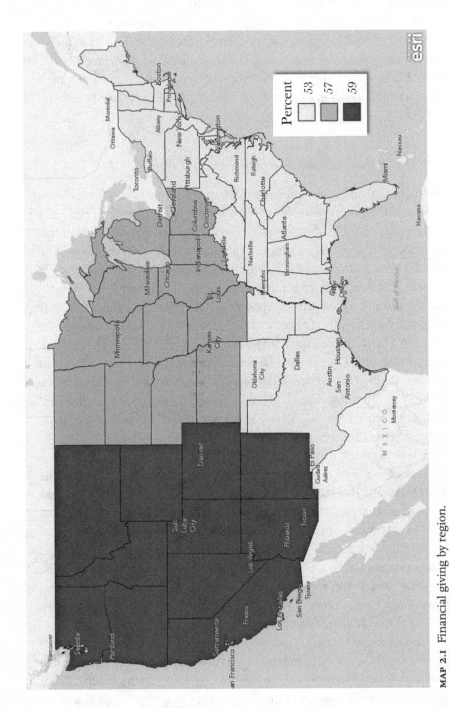

MAP 2.1 Financial giving by region.

Used by permission. Copyright © 2015 Esri, DeLorme, NAVTEQ. All rights reserved.

the median giver amount is $400. Southern givers have a median annual donation of $350, and midwestern givers $300. This means that in order to reach a $2,000 goal, someone could ask four average western givers, five northeastern givers, six southern givers, or seven midwestern givers to donate their average annual donation.

In summary, the landscape of financial giving in the United States shows that more than half of Americans in each region donate money to charitable causes, though wide regional variations emerge in the average amounts of donations. Westerners are more likely to donate money *and* donate higher amounts, on average, than others. Compared to the South, more midwesterners are givers, but midwestern givers donate $50 less annually, on average, than southerner givers. Northeasterners and south-erners participate in financial giving at about the same rate as the average American—just over half donate money. But northeastern givers donate an annual average of $50 more than southerner givers. All in all, there are somewhat different regional patterns for donor rates versus average size of donation, but the West stands out as having the highest financial giving rate and amount.

With that said, simply knowing which region gives the most does not give us the full picture. As we showed earlier, giving rates vary by social statuses, and US regions have different demographics. After we discuss volunteering and political action, we will model regional differences with the social statuses described previously in order to tease apart potential regional culture differences from regional differences in demographic composition.

The Landscape of Volunteering

Before turning to that analysis, we next view levels of volunteering by region and find that there are some similarities to and differences from financial giving patterns. Map 2.2 shows the percentage of the adult population in each region who volunteer: 33 percent of northeasterners and 32 percent of midwesterners volunteer, compared to 25 percent of southerners and westerners. There is no statistically detectable difference between the proportion who volunteer in the Northeast and Midwest, or between southerners and westerners. There is, however, a significant dif-ference between the two clusters: northeasterners and midwesterners are significantly more likely to volunteer than southerners and westerners.

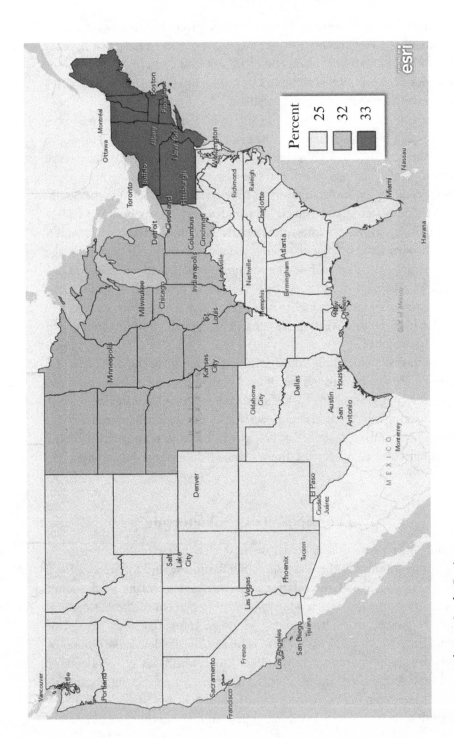

MAP 2.2 Volunteering by Region.

Used by permission. Copyright © 2015 Esri, DeLorme, NAVTEQ. All rights reserved.

Percent

25

32

33

When we examine the amount of volunteer hours in each region, a different pattern appears. Across all regions the median amount of hours volunteered is zero when all Americans are included. Volunteers in the Midwest, West, and South spent a median of 17 hours on charitable causes in the past month. The median in the Northeast is significantly lower, at 11 hours. Residents of the West and South volunteer at lower rates than those of the Midwest; volunteers in these regions average a similar 17 hours in a month. Even though the Northeast averages more people volunteering than the other regions, northeasterners average fewer hours donated than volunteers in other regions. It appears that volunteering contributions are more distributed across the population in the Northeast, and it is the Midwest that has the highest rate and amount of volunteering.

The Landscape of Political Action

Our third pattern is political action, which has a regional pattern similar to that of volunteering, though with lower rates of participation (Map 2.3). There are slight differences between regions in proportions of residents who took political action in the past year. Northeasterners are more politically active than others (23 percent). There is no real difference between the political action participation rate of westerners (21 percent) and midwesterners (20 percent). The proportion of southerners taking political action is significantly lower, at only 16 percent. In comparison, the rate of political action among northeasterners is 1.4 times that of the South.

When we examine the amount of hours devoted to political action in the past month, the median for all regions is zero, much like volunteering. Among activists we find the same pattern as with volunteer hours: the Northeast averages significantly fewer hours in a month (11) than all other regions (17). Effectively, volunteering and political action in the Northeast are more widely distributed, with a greater number of people each contributing lower amounts of political action time. Outside of the Northeast there is virtually no variation in political activity across the United States.

The Landscape of Big 3 Giving Combined

Map 2.4 depicts geographical variation in all Big 3 forms of generosity combined and shows the most distinguishing feature to be that

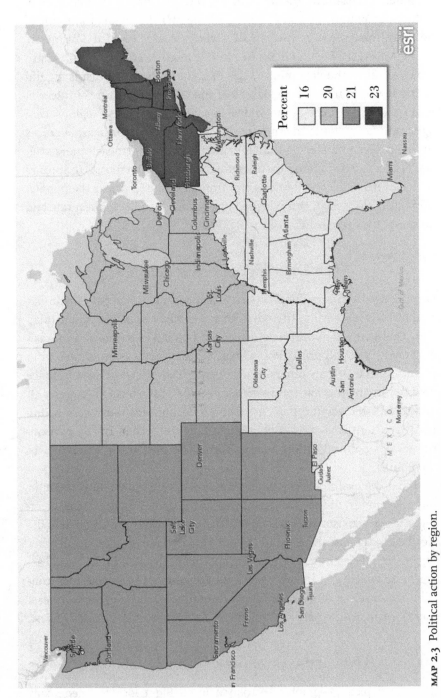

MAP 2.3 Political action by region.

midwesterners (68 percent) are significantly more likely than southerners (64 percent) to be a Big 3 giver. Otherwise there are few regional differences.

These combined findings on Big 3 giving are that, on average:

1. The Midwest has the highest rate of givers.
2. The South consistently has the lowest rates of givers and amounts.
3. The West has the highest rate of financial givers and of donation amounts.
4. The Northeast has the most distributed form of time given, with the highest rates of volunteers and political activists coupled with the fewest hours given per person.

These regional patterns are important to consider given that most research on generosity focuses on one form of giving. Our results suggest that looking at only a single form of giving would be regionally biased, representing the giving preferences most common to certain areas of the country.

All Together: The "Who" and "Where" of American Generosity

To dig deeper into these regional variations we next model them with social status characteristics to tease apart regional demographic differences from regional cultural patterns in giving. The analysis in this section combines chapter 1 findings regarding social status characteristics with results in this chapter on regional giving patterns. We assess the extent to which the "where" patterns of generosity hold, net of "who" gives in each of the Big 3 forms. That is, we answer the question: Do the regional patterns appear to be mainly a result of demographic differences in the composition of residents or cultural norms in giving behaviors? For example, does the fact that southerners tend to be nonwhite, be Republican, and have lower household incomes and education levels on average than other Americans appear to account for the lower southern giving? If so, then we can conclude that the low giving behaviors in the South appear to be a function of the regional demographic characteristics. If not, then there would appear to be a regional normative difference.

This analysis displays the results of models predicting whether people give money, volunteer their time, and take political action, as well as how much money, volunteer hours, and political action hours they donate.[16] For

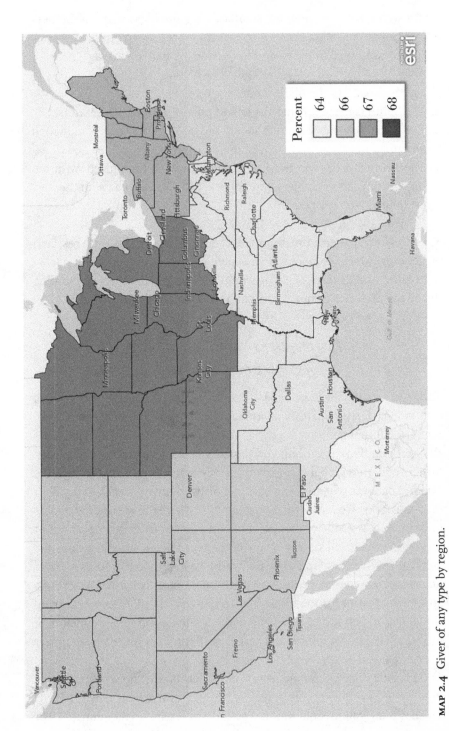

MAP 2.4 Giver of any type by region.

each of the six outcomes, we first model the regional differences. We then add to the models demographic characteristics, to assess whether social status characteristics change the magnitudes of regional variations. Since the South is the region that tends to have the lowest rate of giving, we use is as the baseline for comparison, or reference group. For each giving outcome, the maps indicate whether or not the other three regions are different from the South. Only statistically significant results[17] are displayed in the maps, and darker shades represent areas giving more or less than the South (the reference group)[18] in each of the Big 3 forms of generosity.

Donating Money. The models predicting whether or not someone gives money did not show any significant differences by region. (These maps are not displayed since all regions would be the same color.) When we added demographic characteristics to the models, there also were no detectable differences by region. The results of the model predicting amounts of dollars donated by region also did not show any statistically detectable differences. However, when we added the demographic characteristics into the predictive model, regional differences surface. As Map 2.5 shows, when we hold constant the demographic variations of "who gives," the regional pattern described in the previous section is confirmed. Net of demographic differences, only the West gives significantly larger sums of money than the South.[19] Thus the range of dollars donated in the Midwest, Northeast, and South appear to be about regional differences in demographic compositions. The larger donations in the Northeast, as compared to the South, are likely due to their differing demographics. However, the West influences the amounts of financial donations, net of demographic differences. This indicates that the larger financial donations in the West may be due to *regional cultural differences* not attributable to demographic differences in race, income, education, religiosity, political affiliation, and so on.[20]

Volunteering. Turning to volunteering, we find that residents in the Northeast and Midwest are significantly more likely than southerners to volunteer, but accounting for demographic "who" characteristics significantly changes this picture. Map 2.6 displays the baseline for whether or not residents volunteer by region without any demographic controls added to the model. Once we add these controls, the regional differences are nullified.[21] This suggests that regional differences in volunteering rates result from different compositions of residents, not cultural differences between regions. That is, the regional demographic characteristics of northeasterners and midwesterners explain their higher volunteer participation.

When we look at the number of hours volunteered by region alone (without controlling for demographic characteristics), the same pattern

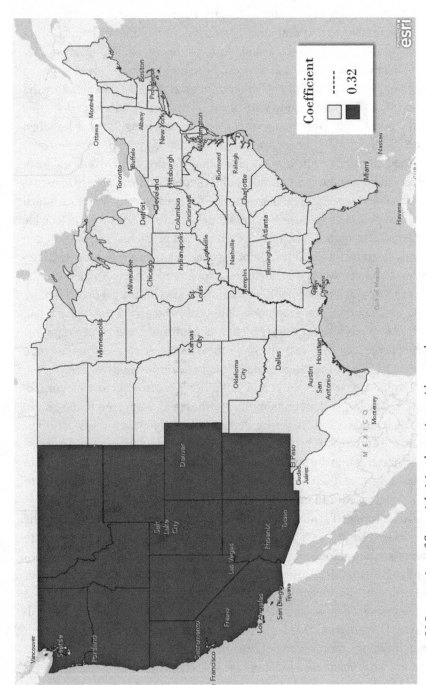

MAP 2.5 OLS regression of financial giving by region, *with controls.*

as in Map 2.6 emerges: the Midwest and Northeast average greater numbers of hours volunteering. However, as Map 2.7 shows, when we add in the social status characteristics, the regional difference of the Northeast persists.[22] This confirms the earlier finding that northeasterners volunteer significantly fewer hours than southerners (11 versus 17 hours in the past month).[23] This indicates there may be regional cultural differences in volunteering, whereby northeasterners generally volunteer fewer hours than southerners, above and beyond demographic differences. We can imagine, for instance, that a culture of "busyness" in the Northeast could cause residents to offer less time to volunteer than other Americans. This is merely one possible explanation for regional cultural differences that these models help indicate exist and are thus in need of further investigation.

Political Action. When demographic differences are not accounted for, participation in political action varies by region, such that northeasterners are more likely to take political action than are southerners (Map 2.8).[24] However, when we include the demographic factors in our statistical model, there is no detectable difference by region alone (map not displayed). The regional differences in political action participation appear to result from the demographics of people living in the Northeast and the South.

However, when we examine the amounts of political action hours given (Map 2.9), we do find regional differences. The pattern is similar to that of the amount of volunteered hours.[25] Namely there is no regional difference detected when region alone is modeled, but when we adjust for social status factors, people in the Northeast donate fewer hours to political action than people in the South (11 versus 17 hours).[26] Again this means that the demographic differences between the Northeast and South do not explain the fewer hours given to political action in the Northeast. These results indicate a regional difference exists in political action among Northeasterners and Southerners.

Overall these statistical models confirm that more people in the Northeast participate in giving time but give less of it per person than people in the South, where fewer people participate but participants give more of their time. Most of the regional differences in participation rates appear to result from differing demographic compositions, while amounts of money and time given may result from different cultural giving norms.

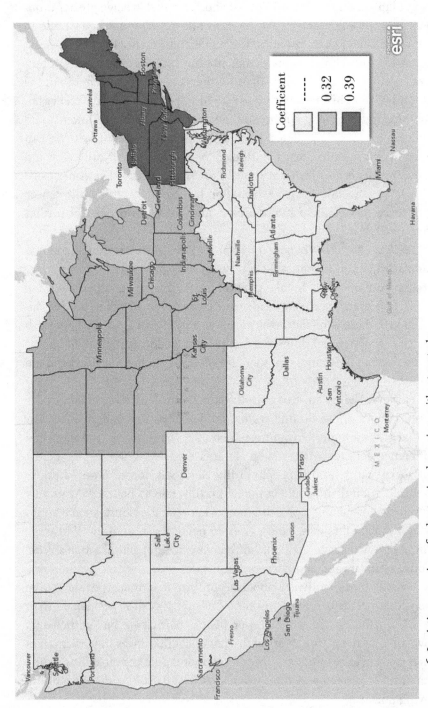

MAP 2.6 Logistic regression of volunteering by region, *without controls.*

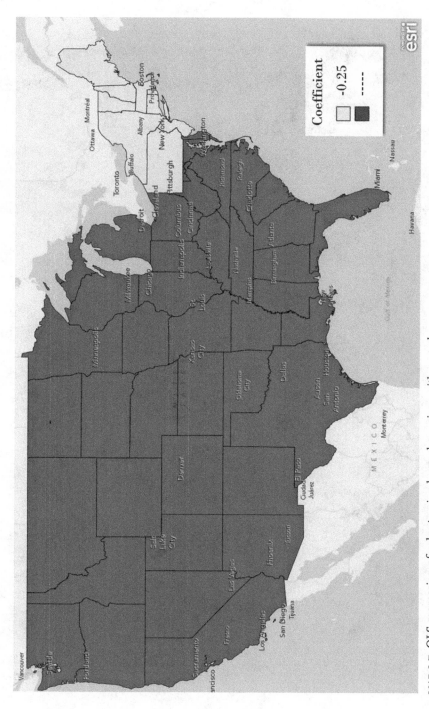

MAP 2.7 OLS regression of volunteering hours by region, *with controls.*
Used by permission. Copyright © 2015 Esri, DeLorme, NAVTEQ. All rights reserved.

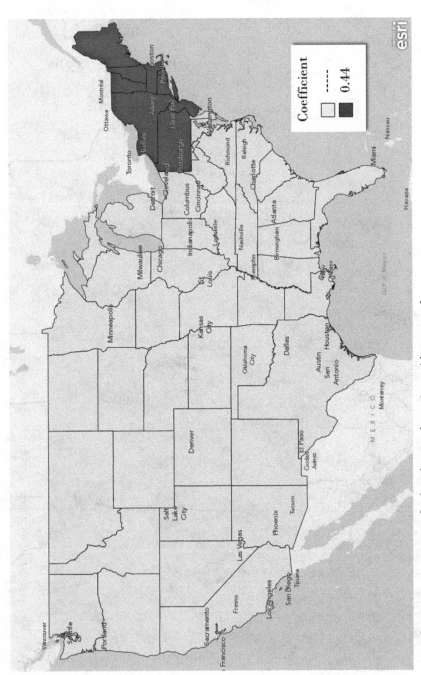

MAP 2.8 Logistic regression of political action by region, *without controls.*

Looking at the Big Picture

In a final regional analysis we model whether Americans participate in *any* of the Big 3 forms of generosity. With and without demographic "who" factors, there were no detectable differences by region (maps not displayed). These analyses reveal that the small differences found earlier are largely due to differences in who lives in these regions.

Together these analyses of Big 3 generosity forms find a combination of demographic ("who") and regional ("where") differences in giving. Westerners are more likely to give money. Midwesterners and northeasterners are more likely to volunteer. Northeasterners are also more likely to take political action. However, northeasterners give fewer hours per participant to volunteering and political action. Some regional differences in giving appear to be about residential compositions and other distinct cultural norms of giving. Specifically participation in volunteering and political action is explained by the Northeast's demographic composition. The participation rates in financial giving as well as amounts of time donated (in volunteering and political action) remain independent of who resides in the region and thus appear to be due to regional cultures.

One implication of these findings is that people can express their generosity through different forms of giving. Often studies on giving limit their analyses to a single form. Such analyses can be misleading because the results may be skewed, catering to the giving form of one region or another. For example, studies focused on volunteering or political action would favor Northeastern giving, while studies focused on financial giving would favor Western giving. Thus the influence of regional patterns (cultural and demographic) could be overlooked in studies assessing only one form of giving.

The Landscape of American Generosity

Looking at the big picture, 90 percent of Americans give through one of the nine forms of generosity described in chapter 1. Of these givers, nearly 75 percent donate through one of the Big 3 forms of generosity: money, volunteering, or taking political action. Having said that, each of the Big 3 forms of giving have regional patterns to them:

- Westerners are more likely to give money and give more of it.
- Northeasterners are more likely to give time but less of it.

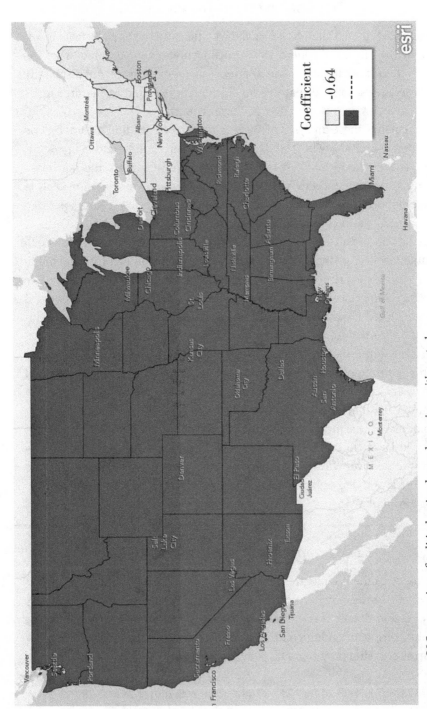

MAP 2.9 OLS regression of political action hours by region, *with controls.*
Used by permission. Copyright © 2015 Esri, DeLorme, NAVTEQ. All rights reserved.

- Midwesterners and southerners have regional demographic patterns to their giving.

Demographic patterns also exist in Big 3 giving, such that, net of other characteristics:

- College graduates are more likely to participate in all Big 3 forms of giving and give larger sums of money.
- Americans who regularly attend religious services are more likely to volunteer and give more hours to it. They also donate larger sums of money but fewer hours to political action.
- Older and married people are more likely to give money than younger people and the unmarried.
- Adults with youth in their household are more likely to volunteer.
- Rural Americans average more volunteer hours.
- Homeowners are less likely to take political action.
- Higher-income Americans are more likely to donate money (and to give greater amounts) as well as to take political action.
- Recession-impacted Americans are less likely to donate money and donate smaller amounts.
- Women are more likely than men to give money, while men are more likely to take political action and to volunteer more hours.
- White, non-Hispanic Americans are more likely to donate money than other racial/ethnic groups, while nonwhite Americans are more likely to take political action.

While giving money, volunteering, and taking political action make up the three major forms of American generosity, they are not all equally prevalent: the majority of people who participate in any one of these forms tend to donate money. And a number of important demographic characteristics and regional variations are related to both whether Americans participate in Big 3 giving and how much they donate.

Case Study Excursus

Having examined our quantitative data on demographic and regional patterns in generosity, we now turn to the qualitative data from our case studies to see how those patterns play out in the lives of individual Americans.

This venture into the lives of our 12 case studies helps to demonstrate the lived experiences of these statistical patterns on the "who" and "where" of American generosity. As evidence of the synchronicity between the quantitative and qualitative findings, we first review the demographic and regional characteristics of our cases.

Many of the demographic and regional patterns in this chapter are evident in the lives of our case studies. In comparing the quantitative findings summarized in Table 2.1, the case studies comport, showing for example that all of the highest givers have at least a bachelor's degree, and many have achieved higher levels of education. Only one of the most generous givers in our case studies (Susan Baker) does not attend religious services regularly, and all but one (Ryan Dewey) are older, married, and in households with youth. Both of our rural southerners (George Nettleson and Regina Buckner) report volunteering a large number of hours. Our leading political activist (Michael Johnson) is male and has a high income, though contrary to the norm for political activists, he does own a home in D.C. All but one (Ryan Dewey) of our highest financial givers have moderate to high incomes. Our cases who were hardest hit by the recession (Tanika Sandaval, Regina Buckner, and Anthony Ross) all give very little to nothing financially (i.e., $20 or less annually). Many of our financial givers are women, and one of the male givers (George Nettleson) credits his wife for their generosity, and one of the female givers (Linda Chesterfield) credits her husband. All of our top financial donors are white, as overall demographic patterns for giving would predict, though our main political action giver (Michael Johnson) is also white.

We also see patterns that align with our survey data on regional giving. One of the highest financial givers (Susan Baker) lives in the West, while the most generous volunteer (George Nettleson) lives in the South, and the top political action giver (Michael Johnson) lives on the East Coast. We have a prototypical northeastern giver (Cindy Phelps), who volunteers but also spends less time doing it than others who donate their time. All but one of the midwesterners (Deon Williams, who is originally from the South) participate in some type of Big 3 giving. These cases illustrate the typical regional patterns presented in this chapter.

The resource-related trends presented in chapter 1 also operate in the lives of our case studies. Three of our four cases who live in or on the brink of poverty (Anthony Ross, Rosa Perez, and Regina Buckner) exhibit very little to no participation in any type of giving besides relational giving, with one of our highest effort-heavy relational givers (Rosa Perez) being in this group. Deon Williams also does not give, and although he is not currently in poverty, its residual effects from his youth still influence him. Likewise, on the other extreme, four of our highest givers across all Big 3 forms of giving (Susan Baker, Linda Chesterfield, George Nettleson, and Michael Johnson) are all either wealthy or comfortably resourced. However, resources are not the end of the story: three of the highest givers (Ryan Dewey, Jackie Sawyer, and George Nettleson) manage to give more than their financial circumstances alone would predict by taking a more systematic approach to their giving and having the support of their religious affiliation to undergird their giving convictions. Similarly one of our highest givers of time (Tanika Sandaval) is able to donate more resources than her limited means would predict, seemingly because her commitment to her children's education fuels her passion.

These cases show that resources can enable or restrain individuals' giving, and also that giving differs by other demographic and regional characteristics. As our survey data showed, a college education, marriage, location, the impact of the recession, and poverty are active influences on whether or not our interviewees could give and how much they could help others. Social statuses and region of residence are part of the landscape of American generosity.

The Role of Financial Resources

Beyond poverty, financial resources also condition giving. The survey data showed that household income influenced donations, but our statistical analyses showed that economic resource availability did not fully explain who gives and how much. As these interviewees further evidence, financial resources do play a role in giving behaviors, but other social factors also play significant roles in understanding who gives and in what amounts.

Susan Baker puts her fairly affluent, well-resourced, classic upper-middle-class position into her own words: "I think I've had a pretty darn normal life. I don't think I've, I haven't had any great breaks, and I haven't had any horrible losses." Likewise Jackie Sawyer describes her more modest but still comfortable circumstances: "I'm proud of the fact that we don't have to struggle financially. That we have things organized. And that we don't really have to think about where's our next paycheck coming from, where is the water bill—how is that gonna get paid, the insurance bill." Michael Johnson described his life overall by saying, "Right now I would say I'm pleased with my life in terms of what I have."

In stark contrast are the voices on the other end of the spectrum, our resource-constrained cases. Regina Buckner attributes her overall lack of giving to "not having enough to support my own family a lot of times." Tanika Sandaval has trouble giving financially and describes how her money situation has been fairly volatile in recent years: "Well at times, you know, cause my income sometimes fluctuates, goes up and down. So, yeah, [it] varies; it changes at times." She describes her general life circumstances this way: "In between, it's been kind of rocky, you know, some little changes within income and stuff like that. But overall, just pretty much [trying] to deal with it. . . . "My situation is kinda like that. I'm in between. So it's kinda, I'm trying to [wait it out and] see how I can make that work." Similarly Anthony Ross explains that one reason he doesn't give is his lack of resources: "I mean, feasibility. If you undergive, then you kind of feel bad about it. If you overgive, then I don't even have enough money for myself. . . . Always the economy, stuff like that will probably affect how much money I can give."

Then there are those who are more middle-of-the-road: they have resources available but feel somewhat constrained. Despite being reasonably economically resourced, Jackie Sawyer still prioritizes being thrifty and says she makes more out of the resources she does have "cause I coupon, and I can find the bargain, and I know where the deals are." She credits this practice for enabling her family to afford a private, religious education for their children: "We're able to send our kids to private school, the Christian school, and not have to worry about how are we gonna pay for Christian school." When reflecting on the overall effect their approach to financial matters has had on their life, she says, "We've made choices through our early parts of our marriage where we didn't do things, so that now we can afford this house, and afford to send our kids to school, and do some of the extra things."

Other interviewees struggle to make ends meet less due to resource constraints than as a result of difficulty managing finances. Linda

Chesterfield, for instance, describes her financial practices: "I feel like I'm borderline financially irresponsible with the day and age of credit cards, 'Oh I can put this on the credit card, but we're paying those balances in full, but we don't have to.' . . . I'm terrible at managing money. Horrible." However, she goes on to explain, "I'm married to someone who's very financially responsible. [He]'s like 'No, you don't ever carry a balance on a credit card.'" Thus it seems that the financial giving that does occur in her household is primarily a result of her husband being a Planned giver who budgets the household finances: "So I don't really put a lot of thought in stuff. I mean, I don't provide; my husband provides. But, I go and get what we need." In their household division of labor he concerns himself with the overall budget and financial giving, while she concerns herself with volunteering and relational giving. This situation seems to work for Linda since she has her husband there to handle the finances, but we can imagine how her situation, and their household giving, could look quite different if this arrangement did not work well.

From these cases we see that resource constraints exist and that they are also patterned by other social factors, including how those economic resources are saved and expended. Likewise some seem to use generosity forms interchangeably, substituting giving time if there is not enough money to donate. We also frequently heard from givers that they usually want to be giving more than they currently are and in some cases are actively seeking ways to do so. In fact participating in these interviews and reflecting upon their current giving levels seemed to be making some reconsider how to make their actions comport closer to their generosity desires.

Residual Poverty

In addition to the ways in which financial giving is patterned by current access to resources, we also see the effects of past or future concerns about money playing a role in current giving practices. Some people hold onto their money due to financial insecurity. Even though from an outside perspective they may be seen as relatively affluent, they perceive themselves as not yet having enough. Recall Cindy Phelps's story about how her parents' divorce and the subsequent economic strain her mother endured caused her to stress about never having enough money put aside. In these cases people worry about the future and believe they need to cling to their money in case they some day come up short. Such insecurity is related to resources, but it can also be related in a way that stems from residual childhood factors. For some the economic deprivation of childhood continues to haunt their current economic situation, coloring their perception of greater affluence today.

Deon Williams is a prime example of someone who, in theory, has resources to give away. He is a single man with a middle-class income who is retired and still in good health. However, he does not think of himself as resourced and instead says, "I try to keep my head above water by staying out of trouble, you know what I'm saying?" He is practicing a basic survival strategy of "keeping afloat" even though he is not in an emergency situation. We link this resource constraint perspective to a residual poverty influence.

Deon's mindset appears to stem from spending his childhood in poverty. It left him always wanting to hold onto and enjoy the resources he has:

> I don't give money away because basically, I'm stingy. And I don't have it to give away. The money I get from my retirement, it seems like it's just enough to keep my head afloat, along with maybe a dollar or two given here, or a dollar or two given there. I mean, really I don't have nothing to give. I don't have nothing to give away, and then plus, like I said, I got a little stingy in me too. I don't wanna use that term *stingy*, I just call it being economical. To make it through the month. It's different when you're getting that check once a month, as opposed to some people get paid weekly, some people get paid biweekly. But when you just get it once a month, it's a whole different ball game.

Deon illustrates residual poverty as a hangover from earlier, less-resourced days that affects life in the present. The habit of holding on tight to resources lingers beyond the time when it is needed as a survival mechanism. The mentality is that the resources could slip away again, and so it makes sense to reserve them. Thus, from an outside perspective, someone like Deon could be characterized as stingy, ungenerous. Yet upon further investigation, the notion of residual poverty reveals a deeper reason for his cautious approach to giving. He may be currently resourced, but his financial fears of the past cast a long shadow over his life, making him cling to his resources as if they were still scarce.

The Role of Time Resources

Like financial resources, availability of time also plays a role in enabling or constraining giving. Many people we spoke with cited a lack of available time as the reason they are unable to volunteer. However, our survey data in chapter 1 show that people clearly do have discretionary time available, certainly enough to spend a great deal of time on shopping for nonessential goods. Our case studies were similar: they all had discretionary time that they could reallocate to giving. One explanation for this discrepancy is the fact that many Americans *perceive* that they are busy. As with money, the perception of having time is in many ways more important than the absolute amount of time that is available. George Nettleson illustrates how someone can actively fight the perception of time constraints. George seems to have found a way to keep himself removed from the time pressures so many other Americans feel:

> I rebel against hurriedness. And I feel that, maybe not your stress, but your hurriedness is something that every individual has control over and should be able to regulate on their own, they have the power to be hurried or unhurried. And I don't do well if I have to be in a hurried and stressful situation for a very long time. I feel I have the power to control that, so I do.

Perhaps it is because he chooses to not view his life as hurried that he and his wife are able to give away so much of their time, despite both being employed and raising two busy daughters. George demonstrates how having discretionary time, like having discretionary financial resources, is partly in the eye of the beholder.

The Role of Religious Resources

The survey we reviewed in this chapter shows that regular religious attendance is one of the key differentiating characteristics of givers, especially of those giving higher amounts. This theme also shows up throughout our interviews, underscoring the role that religion plays in supporting generous behaviors. Multiple interviewees articulated the important role religion plays in motivating them to give.

Religious motivation certainly drives the donations of Ryan Dewey, who explains:

> I give away money again cause of my religious convictions. I feel that is the right thing to do, wanting to model my life after Christ and wanting to do the right thing, and to see the impact it can have in people's lives, see the good things it can do for other people and to help them.

Likewise Jackie Sawyer and George Nettleson both describe their religious convictions as a primary reason for their generosity. These three attend religious services more regularly than the other nine cases, and they also give tremendous amounts.

Religion also appears to play a role in the giving of cases who attend services less regularly. It appears that religious attendance in the formative childhood years (similar to the residual effects of poverty) has provided these interviewees with a long-lasting religious orientation to giving. For example, Tanika Sandaval said this about religion:

> That's your foundation there. That's like a foundation right there. That's something that when you're young, it just shows you the right way, wrong way. That's your morals there, that's your characteristics. The person that you're going to kinda be, those set the ground tone of things, you know? It's a way of life.

She continued, "I think about God every day." Thus although Tanika may not regularly attend church today, it appears her childhood religious foundation underlies her motivation to volunteer.

Michael Johnson attends services semiregularly and says that religion influences his giving—though it seems to have a slightly smaller influence on him than on some of our more regularly attending givers. This could be linked to how he perceives his own dedication to his religion. Michael describes himself as being selective when it comes to following the Catholic Church's teachings:

> I belong to the Catholic Church. I'm, ah [sigh], you know, I go on a regular basis, but I mean there are people who are clearly, you know, more religious or more devout in their views than I am. I'm not

gonna say that I'm a "cafeteria Catholic," but, you know, there's some things that I don't accept to [the] same degree as some Catholics do.

This pick-and-choose mentality is prototypical of the "cafeteria Catholic," an identity that Michael explicitly rejects.

When we asked whether his religious faith shapes or influences his life, Michael replied:

Well, I think it's probably shaped my life in terms [of] the way I look at things politically in trying to help people and the way that I think our policies should treat those who do not have as much, or those who may be disadvantaged in some way. I mean, clearly religion has influenced my thoughts in those regards.

But when we asked how much religion was part of his everyday life, Michael said, "It's a part, but it's certainly not what I would call a major part where I'm spending most of my time. And I suppose the reason for this is I've got so many things to do." The fact that religion plays little part in his everyday life could help to explain why his financial and volunteering amounts are not as high as the models would predict, but he generally fits the trend of religious attenders.

Cindy Phelps, who is even less religiously involved than Michael, describes her religious experiences this way:

I've never really felt a very good sense of belonging in a religious group because my mother was born Catholic and raised Baptist, and then married my father, who is Jewish. So my family tried to raise us Jewish, but my mother not being Jewish. And everyone in my temple was like—well, the kids my age, anyways—were like, "You're not Jewish." So I've never really felt a huge sense of belonging in a religious group.

Cindy's parents tried to raise their children with a religious background, but exposure to so many different religious groups undermined Cindy's long-term commitment to any of them. Nevertheless the values she acquired during those early years still shape her current emphasis on volunteering, despite her irregular religious attendance today.

Religious exposure during childhood does not always continue to influence giving, however. For example, Anthony Ross's only memory of giving goes back to a time when he was regularly attending Mass with his grandmother and mother. The most money he ever remembers giving was to the church when he was a child, but Anthony no longer considers himself a religious person, and says, "I don't really go [to church]. Probably the last time I've been to church was when I was like 15 or something."

Though Regina Buckner still claims to be Catholic, she no longer attends religious services: "I'm Catholic, but other than that, I don't attend church regularly basically anymore." She only goes with her mother when she comes to town. When we asked about her religious beliefs, Regina could not say much. For example, when we asked, "Do you believe in God?," she said simply, "Yes." We then asked, "What is God like to you?" After a long pause, she answered, "A stranger [laughs]. I don't really know." Regina's religious upbringing does not appear to play a role in her day-to-day life or motivate her to give more.

Likewise, Deon Williams thinks of himself as a Christian, but not really religious. At this point in his life he attends church services only a couple times a year when visiting family. He explains:

> To be honest with you, I'm not one of them type of people who run to church all the time, [I don't] spend a great deal in church. But I do live by the church rules. I treat people like they want to be treated, like I want to be treated. Every once in a while I drop to my knees and I thank God for everything he's blessed me with, which he's been good to me. I just live by the church rules. Like I said, I'm not a very religious person, I don't go out preaching about God, and all that stuff, running to church all the time, but I live by those rules.

When we responded by asking why he still goes to church sometimes, Deon said:

> I think it's just the right thing to do; you should go there some-times. Let the Lord know that you come to his house sometimes. See and [for] black folks, church is the Lord's house. So of course you'll go to his house sometimes. Show him some respect, some worship, go to his house.

Thus for Deon religion is a semiannual responsibility, almost like having to pay taxes. Give what is owed, and then move it to the background.

Religion is key to understanding the giving behaviors of some of our cases, who hold a strong moral conviction that giving is part of a religious mission, and it has a lingering effect in those who do not regularly attend today but had exposure during their childhood. These interviewees exemplify the quantitative finding that those who attend religious services regularly are more likely to be givers. In other cases religion plays a smaller, more diffuse role in giving; these people acquired a moral foundation in childhood, incorporated the golden rule and other values into their lives, and then no longer felt the need to be part of a religious congregation in order to sustain those values. For yet other cases religion played some role in their lives in the distant past, but it appears to have little to no bearing on their current giving or their lives in general.

Conclusion: The "Who" and "Where" of American Generosity

Having considered how our case studies confirm and bring greater nuance to our discussions of the "who" and "where" demographical and regional trends in Big 3 giving, we better understand the complexity of giving patterns. From the quantitative data and statistics, we know that someone who is married, college-educated, or regularly attending religious services is more likely to donate money or volunteer than someone who does not exhibit these traits. The interview data help us understand why that pattern exists—and why there are exceptions. Personal histories, current relationships, and perspectives on lifestyle, among other phenomena, are rarely measured on surveys about giving, but they too influence decisions and behaviors. In upcoming chapters we dig more deeply into these factors with data from our survey and interviews.

Across all forms of resources a complex relationship of financial and social resources appears to be operating. Absolute economic deprivation makes it nearly impossible to give. Some people are poverty-stricken to the point that supporting themselves and their families requires their full concentration. Likewise people can be so busy taking care of children or working that they have little to no spare time to give away. Access to religious resources appears to be helpful in maintaining some level of giving. Beyond these baselines, access to resources explains less. Giving patterns among the majority of Americans are best understood within the context of their social status and regional characteristics. In addition we think not all Americans may approach giving in the same way and turn to this in the following chapter.

3

Types of American Givers

VARIATIONS IN APPROACHES TO GIVING

UP TO THIS point we have discussed giving forms and how their rates of participation vary by social status and regional characteristics, providing a picture of the *what, who,* and *where* of American generosity. We have demonstrated that access to socioeconomic resources, social status characteristics, and regional location decipher whether and how much Americans give. We have treated American giving as a uniform process up to this point, but we do not think that all Americans, or even those who share demographic traits, are likely to approach their philanthropic process in the same way. Rather we expect that people practice giving with different strategies (or lack thereof). And their approaches may relate to whether and how much they give. By looking at the different approaches people use in the process of giving, we now ask: *How* do Americans give? To answer this question, we use a statistical technique that groups givers into types based on the approaches they take to giving.[1]

Giving Approaches

To start assessing American giving approaches, we focus on *financial giving.* We do this for two primary reasons: we showed in chapter 2 that most Big 3 givers donate money as part of their giving portfolios, and we think that financial giving may be the process that is easiest to explicate (since people tend to devote some thought to their household's financial processes, deciding whether or not to budget, or whether to save or spend), while also representing processes for other forms of giving. Thus the process of donating money likely exposes the biggest swath of the American picture, illuminating various hues within the spectrum of giving. We investigate these processes in the pages to follow.

To study Americans' giving processes, we asked a series of questions in our survey about people's systems for giving, their cognitive decision making related to giving, and (if they give) the methods they use to determine how much money to give. We identified systems for giving by asking respondents if they follow a regular, structured routine for donating money or if they instead give in a more spontaneous or situational way. To explore cognitive decision making related to giving, we asked if they make a conscious decision to give away more of their money to charitable, religious, or other causes or if financial donations mostly happen without a lot of planning and intention. We also asked them to categorize their methods for deciding how much money to contribute to charitable organizations as (1) spontaneous depending on the situation, (2) whatever seemed affordable for a period of time, (3) a monthly or annual dollar amount, or (4) a percentage of their annual income.

Based on these measures we have three sets of polarities for the giving approaches of most American givers:

1. "Routine" versus "spontaneous" system of giving
2. "Conscious" versus "just happens" cognitive decision making
3. "Predetermined" versus "it depends" method for deciding how much to give

To assess whether and how these giving behaviors cluster together to form certain giving approaches, we employ a fuzzy-set qualitative comparative analysis (fsQCA).[2] These fsQCA models converged on the first two sets of polarities: routine versus spontaneous giving and conscious versus situational decision-making approaches. Responses from the third question on method for deciding collapsed onto these two other approaches: we do not gain any additional information (no unique variation was explained) when we assess the third measure.[3] Thus we focus our assessment of giving approaches on the first two measures. Using those measures we categorize Americans as taking one of four approaches to giving, which we label Planned, Habitual, Selective, and Impulsive.

Figure 3.1 visually represents the ideal types of American giving approaches. There are two dimensions: the x-axis (horizontal) is the system of giving, and the y-axis (vertical) is the cognitive decision-making approach. The four ideal types result from the possible 2x2 combinations of traits. Those labeled Planned givers fall on the left side, with a routine system of giving and a conscious decision to give. Those we term Impulsive givers are opposite Planned givers, on the right side, with a spontaneous/situational approach and a "just happened" decision-making process. At the top are Habitual givers, with a routine system and a "just happened" decision. At the bottom are those we call Selective givers because they make a conscious decision with a spontaneous approach. In sum these types show the following giving configurations:

- Planned: (a) structured/routine system and (b) conscious decision
- Habitual: (a) structured/routine system and (b) "just happened"
- Selective: (a) spontaneous/situational system and (b) conscious decision
- Impulsive: (a) spontaneous/situational system and (b) "just happened"

The resulting typology categorizes as Planned givers those with the most conscious, routine, and systematic process to giving, in contrast to Impulsive givers, who use the most spontaneous, situational, and unplanned giving process. Habitual and Selective givers stand in between Planned and Impulsive; both share one approach each with Planned and Impulsive givers.

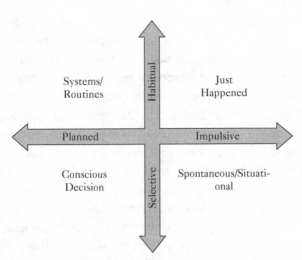

FIGURE 3.1 Dimensions of giving approaches.

Giver Types

We use the fsQCA analysis to test how well this ideal typology of givers actually describes Americans. Though we theorized how the giving systems and decisions would combine into the ideal types presented in Figure 3.1, we must confirm this potential typology, evaluating how well these approaches actually describe American giving patterns.

Based on our fsQCA analysis, the results reveal that most American givers are Impulsive, some are Selective and Planned, and few are Habitual in their giving. Together these four types represent more than 80 percent of American givers. The remaining 20 percent do not fall neatly into one of these four types because they either did not answer enough of the questions to categorize them or they answered in inconsistent ways that did not result in a discernible type. This group of Americans composes a fifth type that we call Atypical givers.[4] And there is a sixth group, nongivers, who have no giving approach. Figure 3.2 illustrates the relative number of Americans taking each type of approach; the size of the circles represents the relative proportion of Americans for each giver type, and the overlap between the circles shows the shared traits between types.

Impulsive givers constitute about 40 percent of Americans who donate money. These givers report that they "just happen" to decide to give money

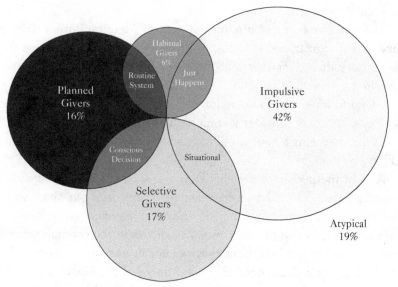

Coverage = 0.839; Solution Consistency = 0.905

FIGURE 3.2 Giver type participation rates.

to a cause and that they give spontaneously, depending on the situation, rather than routinely. Examples of this kind of giver are people who give when they are presented with an immediate situation, such as texting in a $10 donation to emergency relief efforts after a natural disaster, dropping some money into the Salvation Army bucket around the holidays, donating a turkey basket around Thanksgiving, or giving to a charitable cause when their friends or coworkers enter a race and request their support. Impulsive givers may support the same causes from time to time, but they have no sustained, regular, or conscious involvement with giving to charitable causes. Impulsive givers make up the largest proportion of givers of any type and represent nearly as many American givers as the other three types combined.

At the opposite end of the giving process spectrum, *Planned givers* constitute about 16 percent of American givers. These givers describe their giving approaches as routine in system and conscious in decision making. Planned givers have a regular, established routine for giving, and they spend time consciously deciding on their donations, allowing their giving amounts or the targets of their giving to adjust and change. Many Planned givers appreciate "giving feedback": reports or other information from charities on what their donations accomplished. Such feedback is crucial to the conscious decision-making process; without feedback from the charities they sponsor, Planned givers may choose to contribute to a different target.

Habitual givers represent only 6 percent of American givers. Though they have a regular, routine habit of giving, they acknowledge that they do not give their donations that much conscious thought. These givers instead put some thought into developing their routine system, and then they tend to let it run on autopilot. Giving is a regular part of their life activities, and they consider it important, but rarely do Habitual givers give their donations a moment of conscious thought in the midst of their day-to-day lives.

Also in the middle of the spectrum are *Selective givers*, 17 percent of American givers. Selective givers make conscious decisions about where and how much to give, but they do so with a spontaneous, nonroutine approach. In other words, they pick and choose which charitable causes they will support and how much they will donate as requests for contributions arise. Their giving depends on a number of situational factors that they consider in the moment of the request, such as who is requesting it, how they are asked, to what extent they believe in or support the cause, how much the request is for, what funds are available, whether they have made another donation recently, and so on. By its nature this type of giving is more inconsistent (less routine) and can fluctuate over the course of the year depending on situational factors and givers' reaction to them in the moment in time.

About 20 percent of American givers do not fit into one of these four giver types. They are *Atypical givers*, who either did not fully respond to the giving questions or reported combinations of approaches that did not seem to logically cohere (e.g., reporting that they never give on one question but in another reporting that they have a structured routine to their giving). Not all of our survey respondents have reflected on their processes for various social behaviors, and this Atypical type represents those givers who have no discernible approach to giving but still identify as someone who gives. As our Atypical case study, Deon Williams, shows, givers of this type give small amounts and often have more in common with nongivers than they do the primary giver types.

It deserves mention that this typology of giving approaches represents American givers. Approximately 10 percent of Americans do not give at all and therefore fall into a sixth category, *nongivers*. As our case studies will illustrate, many nongivers are struggling to get by and maintain a life without depending on others' support. In this sense the most "giving" thing many nongivers do is try as best they can not to be a burden to others. Nongivers often have more chaotic lives, subsist on the fringes of poverty, or are young and do not yet have established lives and resources.

Generous Behaviors by Giver Types

We have shown how various types of givers approach monetary giving, but how do they approach other forms of generosity? Given that financial giving is predictive of participation in other forms of generosity, we think that the giver typology applies to more than just financial givers. Though the typology is based specifically on questions regarding financial giving, we assessed the extent to which approaches to financial giving are indicative of approaches to other forms of giving. Through multiple robustness analyses using a range of generosity behaviors,[5] we conclusively confirmed the usefulness of the typology in explaining Big 3 giving.

To demonstrate how well our types explain Big 3 giving practices, we present distributions of giver type for each form of Big 3 giving. These

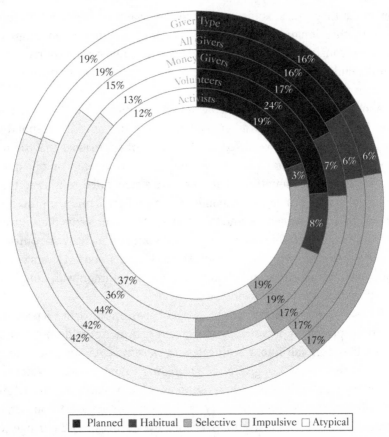

Giver Type
All Givers
Money Givers
Volunteers
Activists

19%
19%
15%
13%
12%

16%
16%
17%
24%
19%

7% 6% 6%

3%

8%

37%
36%
44%
42%
42%

19%
19%
17%
17%
17%

■ Planned ■ Habitual ■ Selective □ Impulsive □ Atypical

FIGURE 3.3 Giver types for Big 3 generosity forms.

data are portrayed in Figure 3.3, a racetrack graphic with nested rings illustrating the giver type distribution for various categories of givers: (a) all American givers, that is, people who give through any of the nine forms of generosity (outer ring); (b) Big 3 American givers; (c) Americans who give *money* to charitable causes; (d) Americans who *volunteer* for charitable causes; and (e) Americans who take *political action* for charitable causes (innermost ring). The second ring from the outside, representing Big 3 givers, shows a distribution of giving types nearly identical to the outer-ring, giver-all model. The middle ring shows that when we look only at those who give money, the proportions are again nearly equivalent; most are within a percentage point or two. The only notable difference is that there are fewer Atypical financial givers.

The volunteering layer (in Figure 3.3, the fourth ring inside the circle) represents the greatest distinction in proportional representation compared to the giver-all model. Planned givers (24 percent) make up a larger proportion of volunteers than of other kinds of givers (16–19 percent). Habitual givers represent a slightly larger proportion (8 percent), and Selective givers a similar proportion (19 percent) than in other giving forms. Volunteers represent the smaller proportion of Impulsive givers (36 percent, as compared to 42–44 percent for other giving forms), and Atypical givers also represent a smaller proportion of volunteers than do activists (13 percent, as compared to 22 percent). The skew of non-Impulsive givers to other types may be due to the difficulty of giving impulsively through volunteering compared to giving through financial donations, since there typically has to be some planning involved in volunteering time.

In political action there are only slight differences from the monetary or overall giver trends. (In Figure 3.3 the innermost ring of the circle represents the proportions of giver types among political activists). There are half as many Habitual political activists as Big 3 Habitual givers and fewer Impulsive political activists. Thus while the giver typology is robustly generalizable to other forms of generosity, there are some statistically minor but substantively interesting variations across giving types, namely that Impulsive givers average less volunteering and political action than donating money and that Habitual givers average less political action than donating money.

Having looked at each of the Big 3 giving types, we now zoom out to view giving in all nine forms of generosity. Figure 3.4 shows participation by giver type across all nine forms of generosity as compared to the average participation (discussed in chapter 1).[6] For donating money, the first set of columns shows that 80 to 90 percent of each type of giver donates money, with the exception of the 60 percent of Atypical givers who participate in donating money at a rate closer to the national average (55 percent). While there are various interesting differences among types within each form of giving, we are focused here on looking across the forms of giving for each giver type. Overall the participation patterns for each giver type show that:

- *Planned givers have the highest participation rates for seven of nine generosity forms.* One notable exception is that Habitual givers participate slightly more than Planned in donating money. Together Habitual and Planned givers participate at higher rates than Selective, Impulsive, and Atypical givers. The other exception for the high participation in giving among Planned givers is the group's average participation in relational

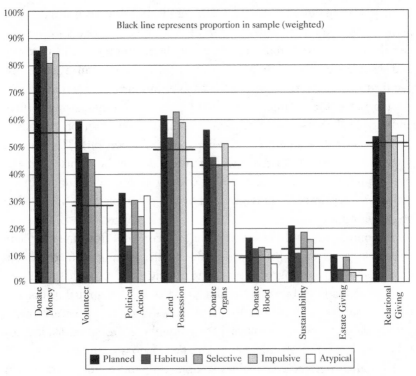

FIGURE 3.4 Generous behaviors by giver types.

giving: Planned givers tend to follow the pattern of participation for Impulsive and Atypical givers, which is near the national average.

- *Atypical givers have the lowest participation rates in all generosity forms except political action.* Atypical givers participate in political action at high rates similar to the participation of Planned and Selective givers.
- *The participation of Habitual givers varies by the form of giving.* Habitual givers donate money and relationally give at high rates. Participation in volunteering and donating blood is moderate and comparable to Selective givers. Participation in lending possessions, donating organs, sustainability, and estate giving is low among Habitual givers. Participation in political action is quite low—in fact lower than the national average. Among these nine forms, the rates of Habitual type participation in each generosity form are lower than that of Planned givers but often higher than Selective, Impulsive, and Atypical givers.
- *The participation of Selective givers varies by the form of giving.* Selective givers politically act, lend possessions, live sustainably, and donate their estate at high rates among the five types. Compared to Atypical givers,

Selective givers donate money, volunteer, donate blood, and relationally give at moderate rates. Selective givers donate their organs at rates comparable to the national average. In general, Selective givers participate in giving at lower rates than Planned and Habitual givers, while generally more than Impulsive and Atypical givers.

- *Impulsive givers often have low giving participation, but there are several exceptions.* For the least effort-heavy forms, namely lending possessions and donating organs, Impulsive givers donate at high rates. Impulsive givers participate in giving money more than Selective givers and in sustainability more than Habitual givers. Across the board Impulsive givers have lower participation rates than Planned givers and often lower than Habitual and Selective givers.

With this analysis we start to see a pattern of "specialization" in generosity forms by the different giver types.

Financial Giving

In laying out the various specializations of giver types, we start by examining the *absence* of participation in financial giving, that is, the percentage of each giver type that donated zero dollars in the past year (Figure 3.5)[7]:

- *Impulsive givers have the highest nonparticipation rate*, with more than 40 percent donating nothing to charitable causes in the past year.
- *Habitual givers have the lowest nonparticipation rate*, with less than 10 percent donating nothing to charitable causes in the past year.
- *Selective, Planned, and Atypical givers have moderate nonparticipation rates*, with around 14 percent people in these groups donating zero dollars in the past year.

Thus while Planned, Habitual, Selective, and Impulsive givers are all more likely than the Atypical to consider themselves givers, Impulsive givers are the most likely to not have donated any money during the past year, while Habitual givers are the least likely.

Next we look at the average amounts of money donated annually, where we also find some specialization among giving types (Figure 3.6). Since people who gave zero dollars significantly pull down the average dollar amounts, we show both the averages including these zero-dollar givers and the averages excluding them. Since high donation amounts can pull *up* the

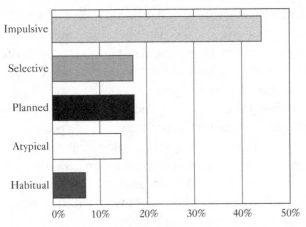

FIGURE 3.5 Nongivers by giver type.

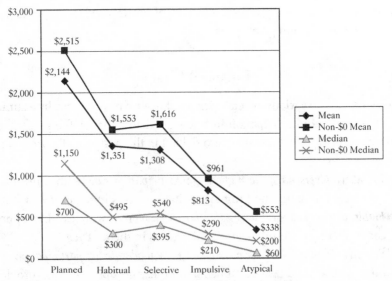

FIGURE 3.6 Average financial giving amount by giving type.

average (mean), we additionally show the median dollar amount given—the midpoint in the range of donation amounts. No matter how we define the average, we find a remarkably consistent pattern: on average Planned givers donate the most money, Habitual and Selective givers give amounts similar to each other but smaller than Planned givers, Impulsive givers give less, and Atypical givers donate the least. Specifically, Planned givers donate:

- An average of $2,000 more per year than Atypical givers.
- More than 2.5 times as much as Impulsive givers.
- More than twice the median average of Selective and Habitual givers.

The donations of Habitual and Selective givers are similar. More Habitual than Selective givers donate, but when Selective type donate, they donate slightly more. Habitual and Selective givers average lower donations than Planned givers but higher donations than Impulsive and Atypical givers. Of the four main types, Impulsive givers consistently rank lowest in their donation amounts, donating:

- About one-third of what Planned givers donate.
- About two-thirds to three-quarters of what Habitual or Selective givers donate.
- More than twice as much as Atypical givers.

Atypical givers average the lowest contributions:

- About half as much as Impulsive givers.
- Two-fifths as much as Habitual and Selective givers.
- A small fraction of what Planned givers donate.

To put this in perspective, the median donated by Atypical givers was $60 to charitable causes.

When we approximate the donation amounts as a percentage of income (not displayed),[8] roughly the same stepwise progression appears, from Planned givers at the top to Atypical givers at the bottom. Overall Americans give a median of 1 percent of household income to charity per year. Impulsive givers are one and a half times as likely as Planned, Habitual, and Selective givers to donate less than 1 percent of their annual income, while Planned givers are nearly three times more likely than Atypical givers to donate greater than 1 percent of their income.

Time Given

A somewhat different pattern occurs for giving volunteer time. Figure 3.7 displays the median amount of hours each giver type contributes per month, both excluding zero-hour givers (pattern bars) and including the zero-hour givers (*). Among those who volunteer:

- Selective givers donate the most time (a median of 16 hours per month).
- Planned givers average about two hours less per month than Selective givers (14 hours per month).

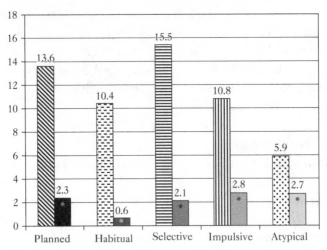

FIGURE 3.7 Median volunteering time by giver type (non-zero and zero medians).

- Impulsive and Habitual givers volunteer about the same amount (11 and 10 hours per month, respectively).
- Atypical givers volunteer less than half as much as Planned givers (6 hours per month).

It is important to note, however, that more than half of Selective, Impulsive, Habitual, and Atypical givers did not volunteer any hours in the past month. When we count the nonvolunteers in the average volunteering time (* bars), we see little difference in hours among the types, with the exception of Habitual givers, who average less than one hour of volunteering by this measure.

There is very little variation among giver types when it comes to time spent on political action (not displayed). So few Americans take political action at all that zero hours is the average across all types. Among those who take political action, however, some interesting trends are evident:

- Impulsive and Atypical givers donate the most time on average to political causes (about 3 hours per month).
- Planned and Selective givers contribute slightly fewer hours to political action (an average of 2 hours per month).
- Habitual givers devote the fewest hours to political action (averaging nearly one hour per month).

Connections and Patterns in Giving. As these findings demonstrate, there is some specialization in generosity forms across giver types. On average Planned and Habitual givers are more likely to give money; Planned givers tend to give greater amounts of money; Planned and Selective givers volunteer more hours; and Impulsive and Atypical givers give more time to political activism. Planned givers outpace all other types in their participation in most forms of generosity. Selective and Habitual givers participate at more moderate levels, though Selective givers do tend to spend more time volunteering and taking political action. Impulsive givers are less likely to participate in nearly all forms of giving behaviors. They do, however, still take political action and have a relatively high rate of financial giving, though their monetary donations tend to be small. By differentiating giving processes into these types we better understand which Americans participate in what generosity forms and to what extent.

Case Study Excursus: Part 1

Before undertaking our quantitative analyses of the characteristics that distinguish one type from another, we first revisit our 12 case studies to illustrate how the different combinations of processes for giving look in the lives of real people and how these processes operate together to form overall approaches to giving. Among our case studies, we have two Planned givers (Susan Baker and Ryan Dewey), two Habitual givers (Jackie Sawyer and George Nettleson), two Selective givers (Michael Johnson and Linda Chesterfield), three Impulsive givers (Cindy Phelps, Tanika Sandaval, and Regina Buckner), one Atypical giver (Deon Williams), and two nongivers (Rosa Perez and Anthony Ross).

Planned Givers

Ryan Dewey describes his overall approach to money this way:

> I generally make [a] decision because I don't want to go in[to] debt, so I try to manage my money carefully so that I don't have to go in[to] debt. . . . I am not really a budgeter, but I do review my finances on a monthly basis. I try to make sure what I'm spending is matching up with what I'm making. I withdraw cash and pay for everything with cash so that I mentally keep track of what I am spending. So those are my practical ways of doing that.

About his financial giving Ryan said, "I think I know my financial situation pretty well. I know my priorities, so I know that I give regularly to the church, and I also give to World Vision, and that is my giving at this point." He enjoys learning about the good that his donations are accomplishing: "I just think that's really exciting because you get a tangible feedback on what your money is doing and you can see that it is actually really helping somebody else's life." When we asked Ryan if he had any particular method for handling his giving, he replied:

> I set aside 10 percent of my income for the church and then the other giving with World Vision. I give to the church on a month-to-month basis and World Vision is through two larger payments twice a year, so it is doing a bit of planning in terms of the World Vision stuff because that is a sorta larger outflow of money at specific times a year, but yeah, *there's that planning aspect of it* [emphasis added].

We followed up to ask how he makes the payments, and he said, "I usually write a check."

In response we asked Ryan if he had any ideas about how this method may affect his pattern or amount of giving, and he said:

> I think I give the way I do because I would like it to be a little bit more visible. I would like to be reminded of what I'm giving. I know one of the options for giving to the church is an automatic withdrawal from your bank account sort of plan, but I like the idea of having to write the check because I feel like it makes you think a little bit more about it. I think it gives you the opportunity to realize that you are grateful for what you have and that you have the opportunity to give money away, so *I think there is a little bit more conscious thought in what you are doing rather than if it is an automatic withdrawal kind of situation* [emphasis added].

Thus while for some it may be desirable not to have to think about giving money, Ryan specifically wants to put conscious thought into his financial planning. He voiced what could be a motto for Planned givers: "I think there is always the tendency that if you don't plan for giving, you are not going to give."

When asked how much she tends to focus on giving, Susan Baker describes a routine system and conscious decision-making process:

We've been married forever now. Originally [early in our marriage] it was like $10 here and $20 there, and we just felt like it was just out of control. We were giving little bits and pieces. And so then [my husband], being the brilliant financial master he is, said, "Okay, we need to focus." So we sat down and brainstormed categories. [We said], "Okay. We have animal causes, we have people causes, we have whatever." So we broke things up into causes and then looked at the various organizations we had been giving to and said, "Let's just pick one. We don't need to give to six different environmental causes, let's pick one, and give them a large chunk of money that's meaningful." So I think about it a lot, but I've tried to stay focused on, we need to be narrow.

Discussing their overall giving goal, Susan said, "I think our goal at one point was we were shooting for $3,000, maybe $2,000. I don't remember. [My husband] figured it out, cause he's the financial wizard in the family. So he figured out what our total giving should be, and then we figured out how to divide it up." Susan describes a cautious approach that typifies our Planned givers:

When I stop and think "Is this a worthwhile organization, and do I really want to give the money, and do I really want to support them?" Then yes, there are certain organizations for which I really do want to give the money. And if I had an infinite supply of it, I would give them much more.

Susan shows how concern for the worthiness of charitable targets requires conscious, reflective thought about where to give to and how much.

Habitual Givers

When asked to describe her personality, Jackie Sawyer said,

I guess [laughs]. I'm very organized, very type-A. It's gotta be written down somewhere; it will happen. If I said I will do it, it will get done, which, again, can be a weakness, in that then "Oh my goodness, I have all this stuff that I have got to get done." But I'll get it done.

Thus her general approach to her life is to be methodical, organized, a list maker. However, when we asked how much she tends to pay attention to her family's financial giving, she replied:

> Not a whole lot. It's probably something that is just automatic and assumed. I mean, we have—we tithe to church, and so that's just an automatic thing that I don't really think about beyond making sure that the check is written every two weeks. . . . For the most part, most of our giving is *fairly automatic and just routine* [emphasis added].

Jackie specifically says she does not want to devote too much conscious thought to their giving:

> *Cause if I thought about it a lot, and I try not to,* I think about how much money there is that I just always have to try and remind myself that it's not my money—any of it. But there's a lot of money that goes out of this house to church and to school, and yeah, it's not money that we need. And so *I just have to always remember that I can't base my thinking on the whole amount, that that part of it has to be just gone, before I ever start figuring out how much money we have* [emphasis added].

She describes her method of and attitude toward financial giving:

> You just keep writing the checks, and eventually it gets easier [laughs]. And you find ways to just live with what you have and come to the understanding and the realization that what you have is enough. So I think that's what probably gradually, over time, makes it easier is that "I don't need that. It's not gonna be life-changing to have that."

Later, in response to how she figures out her giving, Jackie said, "I don't know cause a lot of times I don't really think about it a whole lot." Not spending too much time consciously considering their giving is part of Jackie's strategy. It enables her to give more than she would if she reflected on it too much and started wanting to keep more of the family's money for themselves. This strategy is distinct from that of Planned givers but ends up resulting in the same outcome: larger donation amounts.

It is not important to Jackie to learn specifically what her money is accomplishing: "I don't spend a lot of time worrying about it. . . . *I don't go investigate where my money went* [emphasis added]." When we asked if she gives by check, automatic withdrawal, or cash, Jackie's answer typified the Habitual giver approach: "It's a little of both. Church is checks. Compassion is direct withdrawal. World Vision, that's a direct withdrawal. A lot of times it's writing checks, and then there's a few things that you just pull cash for." The method is clear, obvious, and repetitive. The system is in place, and Jackie sees no need to give it much thought.

This method appears to be made possible in part by the Sawyers' implementation of the Dave Ramsey[9] method for household budgeting, which is taught in a number of religious congregations. Jackie explains:

> It's the Dave Ramsey method. We have a lot of Dave happening in this house. [My husband] has taught the financial peace class, and we've been through it. And so yeah, we're debt-free except the house. . . . We're on pretty much a cash system, although we do use the debit cards, but there are no credit cards in the household.

When asked if there are any factors that prevent them from giving more, she said, "Yep, there's no more dollars in the budget [laughs]. It's pretty much all assigned somewhere." Thus even their inability to give more reflects their habitual approach to their overall budget.

Similarly, when asked how much she pays attention to issues of volunteering, Jackie says, "I think that I don't really pay a whole lot of attention to it. It's just something that happens, and you don't even always think of it as volunteering. Like working at church or doing the stuff for school, *it's just part of what you do* [emphasis added]." From giving money to volunteering time, Jackie reflects a prototypical Habitual giver who has integrated giving into the fabric of her day-to-day life to such an extent that it takes barely any thought to maintain.

George Nettleson exhibits a similar approach to giving. George and his wife are generally savers, focused on saving for their daughters' college education and their own retirement. They have a budget and stick to it. Unlike many Americans with whom we have spoken, however, George and his wife include donations in that budget. They too feel the dread of not "making it" that so many Americans do, and George says, "It seemed like, 'Oh, we're just going to make it. We're just going to barely make it.'

And so I would like to have a nice cushion." When we asked George how he makes his buying and spending decisions, he answered:

> To put it plainly, I buy whatever [my wife] lets me buy [laughs]. Part of the reason we're doing so well is because she has managed our money, and she comes from a long line of people who are good with money and sensible. And I guess I probably should have taken more responsibility over the years, but I just totally trust almost anything that she says around money.

Regarding his financial giving George says:

> *We've always tithed.* . . . I think it's a good thing to do, and it's easier if you just go ahead and decide. *It's kind of freer if you go ahead and decide ahead of time,* "That's going to be my *lifestyle.* That's what I'm going to do." *Rather than when something comes up* you go, "Oh, I don't know. I don't want to give money" [emphasis added].

George seems to be somewhat disparaging of a Selective or Impulsive approach, which would not be as helpful for meeting his giving goals. He suggests that letting his giving run on autopilot better carries out his intention to give. After establishing the routine, the giving does not appear to require much conscious thought: "*Once we give money* to an organization that we feel is reputable, then we pretty much feel pretty good. *We don't get into following up*" [emphasis added].

Selective Givers

Michael Johnson's description of his approach to giving exemplifies the traits of a Selective giver:

> I wouldn't say that I spend [a] great deal of time thinking about it. *I react when the occasion is presented.* I mean, I'll give to the church, and then, let's say, organizations in the field of aging I think are beneficial, university, some disease-related charities, particularly like cancer because my wife died from cancer [emphasis added].

Michael shows that Selective givers share with Impulsive givers a reactive approach to giving. However, he also exemplifies how Selective giving differs from Impulsive: it involves conscious, direct attention to various causes and generally a greater commitment to give in one way or another.

Michael goes on to say that he thinks giving in general is a good thing, despite how his specific donation amounts or causes might fluctuate: "I mean, in terms of saying what is the proper amount, that is a much more difficult thing to assess. But the general proposition that people should give, I think is a good one, and one that I support." He continues to embody the Selective giver qualities by saying:

> I give because I want to. *And in most cases when I'm asked. Well, [in] the vast majority of cases, I would say that I do give.* I get a lot of solicitations. But most of the time I'll do it on my own. In cases when I do not, it's usually not because I'm opposed to the charity; it's just that I've got so many things to do.... It's not that there is any strong feeling against giving to a particular charity [emphasis added].

Here Michael describes the process of being a Selective giver: having a general orientation to give, waiting for opportunities to arise, and then picking and choosing particular causes to support based on interest and available resources.

When we asked Michael, "What are the primary reasons you give money away?," he responded, "*Cause I support a cause*, or I support religion, maybe what the Catholic Church is doing, or the desire to help people who would benefit from what the charity is doing [emphasis added]." He added:

> For the most part I wouldn't say that I've sought out a particular charity to give to. *It's been more passive in the sense that I may get a solicitation, and then I respond....* I wouldn't say that I have any particular method. As I said to an earlier question, I *usually respond to solicitations rather than seeking [them] out.* You know, particular charities [emphasis added].

Michael also demonstrates how Selective givers determine their volunteering:

> I think that it is a good thing to do. I think from a moral standpoint it is desirable, and I personally would like to do more myself. Maybe someday I will have the opportunity to do what I think should be

done.... I have a desire. But it's got to be tempered with what is attainable given my time schedule. And I recognize that it's very limited, at least for now. Maybe later on I will be able to do more.

In discussing how he picks charitable organizations, Michael said:

Well, the church, because it's something that I was familiar with.... And then at school because my daughter had gone to [that school], and this happened to be after she had graduated. When my wife was alive, I mean, we did more.... Since I've been widowed the volunteer work has dropped very, very significantly, and also because I do not have a younger daughter [who is still in school].

Michael said his general approach was to "wait to be asked, more so than seeking out [the opportunities to give]."

Linda Chesterfield is another excellent example of a Selective giver. When asked how much she thinks about financial giving, she replied, "Not a whole lot. I mean, we, he gives to church every week. And then they have a diocesan appeal, with the diocese, once a year, asks for even more money. So I pay attention to the aspect that it's coming out of our finances." She goes on to explain, "I think it's *giving when you can. When it's to a good cause*, it's good. ... *I don't seek it out* [emphasis added]." Linda has not fully bought into the concept that it is important to give money regularly. She continues:

Sometimes you'll see these charities or these drives on TV for muscular dystrophy or want you to give money. [Then I] give money. Sometimes one of my primary thoughts about giving is *If you can give, great. If you can't, like you shouldn't feel obligated to.... I don't pay a whole lot of attention to it* [emphasis added].

Linda describes her giving as primarily a result of her husband's wanting to support their church and his college, coupled with occasional support for charities that her children tell her about or their math-a-thons for St. Jude's.

When describing her method for giving, Linda says, "We talk it out as a family, and if we can afford to do so, great. If we can't ... *It's looking at whether we can afford to do it* or not is a big, you know, decision factor and whether we care about the cause at all [emphasis added]." At the same time, she does sometimes wish she could be more generous:

> Yeah, sometimes I feel like I might be a little bit Scrooge-ish when it comes to just doing the simple things that we do, and I should just give away and not complain. But then there are those times when we were in a financial situation where we could do more. I would like to do more, because some of the causes that I believe in, we don't currently give to.

Thus whether Linda financially gives depends on a situation-by-situation selection process that involves a combination of how much money her family has available at that time and how worthy the cause is or how much she cares about it.

Linda also describes herself as selective when it comes to volunteering. When asked how much she thinks about the issues of volunteering, she said, "*I don't really find myself thinking about it*, unless it's mentioned or people are asking for volunteer help. But I don't sit around just thinking about it [emphasis added]." Almost exactly echoing how she described her approach to monetary giving, she explains, "I think that *if you have the time, and somebody asked you* to volunteer, *and you can*, then *if you've got no good reason not to*, then why not? But I also think if you don't have the time, or the resources, you shouldn't feel obligated [emphasis added]."

Impulsive Givers

As the largest giver type, Impulsive givers represent a broad swath of the American population. Impulsive givers are typified by a spontaneous and situation-based decision-making approach coupled with a giving system that "just happens." Each of our Impulsive interviewees shows us how this approach to giving plays out in daily life.

When we asked Cindy Phelps, the high-powered young lawyer in New York, what she thinks life is all about, she replied:

> I think life is all about being happy. But at the same time, your happiness depends on what are you giving to your community, to other people. How are you helping, giving most of yourself, and things

that you feel passionate about? Trying to make change in the world. Doing things that make things better, make the world a better place.

We followed up by asking, "What are your highest life priorities?" To which she replied, "I want to be happy and financially secure. I want to have a family eventually and have kids. I think my highest priority is just being happy."

Cindy describes herself, though, as "very, very frugal": "I don't spend money, usually at all." This is probably because she thinks of herself as "financially limited." However, she does say she has given money in the past. When we asked her how she has found causes to support financially, she answered, "I get the mailers." She also recounts doing a charitable race with friends: "I didn't really donate much money, but I did my entry fee. I did that with a group of women that I work with in my profession in general. So that also kind of came to me."

One of the main forms of giving that Cindy describes is giving clothes to Goodwill. This happens sporadically, "whenever I clean out my closet." "You just do that kind of on a whim?" we asked. "Yeah, just to clean," she replied. She summarizes her Impulsive approach to giving by saying, "I do it maybe two or three times a year, *whenever I have the ability, or whenever I have some extra cash* [emphasis added]." Despite her current approach to giving as opportunities come, Cindy says, "But should I be better off in the future, which I hope to be, I will give more as my income goes up."

Despite her spontaneous and irregular approach to financial giving, Cindy does volunteer weekly. Every Tuesday after work she volunteers in an after-school program for low-income youth. When asked whether she thinks volunteering is important, she said, "I think people should if they have the time, but then I understand that there are people who don't have the time." She describes her reasons for volunteering:

> I think it's because I'm so grateful that [the] things that have hap-
> pened to me in my life [are the things] that I'm grateful for. I should
> show or give back, show that I am grateful for this and give back to
> the community and perpetuate the "pay it forward" kind of thing. . . . It
> makes me feel like I'm giving back to my community, and I like that.

She goes on to explain that she got involved when she was new to town, "and I wanted to meet new people and it was a good organization to both meet new people and volunteer time."

In summary, Cindy practices some forms of generosity, the most notable of which is volunteering a few hours in a weekly after-school program, along with some occasional financial giving and sporadic clothing donations. At the end of the interview she said, "I would like to think when I'm older, and have more money, and I have probably more free time, that I would give more. That I would be able to." Cindy is a typical Impulsive giver, someone who is generally pro-generosity, certainly not opposed to it, and who gives from time to time as specific requests arise. Impulsive givers see themselves as not having enough time or money to contribute regularly and have a less than enthusiastic overall commitment to giving, resulting in sporadic participation as occasions and requests arise.

We asked Tanika Sandaval, the single mom of three boys in Los Angeles, "How much do you tend to think about or pay attention to the issue of financial giving?" She replied, "Hmm, [if] it's just something that really touches my heart, really. If I can do things, I would love that." When we asked whether or not giving money is a moral duty, she said, "That's the in-between. I go in-between." We followed up by asking, "What would it take for you to give away more money?" She said, "I guess my sources is limited now. So I guess if I had more, and I was able to do it, then I would." She continued, "It's not so much the budget, like if I see someone who need it, or really—I'll help, like food or something like that, someone may not have food. I would go and take the meat out, groceries out, give it to them—so yeah." Though she seems generally open to giving money away for charitable causes, she explains, "You have to watch that kinda stuff too, because if you gave everyone—say a hundred people a dollar—then how much is that gonna cost you. But you have to be practical. [If] it's for a cause and I see it's going to something, I don't mind doing that."

As for how she selects a target for giving, Tanika explains, "If they are [receptive] to it and they feel like they appreciate it, genuinely appreciate it, to me, I feel like I'm gaining." She continued, "It feels good when you know you can help somebody, it does." We see from this that one situational factor of her giving approach, in addition to the availability of funds, is the extent to which she believes that someone will benefit in the moment of the gift. Though she volunteers frequently at her children's school, it seems that her approach to volunteering is also Impulsive. When Tanika describes how much time she gives to the school, she says, "*It kinda varies* [emphasis added]," and explains that she will attend meetings and help out as a liaison if she is approached by school administrators or other parents. The chances that she will agree to volunteer when asked to do so appear to vary based on factors such as her available time and how much she likes the person asking her. Thus Tanika does not consider giving until the situation presents itself, and when the situation arises, the decision to give "just happens" in the moment depending on how she is feeling that day about her ability to give.

Regina Buckner describes her household's overall approach to money matters as operating on a need basis: "Whether it's something we need. If we don't need it, and we don't have the money, we usually don't get it." On the topic of financial giving she says:

> I can't say that I think a whole lot about it. I know, when we see the red [Salvation Army] kettles, I usually let the girls take whatever pocket change that we have. And they absolutely love putting the coins into the bucket, so I let them do that. And then we'll get phone calls from all sorts of charities, especially around tax time, when of course they know everybody's getting their money [laughs]. And then I'll usually give a little bit to different ones.

When we asked how she finds out about options for giving, Regina explained, "Usually I get a phone call, or a letter in the mail. And if I can look back at the paperwork that they send me and make sure it's a legitimate charity, then usually I will send them a little bit, if I have it." In summarizing her approach to giving away money, she says, "*I usually give a little bit to anybody that asks*, though I prefer to give more to the ones that, I know will touch somebody I know or are like myself [emphasis added]." This is the Impulsive process: she gives when asked, spontaneously, without reflective, conscious thought or planning. However, unlike some of the more resourced interviewees in the Impulsive category, Regina is just trying to keep her head above water financially and has little to give away.

Atypical Givers

Atypical givers represent a group who claim to give but do not exhibit any specific approach to giving, and who often lack discernible patterns in other categories. They are "sorta" givers who share some characteristics with Impulsive givers but others with nongivers. Mirroring the rarity of Atypical givers nationally, our case studies produced only one individual who met this type's criteria: Deon Williams.

Deon describes his overall approach to money in this way: "I am the worst money manager in the world. I get like almost $2,100 a month, and by the time the end of the month come, I'm damn near flat broke. I spend my money on impulse. If I need this, I go get it, if I need that, I go get it." This sounds very similar to our Impulsive givers. In fact Deon describes his approach to giving this way: "Actually, it's a *spur of the moment type thing* when I give to charities. It's not like I write checks and mail off monies to this, that, the other [emphasis added]." He continues:

> Okay, when I say spur of the moment things, like I'm riding down the street, and you can see the fire department standing on the side with the boots. You throw money in the boot or something, help people, something like that. It's just a spur of the moment type thing when I give.

Here Deon sounds exactly like an Impulsive giver, but he did not answer the questions on the survey in the same way. In his survey responses to the giving system and method questions, he answered that he does not give money away for charitable causes and that his approach to giving is spontaneous. There was an option on the survey to respond to the approach question "Do not give money away," yet despite answering the prior question by saying he did not give away money, he answered the approach question by describing his approach as spontaneous. We presume that this set of answers results from having such low participation in giving that he does not really have an approach. We suspect that Deon did not count the fire department giving on the survey, for example, because the donation was pocket change. His participation is likely low enough that he does not always register it as giving. This is different from Impulsive givers, who are cognizant of their nonroutine, nonreflective giving but still identify as givers.

Nongivers

Describing her overall approach to money matters, Rosa Perez says, "I go by budget. I write everything down, how much everything is, and I was always taught to take care of my bills before my entertainment or anything like that. So if I have something [left] over, for fun time, then I'll do that.

But if I don't, I don't, and move on." It is a challenge for her to have money left over, to save at all, let alone to give away money.

Rosa says she really has no method for giving, other than occasionally bartering down a giving request: "No, *I don't really think about it.* When I was working and I got the stuff in the envelope—cancer this and stuff like that, I was giving them like $20. Even though they asked for $35, I'll give them $20 [emphasis added]." After she made that donation, she became frustrated by the repeated contact: "Yeah. But then [they] just kept mailing me and mailing me and mailing me and mailing me nonstop. And I'm just like, I don't have it. Like right now I don't have it. So *when I get it in the mail I rip it up cause I don't have it* [emphasis added]." When we asked her to summarize her overall approach, she said, "I would say *if I had it, I would give it* [emphasis added]."

Anthony Ross is also a nongiver. Discussing his overall approach to financial matters, he says, "Managing my money, let's see. Not over-drafting. Buying food, there's not a lot of things to buy." He has no approach to giving since he is not currently engaged in any giving that he recalls. However, he explains that were he to give, his process would be Impulsive: "*It's something that I don't think about on a common basis.* Something that is kind of impulsive, something that hits me. Impulsive. *Out of nowhere.* Like, *if someone's asking for money, then you make a judgment call.* It's not something I really think about [emphasis added]."

In summary, Americans' approaches to giving fall into six distinct types—Planned, Habitual, Selective, Impulsive, Atypical, and nongivers—based on two sets of polarities. Each of our case studies shows how the various combinations of giving processes play out in the lives of ordinary people. Now that we have provided real-life illustrations of these types of givers, we resume our quantitative analyses on the relationships between giving approaches and outcomes.

The "Who" of American Giver Types

Now that we have illustrated the giving processes of our 12 case studies and have some sense of each giver type's generosity behaviors, we examine who these different giver types are. Here we explore how the different social status characteristics that we discussed in chapter 2 apply to giver types.[10] Figure 3.8 shows the distribution of demographic characteristics across giver types. The notations in the top of the bars represent whether there is a statistically significant difference compared to Atypical givers.[11]

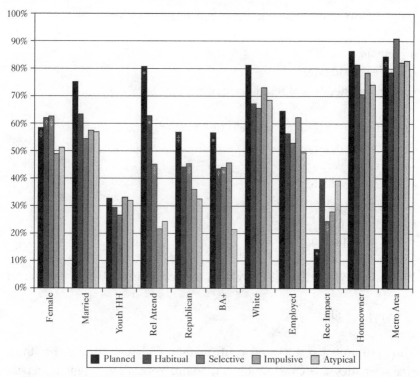

Note: † p<.1, ‡ p<.05, *p<.01

FIGURE 3.8 Participation differences by giver type.

These differences are independent of the other characteristics. For example, differences regarding female participation in giving hold constant any differences in income by gender.

These statistical analyses reveal patterns of social statuses for each group. Overall we find a linear relationship between income and giving type. Planned givers have the highest household income on average, followed by Habitual, Impulsive, and Selective givers. All four of these types have significantly higher incomes, on average, than Atypical givers. We also find that Planned givers are more likely than Atypical givers to be:

- Female
- Regular attenders of religious services
- Republican
- Residents of urban areas
- College graduates
- Not as impacted by the recession

Habitual givers are more apt than Atypical givers to be:

- Female
- College graduates
- Regular attenders of religious services

Compared to Atypical givers, Selective givers are more often:

- Female
- College graduates
- Regular attenders of religious services
- Republican
- Not as impacted by the recession

Impulsive givers are more likely than Atypical givers to be:

- College graduates

Thus our initial results and confirmatory analyses indicate that three characteristics are consistently important: education, religious service attendance, and income.[12] These three measures are the most meaningful social status indicators for differentiating giver types.

To study how these three key characteristics (education, religious attendance, and income) relate to giver types, we plot a series of predicted probabilities in Figures 3.9. These predicted probabilities show the role that these three malleable social status characteristics play in differentiating the four main giver types from Atypical givers. They are malleable in contrast to characteristics that givers can not change, such as age, gender, and the impact of the recession. But income, religious service attendance, and educational attainment are characteristics that Americans exert some control over. They are also the ones that are most likely to fluctuate over the course of life. Thus we focus on these three traits to understand their important role in differentiating giver types and to highlight how giving processes interact with life changes and social contexts over the life course.

Household Income and College Degree

The first series in Figure 3.9 pictures our data on that relationship by giver types (a=Planned, b=Habitual, c=Selective, d=Impulsive),

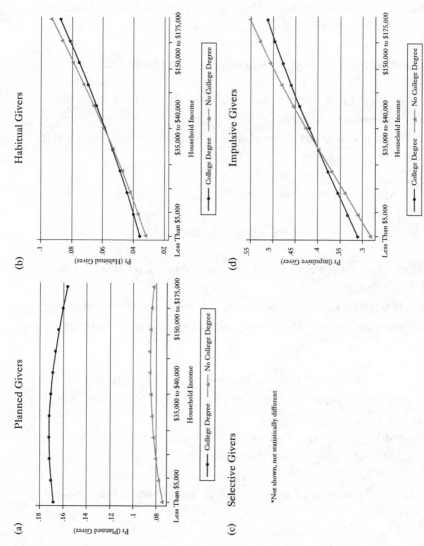

FIGURE 3.9 Predicted probabilities by household income and college degree for each giver type (a=Planned, b=Habitual, c=Selective, d=Impulsive).

controlling for all the other social status characteristics described previously.[13] Household income is depicted along the x-axis and covers the entire range of 19 income brackets, with the lowest bracket on the left and the highest on the right. Attainment of a four-year college degree is depicted by the different lines. The y-axis represents the predicted probabilities for being a giver of each type based upon the varying education and income levels.

The results in Figure 3.9(a) show that being a Planned giver is:

- More likely for Americans with a college degree than those without (10 percentage point gap).
- Fairly unrelated to income level (the association is small, as shown by the relative flatness of both lines).

Thus having a college degree makes someone significantly more likely to be a Planned giver.

As Figure 3.9(b) illustrates, being a Habitual giver is:

- More likely for Americans with higher income levels than those with lower income.
- Fairly unrelated to college degree status (the two lines representing different education levels are very close to each other and overlap in places).

Thus the likelihood of being a Habitual giver is largely distinguished by income: the greater the household income, the greater the chance of someone being a Habitual giver.

Impulsive giver results pictured in Figure 3.9(d) are similar to those of Habitual givers. Being an Impulsive giver is:

- More likely for Americans with higher income levels than those with lower income.
- Fairly unrelated to college degree status.

There appears to be a moderate relationship of college degree with income level in predicting Impulsive giver types: an American with a high income and no college degree has a larger probability of being an Impulsive giver than one with the same high income and a college degree. Conversely an American with a low income and a college degree has a slightly higher probability of being an Impulsive giver than one with a low income and no college degree.

The relationship between household income level and college degree attainment is similar for Habitual and Impulsive givers: *higher incomes relate to a greater likelihood of being either a Habitual or Impulsive giver.* The relationship between household income level and college degree attainment for Planned givers is different: college degree status is a key differentiator, regardless of income level. There was no difference between the interaction of income and college degree for Selective and Atypical givers.

Household Income and Religious Attendance

Next we examine how household income and religious attendance relate to giver types, as seen in the series of models pictured in Figure 3.10. These figures represent the full range of income brackets along the x-axis and predict the likelihood of being the specified giver type along the y-axis. The lines in these figures represent regular religious service attendance. These figures split givers into two groups based on religious service attendance: "religious regulars" (those who attend once a month or more, shown by the dark line with square markers) and "not religious regulars" (those who attend less than once a month, shown by the light line with diamond markers).[14]

The results in Figure 3.10(a) show that being a Planned giver is:

- More likely for religious regulars than not religious regulars (by a gap of 25 percentage points).
- Fairly unrelated to income level.

Thus the likelihood of being a Planned giver is largely distinguished by how often someone attends religious services: attending them regularly makes the chances of being a Planned giver significantly higher.

Habitual giver results are pictured in Figure 3.10(b). Being a Habitual giver is:

- More likely for religious regulars than those who are not religious regulars.
- More likely for Americans with higher income levels than those with lower income.

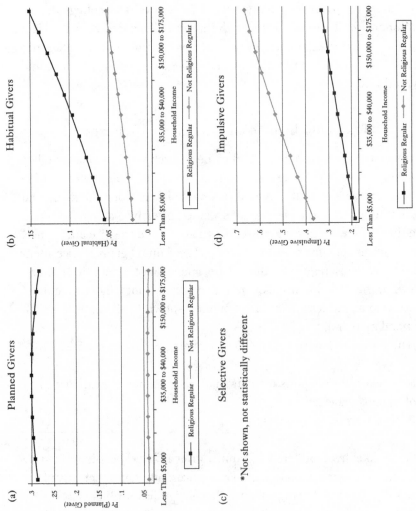

FIGURE 3.10 Predicted probabilities by household income and religious attendance for each giver type (a=Planned, b=Habitual, c=Selective, d=Impulsive).

Thus regular religious service attendance and high income are both related to a greater likelihood of being a Habitual giver.

The results in Figure 3.10(d) are similar for income and inversed for religious attendance, showing that being an Impulsive giver is:

- More likely for those who are not religious regulars than for religious regulars.
- More likely for Americans with higher income levels than those with lower income.

Thus the likelihood of being an Impulsive giver is largely distinguished by income and religious service attendance.

The income relationships in Figure 3.10 remain basically the same as in Figure 3.9: higher incomes relate to a greater likelihood of being either a Habitual or an Impulsive giver but do not change the likelihood of being a Planned giver. However, the relationship between regular religious attendance, income, and giver type varies. Regular religious attendance makes someone more likely to be a Planned giver, regardless of income level. Regular religious attendance is also a key differentiator for Habitual and Impulsive givers, but income level matters. Americans are significantly more likely to be Habitual givers if they are religious regulars and have higher income, while they are more likely to be Impulsive givers if they are not religious regulars and have higher income. There was no difference in the interaction of income and regular religious attendance for Selective givers in comparison to Atypical givers.

Religious Attendance and College Degree

In a final set of analyses, depicted in Figure 3.11, we focus on the relationships between college degree and religious attendance in differentiating giver types. In this series of charts we evaluate the full range of frequency of religious service attendance (unlike in Figures 3.9 and 3.10, where this was a dichotomous measure classifying people simply as regular or not regular) in tandem with educational attainment (having vs. lacking a four-year college degree). Religious attendance increases in frequency along the x-axis, with values ranging from never (left) to more than once a week (right).[15] Education level is depicted via the lines (having a college degree is represented by the dark line with circular markers, while lacking one is represented by the light line with triangular markers). The y-axis

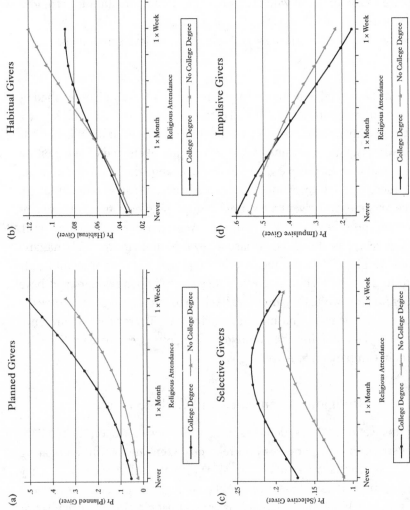

FIGURE 3.11 Predicted probabilities by religious attendance and college degree for each giver type (a=Planned, b=Habitual, c=Selective, d=Impulsive).

displays the predicted probabilities for being each giver type based on the religious attendance and college degree attainment.[16]

The results in Figure 3.11(a) show that being a *Planned giver*:
- Increases in likelihood as religious service attendance increases.
- Is more likely for college graduates than those without college degrees at every level of religious attendance.

This relationship is positive, which means that the likelihood of being a Planned giver increases in magnitude with more frequent religious service attendance.

Habitual giver results are pictured in Figure 3.11(b). Being a *Habitual giver*:
- Generally increases in likelihood as religious service attendance increases.
- Is unrelated to college degree attainment among infrequent religious attenders.
- Is more likely for frequent religious attendance among those *without* a college degree.

Thus attending religious services at least two times a month affects the likelihood of being a Habitual giver to a greater extent if someone does not have a college degree.

Selective giver results are pictured in Figure 3.11(c). Being a *Selective giver*:
- Has a curvilinear relationship with religious attendance. The likelihood is higher among moderate attenders than higher or lower frequency attenders.
- Is more likely for college graduates, especially those with moderate attendance.

Thus those who attend religious services semifrequently and have a college degree are the most likely to be Selective givers. Interestingly it appears that for this type of giver, religious service participation may also be selectively engaged, mirroring the giving behaviors of the group.

Impulsive giver results pictured in Figure 3.11(d) show that the likelihood of being an *Impulsive giver*:

- Has an inverse relationship with religious attendance, such that more frequent attendance relates to a lower likelihood of being an Impulsive giver.
- Is most likely for college graduates with low attendance.
- Among those with frequent religious attendance, is more likely for those without a college degree.

Thus college graduates who never attend religious services have the greatest likelihood of being Impulsive givers, while graduates who attend frequently have the lowest likelihood.

Combined the results of the analyses in Figures 3.9 to 3.11 indicate that being a Planned giver is more closely related to having a college degree and attending religious services frequently than to income. Habitual givers have the strongest relationship with high income levels and regular religious attendance, especially when someone has both characteristics, with college degree being less relevant. Selective givers have the strongest relationship with college degree attainment and moderately frequent religious service attendance, especially when someone has both characteristics, with income being less relevant. Impulsive givers are most often those who attend religious services infrequently or never and those with higher income, especially when someone has both characteristics, and college degree matters slightly.

Case Study Excursus: Part 2

To put these findings about giver types and social status characteristics into the context of real lives, we briefly revisit a few of our case studies. We look at how our key social status characteristics (income, religious attendance, and college degree) shape our givers' practices and lives.

Planned Givers

Our statistical models showed that attending religious services regularly and having a college degree are linked with a higher likelihood of being a Planned giver, and Ryan Dewey shows both traits. He is currently in a doctoral program and frequently attends religious services. Recall that he gives a great deal of his modest income to charitable causes, in addition to regularly volunteering during his little free time. Ryan describes his reason for giving so generously:

> I give away money again cause of my religious convictions. I feel that is the right thing to do, wanting to model my life after Christ and wanting to do the right thing, and to see the impact it can have in people's lives, see the good things it can do for other people and to help them.

Thinking back to the way that Ryan describes the conscientious thought he devotes to his giving practices, it is also evident that his high education affects how he approaches giving.

Habitual Givers

The combination of attending religious services very frequently and having a high income—a combination common to Habitual givers—is exemplified in Jackie Sawyer. She and her husband make nearly twice as much money as Ryan does (the income difference), but they also attend church frequently. Jackie explains her generous giving:

> I think it's part of my belief system. Again, that none of it is mine and that, therefore, I am obligated to at least give the 10 percent, if not more, because that's what God asked for.... But I think it comes back from my basic belief system that the Bible tells me I should tithe, and so that's what I'm gonna do, without asking or questioning.

Though Jackie and her husband do have college degrees (a factor that does differentiate likelihood of being a Habitual giver), we can see how their giving process—in which Jackie says she intentionally does not give much thought to their financial donations—is less connected to higher education than the typical giving process of Planned givers.

George Nettleson also exemplifies how regular religious practice can play a key role in being a Habitual giver. He is a practicing, churchgoing Baptist, and his religious faith clearly underlies his conviction to give generously. George believes in the authority of the Bible and as such thinks that tithing is part of a Christian life. He says, "I want to tithe because faith is part of my lifestyle.... The tithe is a no-brainer. It's there." This is a classic Habitual approach to giving based on following the concept of the tithe.

Selective Givers

Our Selective givers, Michael Johnson and Linda Chesterfield, both attend religious services significantly less frequently; they are selective in their approach to religious involvement as well as giving. They both had a religious upbringing in the Catholic Church but do not consider faith as key to their day-to-day lives, as do the two Habitual givers. However, they have very high incomes, higher in fact than most of our Habitual and Planned givers. And they both have college degrees, reflecting the bump in the middle of Figure 3.11(c) that shows the high likelihood that those with college degrees who attend religious services semiregularly will be Selective givers.

Impulsive Givers

True to the predicted probability patterns, our three Impulsive givers—Cindy Phelps, Tanika Sandaval, and Regina Buckner—all attend religious services infrequently or never, and two have moderate income. None of these Impulsive givers names religious beliefs as a major motivator for their giving participation, though they all have had some religious exposure in their youth. Educational attainment appears not to play a major role in differentiating these cases, as they span the range from having a high school degree only, to some college, to an advanced degree.

Atypical Givers

Our Atypical giver, Deon Williams, does not have a college degree, has a modest income, and does not attend religious services regularly. He did, however, have some religious influence in his youth, which could be part of what differentiates him from being a nongiver. Though his income level is moderately high, he is the case we described previously as having residual poverty from his childhood that appears to dampen restrict his potential engagement with more generous giving.

Summary

Our case studies generally exemplify the trends we found in this chapter regarding the role of social status characteristics in differentiating giver types, including the trends of the predicted probabilities. The one notable exception to this is Susan Baker, our Planned giver who never attends religious services. Her high education level and moderate income, however, do mirror our predicted probabilities.

Conclusion: The "How" of American Generosity

In studying how Americans approach giving, we discovered that they fall into four primary types of givers with distinct habits, levels of giving, and generous practices. The most notable highlights are that Planned givers tend to outpace all other givers in their generosity participation. Habitual givers are also often very generous. Selective givers exhibit a bit of a giving plateau, rarely matching the generosity of Planned and Habitual givers. Impulsive givers tend to be the lowest givers of the four types. Atypical givers blend Impulsive and nongiver patterns, insofar as they retain a minor giving identity but have no discernible approach to their giving.

Our case studies articulate how these giving processes work in the daily lives of ordinary Americans. As both the case studies and the quantitative analyses demonstrate, giver types have distinct approaches to financial giving that explain differences in other forms of generosity. These giver types also exhibit different social status characteristics, with some of the most prominent patterns being in the interplay of college degree attainment, religious service attendance, and annual household income.

In examining the intersection of these three mutable characteristics, we illustrated a more nuanced picture of American generosity. People who have college degrees and are highly religious appear to be more likely to be Planned givers, but income does not distinguish Planned givers. Higher income and frequent religious service attendance, but not having a college degree, are linked to a higher likelihood of being a Habitual giver. Selective givers are more likely to have college degrees and moderate levels of attendance at religious services, while income level matters less. Americans who do not regularly attend religious services and have higher incomes, especially if they also have college degrees, are most likely to be Impulsive givers. Combining the results of this chapter with the findings of the previous chapters, we can see that Americans group together in their approaches to giving, and that approaches relate to giving outcomes.

One goal in identifying and investigating these approaches to giving is to enable ourselves and other scholars to more readily discuss the different kinds of American philanthropy that exist in the general public. Rather than treating all American givers as one group and comparing them only to those who do not give, this more nuanced approach allows us to better understand different shades of philanthropic giving. These analyses have numerous implications for charities, which can tailor their strategies, campaigns, and appeals according to the form of generosity they are requesting and the type of giver they hope to reach.

We do want to note that nothing in this analysis is meant to imply that one type of giver is necessarily "better" than another. Some may be more likely to give greater amounts than others or more likely to respond to certain types of fundraising strategies, but all of these givers share in common a willingness to give to charitable causes, and all should be respected as the potential giver base from whom contributions can be drawn. It is also important to reiterate that these giver types are not necessarily fixed and immutable; it is quite plausible to imagine that people change types throughout the course of their lives as their resources change. There could even be a life-course trajectory to giving approaches that may move someone from one type of giver to another depending on a change in their commitment to giving. For example, people may change their process of giving due to negative experiences with giving. Identifying the different types of givers, as we have done in this chapter, makes exploring these questions possible. We have here developed the picture of how Americans participate in a range of philanthropic behaviors, coupled with who gives and how much. In the next chapter we turn to why Americans give.

4

Personal and Social Orientations to Giving

A SOCIAL PSYCHOLOGICAL APPROACH

UP TO THIS point we have painted a picture of *how much* Americans participate in different forms of generosity (chapter 1), *who* gives from different social statuses and regional locations (chapter 2), and *how* Americans approach their giving (chapter 3). In this chapter we ask: *Why* do people give? What orients them to give at all? We have established that they need to have resources to give away, that their socioeconomic status and regional location make them more or less likely to give, and that the approach they take to their giving affects whether and how much they give. But *why* is one person more likely to give than another?

In this chapter we begin to answer that question through the lens of social psychology theories. We will describe the survey questions we use to measure how personal and social orientations relate to giving and explore how seeing oneself as a generous person relates to giving behaviors. Our case studies will illustrate how these factors play out in real life.

A Social Psychological Approach

As American givers navigate a range of possible life orientations, they create dynamic personal and social lives. Using social psychological theories,[1] we believe that generous actions are likely shaped by ongoing personal and social processes. Americans have a range of personalities and respond to their social environment in a variety of ways. Over time these interactions provide feedback to each person about his or her role in society, feedback that shapes distinct orientations toward one's social life and one's identity within it. We suspect that the importance of generosity in people's lives is situated within this intrapersonal context. This context includes people's perceptions of their relationships with others; how people perceive their social context and how they view their role in the world are key, we believe, to understanding people's generous actions.

So what kinds of personal and social orientations affect people's interest in giving away their money, time, and possessions? How do intrapersonal orientations extend beyond people's demographic and cultural backgrounds to explain why some people act in certain ways and others do not? In the field of sociology we often focus on people's social status characteristics to the neglect of their intrapersonal orientations. The former may tell us who an actor is, but we must study the latter to explain why people give.

People vary within any social category (gender, ethnicity, socioeconomic status, education level, marital status, or age). In each demographic group, some are quiet-natured while others seem to never stop talking; some love trying new things while others want the comfort of the familiar; some are generally happy and others seem to never be happy no matter how good they seem to have it. Some love to be around people and others hate being in a crowd; some think about social issues or charitable causes constantly, while others never think about them. We meet all these variations of people, and many more, in our day-to-day interactions.

In this chapter we incorporate intrapersonal orientations into our analysis of why some people choose certain philanthropic actions and others do not. Our interdisciplinary backgrounds in sociology, psychology, social psychology, social work, and education shape our understanding of these social psychological influences on people's behaviors. Like many interdisciplinary endeavors, this portion of the journey may feel a bit outside of the disciplinary-trained readers' comfort zone, insofar as we seek to move beyond traditional disciplinary-specific conventions. A sociologist might wonder, for example, why we include a measure of anxiety in our analysis of generosity. Ample evidence from other disciplines (e.g., psychology) suggests we must include this measure and others like it to adequately understand human behavior. The case studies help illustrate the importance and interaction of these factors. Americans' lives and beliefs cannot be neatly divided into disciplinary categories for the purpose of analysis. Pushing beyond such constraints can lead us to interpret the world in a different light and provide new insights into the subjects we wish to understand.

This study in generosity specifically aims to connect the myriad disciplines in a comprehensive way so that we can gain such insights across our disparate and specialized pursuits. We do not claim to do justice to the full range of social psychological findings on the topics we cover. We value theoretical insights from other disciplines and incorporate many of them into the following analyses in an effort to transcend some disciplinary constraints, bridge the academic-practitioner divide, and further our understanding of "big question" topics such as human generosity. As one of our goals in this chapter, we seek to bring together insights from disparate but complementary disciplines to begin a discussion of how the personal and the social come together to explain American generosity.[2]

Before we move on, we provide a bit of background on how we arrived at the intrapersonal measures that are the focus of this chapter. As part of our survey we assessed a wide array of social and social psychological measures that other research shows are related to generosity. Respondents to the survey were asked to assess many of their intrapersonal characteristics: level of depression, extroversion-introversion, locus of control, level of social trust and social solidarity, and a host of other characteristics. There were more than a hundred questions assessing respondents' orientations to their personhood, personal life, interpersonal dynamics, social life, and generous actions to help others. We asked about these intrapersonal characteristics in a variety of ways so as to gain a deeper understanding of each respondent. It is with these measures that we discuss and investigate people's orientations as they relate to generosity.

In the pages to follow, we paint a portrait of the intrapersonal orientations by:

1. Analyzing key intrapersonal orientations
2. Investigating how intrapersonal orientations relate to giving behaviors
3. Exploring how intrapersonal orientations contribute to a generous self-identity

Personal and Social Orientations

Personal and social orientations (Table 4.1) were assessed using 25 subtopics that were measured with 109 questions (see Appendix Table A.4.1 for the full list of questions). Admittedly the list is rather long, but a great many of these subtopics overlap. Once we establish this overlap, we will proceed with a group of factors that conceptually encapsulate these similarities.

Personal Orientations

We categorize personal orientations as generally encompassing personality and well-being, values and morals, and life dispositions. They are depicted in the left column of Table 4.1.

The first group of personal orientations are personality and well-being disposition, which we examine using five characteristics that may relate to a generous personal orientation:

1. Extroversion and introversion: the extent to which people are outgoing and talkative in larger group settings.

Table 4.1 Personal and social orientations (107 measures)

Personal Orientations	Social Orientations
Personality & Well-Being	**Relational Styles**
✓ Extrovert-Introvert	✓ Relational Attachment
✓ Sensation Seeking/Impulsivity	✓ Empathy
✓ Locus of Control	✓ Hospitality
✓ Behavioral Anxiety	✓ Human Family
✓ Depression	**Social Milieu**
Values & Morals	✓ Experience of Caring Ethos
✓ Materialism	✓ Experience of Selflessness
✓ Consumerism	✓ Belief in Reciprocity
✓ Moral Relativism	✓ Trust in Generosity Systems
Life Dispositions	**Charitable Giving**
✓ Gratitude Outlook	✓ Responsibility to Be Generous
✓ Prosperity Perspective	✓ Willing to Give More
✓ Sucker Aversion	✓ Awareness of Giving Options
	✓ Know about Generosity Outcomes

2. Sensation-seeking and impulsivity: the extent to which people seek out activities for stimulating excitement.
3. Intrinsic or extrinsic locus of control: the extent to which people feel in charge of their own destiny, thinking that what happens to them is within their control.
4. Behavioral anxiety: the extent to which people worry about evaluation of others and inhibit their behaviors to conform to perceived expectations.
5. Depression: the extent to which people experience regular or intense sadness that impedes their participation in day-to-day activities.

Studies in psychology, social work, and social psychology consistently find these factors to be key orientations that can be evaluated along a continuum from low to high levels.[3] We think these orientations play some role in people's giving actions.

Our second group of personal orientations concerns values and morals disposition, using three characteristics we think relate to a generous personal orientation:

1. Materialism: the extent to which people aspire to own, or admire people who own, material things.
2. Consumerism: the extent to which people value purchasing and possessing items, enjoy shopping, and see buying as a moral good.
3. Moral relativism: the extent to which people believe that there are no hard-and-fast rights and wrongs in life, universal moral standards do not exist, and morality is a personal decision for each individual based on what brings him or her pleasure.

In studies on morality and values, these three beliefs are found to be highly predictive of people's underlying personal orientations to what is good, what holds value, and what people believe they should be and do.[4] We therefore think that orientations toward these three values relate to generosity outcomes.

We also include life dispositions among the personal orientation measures. These dispositions refer to three attitudes that can color our interpretations of life experiences:

1. Gratuitous outlook: the extent to which people are grateful for what happens to them in life, feeling they are blessed.

2. Prosperity perspective: the extent to which people believe that their life is full of abundance, that there is always enough to share with others—even more than enough—regardless of how many material resources they actually have.

3. Sucker-aversion: the extent to which people are actively concerned about being taken advantage of and feel the need to prevent that outcome.

The literature on generosity, especially from studies on religious giving, shows that these outlooks color giving attitudes.[5] We therefore think that these life dispositions relate to generous actions.

We think personality and well-being, values and morals, and life dispositions represent a good range of Americans' personal orientations and will help explain why people give.

Social Orientations

In addition to studying people's internal perspectives, we also consider their orientations to social interactions. Who people typically engage with in the social world may matter for generosity outcomes. As the right side of Table 4.1 shows, we grouped our measures of people's social orientations into three categories: relational styles, social milieus, and charitable giving orientations.

We describe people's general relational styles with four measures:

1. Relational attachment: the extent to which people feel comfortable being close to others in relationships.

2. Empathy: the extent to which people feel concern for the suffering of others.

3. Hospitality: the extent to which people are generally inviting of others.

4. Human family: the extent to which people believe all human beings belong to one common family.

We expect these general relational styles to push people toward different forms of and approaches to giving.

Social orientations also include "temperature readings," so to speak, of the social milieu. We assess how people experience their social environment using four measures:

1. Caring ethos: the extent to which people experience themselves as being in an ethos (a social environment) that is generally caring.
2. Selflessness: the extent to which people see others as generally selfish or selfless.
3. Reciprocity: the extent to which people perceive their social reality as one in which people both give and receive.
4. Trusting in generosity systems: the extent to which people think that nonprofit organizations and their leaders are generally deserving of trust.

Together these characteristics capture how people orient themselves in their social environment, and we think they will relate to giving outcomes.

Likewise the specific orientations people have toward charitable giving can shape their participation in generosity. Four aspects of charitable giving orientations are:

1. Responsibility to be generous: the extent to which people feel responsible for giving as opposed to expecting wealthy others to be solely responsible.
2. Willingness to give more: the extent to which people believe obstacles or hindrances prevent them from giving more generously.
3. Awareness of options for giving: the extent to which people know about the specific kinds of targets toward which people can contribute.
4. Knowledge about generosity outcomes: the extent to which people receive feedback about the impact of their contributions, what kinds of outcomes they have.

This last set of characteristics focuses directly on orientations particular to generosity and charitable giving. We propose that these social orientations, similar to the personal orientations, can color the way people interpret their life experiences, including experiences related to generosity. Together these measures assess the extent to which people orient themselves (at least at the present moment) primarily toward separating and protecting themselves from others or toward being open to and desiring high engagement with others.

Since we have a representative sample of Americans, we are confident that our survey respondents represent the wide array of orientations across different life stages. We will analyze how various personal and social orientations help to explain generosity behaviors: whether people give, the amount they donate, their approach to giving, and the form in which they give.

Key Personal and Social Orientations

We focus here on a snapshot of personal and social orientations. Responses to each group of items were consistent, giving a solid measure of the most relevant characteristic, such as the extent to which someone was more extroverted or more introverted. With remarkable consistency, we found the items to identify the 25 aspects of respondents' personal and social orientations (see Appendix Table A.4.2.a for full details).[6] Suffice it to say that multiple iterations of modeling reveal consistent underlying, latent dispositions. For simplicity of presentation, Table 4.2 lists the most representative item for each of the 25 characteristics.[7]

Because some of these characteristics likely hang together across domains, we hypothesized, empirically investigated, and reliably verified the clustering characteristics signals underlying factors that help explain who gives, how much they give, and what approaches they take to giving.[8] We present only one representative analysis of the many we performed and cross-checked (see Appendix Table A.4.2.a for full details).[9]

Seven Principal Social Psychological Factors

Our investigation identified seven principal factors representing the swath of social psychological characteristics. Based on our theoretical understandings of the identified clusters, we label and describe these factors here (see also Figure 4.1):

1. *Social Solidarity* is the idea that we are "all in it together" as a neighborhood, nation, society, or human race. Social Solidarity is primarily associated with feelings of empathy, attachment, hospitality, and social connection to others, as Figure 4.1(a) shows. We think that feelings of social solidarity will positively correspond with generous actions since we expect them to prompt someone to care for the social world they see themselves in.

2. *Life Purpose* is the idea that "I am here for a reason" because life is headed toward some goal. This factor is primarily associated with lower levels

Table 4.2 Key personal and social orientations (25 measures)

Personality & Well-Being

Extrovert-Introvert	Talkative	I am talkative.
Sensation Seeking/ Impulsivity	Risk-Taker	I like exciting experiences, even if I break the rules.
Locus of Control	Intrinsic-Control	What happens to me in the future mostly depends on me.
Life Purpose	Goal-Directed	My life often lacks clear goals or sense of direction.
Behavioral Anxiety	Anxious	I feel worried or upset when I think somebody is angry at me.
Depression	Depressed	In past 12 months, how often have you felt sad or down?

Values & Morals

Materialism	Materialist	I admire people with expensive homes, cars, and clothes.
Consumerism	Consumerist	I buy less than I can afford to resist consumerism or to help others.
Moral Relativism	Relativist	Morality is relative—there are no definite rights and wrongs for all.

Life Orientations

Gratitude Outlook	Grateful	I am grateful to a wide variety of people.
Prosperity Perspective	Abundant	I know I enjoy more material abundance than others in the world.
Sucker Aversion	Unwary	I often worry about getting a bad deal or being taken advantage of.

Relational Style

Relational Attachment	Attached	It is easy for me to become emotionally close to others.
Empathy	Empathetic	Other people's misfortunes do not usually disturb me a great deal.

Table 4.2 Continued

Hospitality	Hospitable	In relationships, at being open and hospitable, what kind of person are you?
Human Family	Connected	I feel connected to other people because we are all members of one human family.

Social Milieu

Experience of Caring Ethos	Care Ethos	Growing up, I found most people around me to be stingy/uncaring.
Experience of Selflessness	Selflessness	People mostly just look out for themselves.
Belief in Reciprocity	Reciprocity	Givers benefit just as much as receivers.
Trust in Generosity Systems	Trustworthiness	Most leaders of nonprofits are trustworthy about money.

Social Milieu

Responsibility to Be Generous	Obligated	I feel responsible only when I have extra to give.
Willing to Give More	Objectionless	I have problems/objections about giving money that keep me from giving more.
Awareness of Giving Options	Aware	It is obvious who needs money and how to give to them.
Know of Generosity Outcomes	Informed	I read reports describing the good things my money accomplished.

of depression, higher levels of goal direction, and lower levels of anxiety about the judgment of others (Figure 4.1(b)). To a lesser extent this factor also corresponds with higher levels of an intrinsic sense of control. We think that perceptions of a life purpose will positively correspond with generous actions because we expect them to prompt people to act on their purpose for living by helping others to make the world a better place.

3. *Collective Conscious* represents an awareness of shared purposes and a mentality of "we are all here to help each other." It focuses on giving thought or attention to the ways one's actions can serve common goals

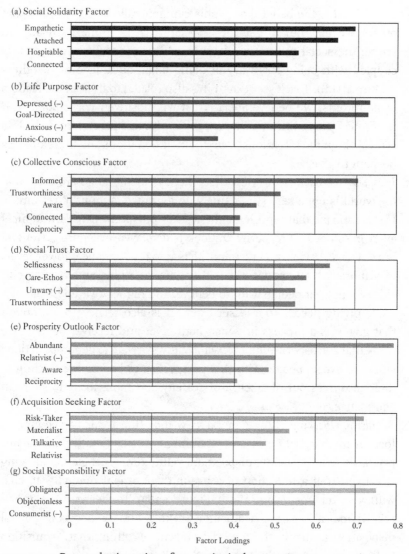

FIGURE 4.1 Personal orientations factor principal components.

that extend beyond the individual. Collective Conscious is primarily associated with the charitable giving characteristics of having awareness of generosity needs, trust in nonprofit leaders, and awareness of giving options (Figure 4.1(c)). To a lesser extent being socially connected and believing in the reciprocity of giving are also part of this factor. We think that Collective Conscious will positively correspond with generous actions since we expect it to inspire people to act in a socially directed way rather than an egoistic way.

4. *Social Trust* is the belief that people can generally be trusted and that others are not "out to get you." Social Trust is primarily related to seeing the social milieu as relatively selfless (nonselfish) and caring, coupled with being less wary of being taken advantage of by others (Figure 4.1(d)). To a lesser extent it is also related to trust in the leaders of nonprofits. We believe Social Trust will positively correspond with generous actions since we expect people with this perspective to be less cynical about the intentions or use of their donations and therefore less hesitant to give.

5. *Prosperity Outlook* is the view that "there is plenty to go around," that the world is not a zero-sum game with a limited amount of resources. Instead the pie that represents the world's prosperity can grow to meet everyone's needs. Prosperity Outlook is displayed in Figure 4.1(e) and is related to having a perception of material abundance, lower levels of a morally relativist view that there are no rights and wrongs outside of whatever people want to believe, and higher awareness of charitable giving needs. To a lesser extent it is also related to the notion that giving is a process in which both giver and receiver benefit. We think that a Prosperity Outlook will positively relate to generous actions since we expect people with this perspective to be less apt to cling to their resources out of a sense of scarcity and more likely to share in abundance.

6. *Acquisition Seeking* is the general view that "life is for the taking." It focuses on material thrills and attainment. Acquisition Seeking relates primarily to a risk-taking disposition, valuing material gain, and being talkative (itself a reflection of a live-in-the-moment mentality to chat with whoever crosses one's path; Figure 4.1(f)). To a lesser extent moral relativism is also part of Acquisition Seeking, and it reflects the general disposition to live in the material present. We think that Acquisition Seeking will negatively correspond with generous actions since we expect thrill-seeking and material desires to correspond with less giving to others.

7. *Social Responsibility* is the conviction that "we are all our brother's (or sister's) keeper," that we are all responsible for each other. The Social Responsibility factor is displayed in Figure 4.1(g). This factor is primarily related to the charitable dispositions of feeling personally obligated to give (not just when one has extra resources), coupled with a lack of major objections to giving, and having a nonconsumerist mentality

that does not focus on buying and owning goods. We think that Social Responsibility will positively relate to generous actions since we expect people who feel responsible for others to act on that belief and be generous on others' behalf.

The seven principal factors in Figure 4.1 represent a picture of social psychological orientations that we think will help to explain the puzzle of differential American generosity. These factors consistently describe Americans' underlying clusters of patterns across the 25 personal and social orientation characteristics. Combined, they represent the various kinds of Americans who may be more or less personally inclined to give. These factors also play key roles in the lives of our 12 case studies.

Orientations to Generosity

Next we assess the billion-dollar question (pun intended, since American giving is a billion-dollar industry): To what extent do personal and social orientations explain different rates of philanthropic behavior? We evaluate how these social psychological explanations relate to the following outcomes:

- Giving money (or not)
- Amounts of money given (logged)
- Giver types (as described in chapter 3)

Out of the seven social psychological factors, five are associated with being a giver, as Figure 4.2 shows: Social Solidarity, Collective Conscious, Prosperity Outlook (by a significantly greater magnitude than the other associations), Acquisition Seeking (negatively associated), and Social Responsibility.[10] We display only the statistically significant results in Figure 4.2, and the models control for all the demographic and resource measures discussed in the previous chapters (see Appendix Table A.4.2.b for full details).[11]

Four of the same five orientations are also related to giving larger amounts of money: Collective Conscious, Prosperity Outlook, Acquisition Seeking (negatively related), and Social Responsibility. Life Purpose also

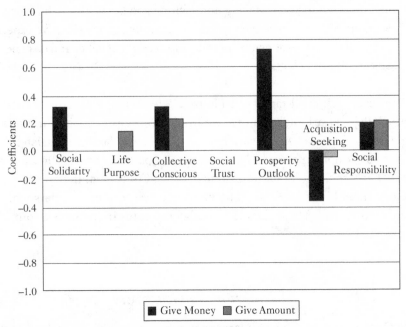

FIGURE 4.2 Personal orientation factors and giving.

associates with the amount of the donation. Social Trust, however, does not appear to be significantly related to people's propensity to give or to their giving levels.

Together Collective Conscious, Prosperity Outlook, and Social Responsibility, as well as lower Acquisition Seeking, differentiate financial givers from those who do not give and relate to greater donation amounts. Social Solidarity differentiates financial givers but does not relate to giving amounts, whereas Life Purpose relates to greater donation amounts but not to whether or not someone opts to make financial donations.

Employing a multinomial logistic regression (see Appendix Table A.4.3 for full details) similar to the one we used in chapter 3, we compare the four distinct giver types—Planned, Habitual, Selective, and Impulsive—to Atypical givers.[12] These social psychological factors do differentiate giver types from one another, though it is important to remember that our comparison of giver types excludes nongivers. Figure 4.3 displays the statistically significant factors related to the giver types, incorporating all previously discussed control measures. In the results below we compare each giver type to Atypical givers.

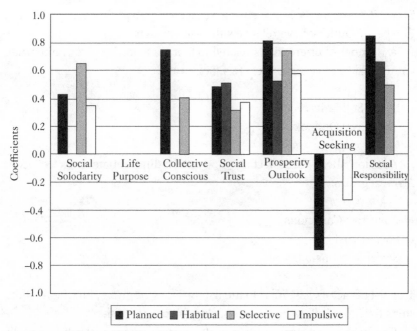

FIGURE 4.3 Personal orientation factors and giver types.

Of the seven social psychological factors, six help explain differences between Planned and Atypical givers:

- Social Solidarity
- Collective Conscious
- Social Trust
- Prosperity Outlook
- Social Responsibility
- Less Acquisition Seeking

Some of these factors also relate to other giver types' difference from Atypical givers, but the relationships are often strongest for Planned givers. Life Purpose is the only factor that is not a statistically significant differentiator between Planned and Atypical givers.

Compared to Atypical givers, Habitual givers are identified by differences in:

- Social Trust
- Social Responsibility
- Prosperity Outlook

Social Responsibility is the strongest factor here, while Social Trust and Prosperity Outlook have relatively the same weight.

A number of orientations related to being a Selective giver rather than an Atypical one. The strongest two factors are:

- Social Solidarity
- Prosperity Outlook

In addition these three factors moderately differentiate Selective from Atypical givers:

- Collective Conscious
- Social Trust
- Social Responsibility

This list of factors is similar to the list for Planned givers, but the relationships for Selective givers are less strong for several of them.

Compared to Atypical givers, Impulsive givers are differentially identified by:

- Prosperity Outlook (at a magnitude comparable to that of Habitual givers)
- Social Solidarity
- Social Trust
- Lower Acquisition Seeking (moderately)

The weight of influence of these four factors is lower than it is for most other giver types.

Prosperity Outlook and Social Trust differentiate all four types of givers from Atypical givers. Social Solidarity differentiates all except Habitual givers, and Social Responsibility differentiates all except Impulsive givers. Collective Conscious differentiates Selective and Planned from Atypical givers, and lower Acquisition Seeking differentiates Impulsive and Planned from Atypical givers. Life Purpose does not significantly differ among giver types. These results suggest that different types of givers are motivated by different social psychological orientations. That is, social psychological factors help to explain which Americans take what approach to giving.

Summary of Personal and Social Orientations to Giving

Our first two analyses in this chapter show that social psychological orientations partially explain why Americans participate in giving with different rates, amounts, and types of approaches. Even after controlling for social status measures, our data show that personal and social orientations of Americans shape the extent to which and the ways in which they engage in generous activities. We identified seven key personal and social orientation factors: Social Solidarity, Life Purpose, Collective Conscious, Social Trust, Prosperity Outlook, Acquisition Seeking, and Social Responsibility. In assessing how these relate to giving patterns, we find that each social psychological factor affects some aspect of the giving process.

No single factor among the seven consistently stands out as having the strongest relationship to giving. Instead all matter in different ways. Table 4.3 summarizes the findings by depicting which factors play a significant role in each kind of giving outcomes: whether people give, whether they give large amounts, whether they take a certain approach to giving, and which type of approach they take (Planned, Habitual, Selective, or Impulsive).

- *Givers and nongivers*
  - Strongly differ on Prosperity Outlook and Acquisition Seeking, which is lower among givers
  - Moderately differ on Social Solidarity and Collective Conscious
  - Slightly differ on the extent of Social Responsibility

- *Those who give higher amounts and those who give less*
  - Strongly differ on Prosperity Outlook, Collective Conscious, and Social Responsibility
  - Moderately differ on Life Purpose (the only outcome for which this factor is significant)
  - Slightly differ on Acquisition Seeking, which is lower among more generous givers

- *All four giver types and Atypical givers*
  - Strongly differ on Prosperity Outlook
  - Moderately differ on Social Trust
  - Moderately differ on Social Responsibility (except Impulsive)

- *Each giver type also shows some distinct patterns, compared to Atypical givers*
  - Planned givers are high on nearly all orientations and are most differentiated by Social Responsibility and Prosperity Outlook.
  - Selective givers have orientations similar to Planned givers, but Acquisition Seeking is not significant.
  - Habitual givers are dominated by Social Responsibility, and Prosperity Outlook and Social Trust also play a role.
  - Impulsive givers' orientations are a milder version of Selective givers', except that Collective Conscious and Social Responsibility are not significant.

With varying levels of influence, Prosperity Outlook and Social Responsibility appear to be the social psychological orientations that most commonly underlie financial giving. An orientation of a Collective Conscious is also quite common. In general, however, we see that many of the motivations for Americans to open their pocketbooks are different from the motivations that determine how much they give. As we have found in previous chapters, to adequately understand generosity we need to consider more than one factor.

Case Study Excursus: Part 1

To put these social psychological orientations to generosity within the context of real lives, we revisit our 12 case studies and describe how they make meaning of their personal orientations to giving. All our cases have their own unique combination of personal and social orientations explaining why they take the approaches they do to their generosity. We pick a representative of each of the giver types to describe their social psychological orientations. For each, we describe the seven factors related to giving as well as the 25 characteristics that make up those factors. The interplay of resources with these orientations will also become apparent in these stories. The result is a demonstration

Table 4.3 Primary social-psychological generosity factors (7 primary factors)

Giver vs. Nongiver

- Prosperity Outlook**
- Acquisition Seeking (Less)**
- Social Solidarity*
- Collective Conscious*
- Social Responsibility

Higher Giving Amounts

- Prosperity Outlook**
- Collective Conscious**
- Social Responsibility**
- Life Purpose*
- Acquisition Seeking (Less)

Giver Type (any) vs. "Other" Giver

- Prosperity Outlook**
- Social Trust*
- Social Responsibility (except Impulsive)

Planned Giver:	Habitual Giver:	Selective Giver:	Impulsive Giver:
Collective Conscious		Collective Conscious*	
Acquisition Seeking (Less)			Acquisition Seeking (Less)
Social Responsibility**	Social Responsibility**	Social Responsibility*	
Social Solidarity*		Social Solidarity**	Social Solidarity
Prosperity Outlook**	Prosperity Outlook	Prosperity Outlook**	Prosperity Outlook
Social Trust*	Social Trust	Social Trust	Social Trust

* Moderate influence; ** Strong influence

of how different orientations and life experiences explain giving behaviors.

Susan Baker: Upper-Middle-Class "One and Done" Los Angeleno

Planned giver Susan Baker reflects that giving type's general trend of giving a large amount and having high social psychological orientations for being a giver. True to form as a Planned giver, Susan has a high level of Social Responsibility and Collective Conscious and also evidences the relation of high Life Purpose and giving greater amounts.

Social Responsibility (Highest)

On social responsibility Susan scored nearly the highest of all our survey respondents. During the interview she told us:

> I think everyone should volunteer. . . . I think everybody needs to give back. I think that volunteering time, I think everybody can afford some. And I think it's critical for our community that everybody does some. Because it's a way to actually touch and feel other people, and have a stronger community.

Susan describes a strong sense of personal responsibility for helping others through giving time to charitable causes. She voices a clear moral conviction that volunteering time for others is the right thing to do.

Collective Conscious (High) and Social Solidarity (Low)

Susan describes her general approach to humanity:

> I go back and forth on that one. That's really funny about me. On the one hand, I believe pretty strongly in that "it takes a village." But ultimately I think everybody's responsible for himself. I don't think anybody should rely on anybody else to help them, but I also think that it's an important human characteristic to take care of other people.

Here Susan evidences having a high sense of Collective Conscious, the idea that "it takes a village." But at the same time, she exhibits a lower sense of Social Solidarity, in that it concerns her to think that people would rely on others to take care of them. Interpreting this in light of her high Social Responsibility suggests that she wants others to feel individually responsible, and thus she moderately orients herself to a "we're all in it together" mentality.

Life Purpose (High)

Susan has a high sense of purpose in life, especially insofar as she believes in the importance of making a difference in the lives of others.

She tells us her purpose is "doing the best I can with the limited skills I have" and describes her priority as "just to be the best person you can be with whatever you've been given. And the 'do no harm' motto, or whatever." Susan tells us that a good life for her would be if she "can look back and say 'I made a difference in one child's life.' Or two children's life. Hopefully not just my own. And if somebody turned out better by some societal definition of better . . . Then I'll think that I did a good job." Her Life Purpose is summarized as "Making the world a better place. Convincing people to think before they act in things that are important to me."

Social Trust (Moderate)

With regard to a sense of social trust, she said, "I think in general I'm a fairly trustworthy person. Like, I trust most people to, if they find my wallet lying on the street, to pick it up and do the right thing with it." This statement makes it sound like Susan should have ranked herself very high on a sense of Social Trust, but later in the interview she discussed her trust in giving targets. About this characteristic of Social Trust she said, "When it comes to giving money, I'm much more in the trust category. I've done my research. I'm gonna give you my money. I'm gonna trust that you're gonna use it appropriately. When it comes to my time, I feel like I'm partially responsible, so, yeah." Susan shows that while she generally trusts people to do the right thing, she evidences some wariness in the targets of her giving since she does background research on them rather than trusting them blindly.

Prosperity Outlook (Moderate)

Though Susan does not spend much time in her interview describing her Prosperity Outlook, she mentions it in various ways throughout. For example, she interjects at one point, "I think I got a nicer husband than I probably should have, and my kid's incredibly well-behaved. I got lucky there." Thus though she does not have the "overfilling cup" that some of our highest Prosperity Outlook interviewees describe, she does generally believe that she has received the better end of things in life, at least to some extent.

Acquisition Seeking (Low)

Susan is very low in her Acquisition Seeking orientation, saying, "Oh, we have plenty of junk. We have more than we need." She gives a specific example: "We both have 10-year-old cars, and neither of us have any big desire to have a new one. So, we're good." This is the picture of a low orientation to Acquisition Seeking, in which material possessions are considered unimportant and there are no major desires to acquire more possessions.

In many ways Susan is a prototypical high giver with a Life Purpose oriented to bettering the lives of others. She displays many of the strong personal orientations related to being a Planned giver and demonstrates how these factors produce a consistently high giving level.

Jackie Sawyer: Thrifty, Type-A, Religious, Midwestern Mom

Jackie Sawyer is one of our Habitual giver cases who, along with her husband, gives high amounts of money. She exhibits the high Life Purpose of many high givers, and she well represents the Habitual giver orientations of a moderately high Prosperity Outlook, Social Trust, and Social Responsibility relative to Impulsive and Atypical givers. At the same time, she evidences these orientations to a lesser extent than the Planned givers.

Life Purpose (High)

Jackie has many of the characteristics and outlooks that define a strong Life Purpose. About where her life is headed she says, "I tend to not really worry about a whole lot." She elaborates, "I'm not a depressed person, so there really hasn't been anything that's really made me super sad. Yeah, and I really—I don't live in [a] sad world. I try to avoid [a] sad world." In this way Jackie exemplifies the low level of depression in the Life Purpose factor. She goes on to talk about her perspective on life: "I tend to—I tend to be a content person, a half-full person versus a half-empty person. When I look at what I have, I'm very thankful for what I have versus always wanting more." In terms of the most important things in her life, she says:

> Most important things in life. Well, because I'm a Christian, I really believe that one of the most important things is to maintain a relationship with Jesus. And to actually cultivate that, which I'm not doing a very good job of. But then, as a part of that, then to live that out in my life; to be a reflection of Christ in his life, and to love

others.... There's all kinds of important things in life, but they're all supposed to, and do, come out of that relationship; like being a good mom, or being a good wife, and being a good employee and an honest employee, and to have high standards for myself, as far as honesty and integrity.

When asked how she has come to this orientation, she replied, "Growing up in a Christian home, being taught from a young age, reading the Bible from a young age."

Jackie describes herself as having a fairly good amount of control. I'm a control freak. I gotta have some control." She continued, "I know I don't control it all, but I think I control how I respond and how I, you know, what the effect is. So, yeah, I'm not total control, but I'm probably fairly close." She elaborates:

Well, for the most part, it means that I choose my attitude too. I mean, that's definitely my mantra. And I don't quite know how to preach it to my daughter, but that you have to choose to look at the glass as half-full instead of choosing to always look at it as half-empty. That you choose how you respond to what happens to you because you don't always get to choose what happens to you.

Prosperity Outlook (High)

As someone who intentionally views the world optimistically, Jackie has a high Prosperity Outlook:

I'd say I probably look more at the positive side of things, the blessings that we have, the abundance that we have, the excessive amount of stuff, and—that we're able to have. So, I guess I—again, back to the whole glass half-full versus glass half-empty, it's always half-full or even better, in my world.

She continued by saying that everything in her life is not perfect, but she chooses to make the best of circumstances, regardless of what they are:

You can look at things like, I don't know, your job and the fact that I have a job—[my] hours [were] cut from full time down to four days a week, when we weren't—we sort of knew it was coming, but weren't 100 percent sure it was coming, and you can look at that as, "Oh my goodness, what are we gonna do?" Or you can look at it like, "All right, cool. Now I get to go part time, and I'm gonna have a day off." So I guess that's one situation, where I could say that I definitely was—we had some premonition, so it wasn't an end-of-the-world thing for us. There were contingencies in place, and we knew that it wasn't going to be a huge burden.

Jackie discusses her relative affluence, as compared to poverty in the world, by saying:

I often wonder why I got to be born white and middle-class and not black, inner-city, with nothing. . . . Worldwide I think [poverty is] a huge issue. And it's just amazing when you look at the dollar a day, and how many people in the world live on less than a dollar a day, and how we can't even fathom that.

This quote exemplifies Jackie's general habit of concentrating on the abundance that she does have and not dwelling on what she wishes might be better. In discussing her attitudes toward gratefulness and gratitude she said, "I'd be more of the lots-of-things-to-be-thankful-for kind of person." When asked how her life has turned out compared to her expectations she replied, "I'd say pretty much what I thought it would be." Jackie chooses to view the cards she has been dealt as perhaps not the highest hand ever dealt but good enough to stay in the game. This abundance view of her life is related to why giving is such a priority for her:

I think that we're in a better position than a lot of people our age are, in that we're able to give as much as we are, because of choices that we made early on and not getting in over our heads and trying to keep up with the Joneses. So I think that we probably have, potentially, a slightly greater ability than many people in our age demographic to give.

Here Jackie demonstrates the direct connection between her Prosperity Outlook orientation and her high giving. Her statement also shows a low Acquisition Seeking orientation, discussed more below.

Social Responsibility (Moderate)

Jackie rated herself as having a moderate sense of Social Responsibility. She evidences how Habitual givers' orientation is high enough to differentiate them from Atypical and Impulsive givers but is not as high as other givers. She definitely feels personally responsible for giving, as part of her Christian identity. At the same time, when asked about whose responsibility it is to ensure her financial giving is being used well, Jackie says, "I would say most of the responsibility shifts. I think it's my responsibility to make sure that where I'm giving is the direction that I want to give in too, but then, once it's given, it's not mine anymore to go, 'Ooh, I'd like to do it this way' or 'I wish it would have happened that way, instead.'" Here Jackie markedly differs from the perspective of Planned givers, who describe a sense of responsibility to follow up and learn about the outputs of their giving. Jackie feels obligated to give but does not feel she needs proof of or feedback about its use.

Jackie also evidences an attenuated sense of Social Responsibility when she discusses volunteering. When asked if she enjoyed the volunteer work she does, she said, "A lot of times, I enjoy it. There are certain times where I'm like, 'Oh, couldn't somebody else just do it?' But I feel, again, an obligation that if—many hands make light work." Thus she feels somewhat burdened by her sense of responsibility. Giving does not provide her with the sense of fulfillment that it seems to provide Planned givers, but the sense of social responsibility clearly still motivates the giving.

Social Trust (Moderate)

When asked if she thought most people are pretty good and trustworthy, Jackie replied, "For the most part, yes." And when asked if she trusted the targets of her family's giving, she said, "At this point, we pretty much trust the targets of our giving, or the money wouldn't be going there." However, she also describes some ambivalence about trusting people: "That's a gray area. For the most part, I trust people, but there have been incidents in the last several—well, yeah, an incident in particular in the last couple years that have really caused me to be not quite as blanket-trusting as what I used to be." She explains:

> I didn't used to really worry about things like sleepovers and friends' parents, and some of that stuff, because I grew up in such a small

community where everybody knew everybody—that you just kind
of, you know, everybody knew everybody's parents. Everybody
either went to [the same] church or school, or you spent a lot of
time with the same group of people. So, I think that formed into
my background.

She goes on to describe some incidents that have made her call that into
question. One involved her daughter's friend's father suddenly getting
arrested, startling Jackie, who had trusted him: "That kind of makes you
go 'Hmm,' and makes you question everything that you've ever—the trust
that you just blankly gave. You have to think about it, and you have to be
aware, and I guess question more than what I used to." This experience
helps show how these orientations are dynamic and can change over time.
It sounds as if Jackie used to be high on Social Trust but has attenuated it
due to this experience. This helps us understand why she can be moderate
on Social Trust even though she is highly trusting of her giving targets. If
Jackie had started out with a moderate degree of Social Trust before this
incident, she may have become more wary, with little Social Trust, as some
of our other interviewees are.

Social Solidarity (Moderate) and Collective Conscious (Moderate)
Jackie demonstrates how having a moderate sense of Social Solidarity and
Collective Conscious relates to the characteristics of a guarded, more introverted personality. When asked to describe her comfort level with relationships, she evidenced a moderate attachment by saying:

Yeah, I'd be not the first one to jump into a deep relationship, if
you ask my husband how long it took for our relationship to go
anywhere. So, yeah, I tread lightly in those waters. And that may
be part of the whole—why I'm not so connected is because I don't
dig really deeply into some of those. I mean, I have a couple people that I have very deep connections with, but beyond that, yeah
no. Not so much.

Jackie's empathy balances this introversion: "I'm definitely an empathetic person. How come I always end up with many things on my calendar? Because, if I can help somewhere, I try to help somewhere."
She continued, "Yeah. Yep, I am thankful and happy when I can help

somebody out and do something, spend some time lightening someone else's world."

Jackie continues describing her moderate sense of Social Solidarity by saying that she is unsure of the impact she has on others: "I'm not probably one to think I can make huge amounts of change. Again, I can change my world, but to think I'm gonna make any huge, global change, or any national change, that's not really in my realm of things I strive to do on a daily basis." Thus she tends to feel generally connected to people, has a high degree of empathy, but is a little guarded interpersonally and a little less generally socially attached than our highest Social Solidarity–oriented interviewees.

True to form as a Habitual giver, she does not differentiate from an Atypical giver's average level of Collective Conscious orientation: "I guess I'm kind of a middle-of-the-road person. Not so sure it takes a whole village, but it probably takes more than just a family to raise kids. I guess I feel some responsibility to all of mankind."

Acquisition Seeking (Low)

Jackie's high Prosperity Outlook appears to be connected to her low Acquisition Seeking orientation. To make financial decisions, she says, she and her husband ask themselves, "Do we really need it? Is it in the budget?" This comes down to an approach in which they "look at wants versus needs." For example, she explains, "We live in this house, so I don't think we really live simply, but we don't have a need or a want for a lot of luxury items. Again, mostly we have the basic stuff." This recognition that the resources they have are sufficient to address their basic needs seems to allow her and her husband to focus on their abundance and give heavily to charitable causes.

In summary, Jackie is a prototypical Habitual giver who has high enough Social Trust, Prosperity Outlook, and Social Responsibility orientations to differentiate her from an Atypical or Impulsive giver. At the same time, her orientations are not as high as they are for our Planned givers, nor are they coupled with a high sense of the other orientations. In fact it seems that her lower orientations to Collective Conscious and Social Solidarity partially explain why she does not feel the need to put regular thought into her giving approaches: the feedback from giving is less important to her because she does not feel it is her responsibility after she donates. Once again we see in Jackie how a high degree of Life Purpose, especially in feeling called to better the lives of others, is related to high giving levels.

Linda Chesterfield: Midwestern Soccer Mom Puts Family First

Linda Chesterfield is a prototypical Selective giver and in many ways fits the average case for that giving type, scoring in the moderate range on all her intrapersonal orientations. Remember that Linda and her husband give moderate amounts of money and time but would likely not give any money if the decision were solely up to Linda. In line with this, Linda scored low on Life Purpose, as do many of our donors who give small amounts. Moreover she scored high on Acquisition Seeking, which relates to less giving.

Acquisition Seeking (High)

Linda describes herself as "pretty much living the life that I want to live." However, she goes on to say:

> I wish we had more time. And, this is going to sound terribly greedy, but I wish we had more money, just to do things. Outside of essential things, I'd like to have some fun. Just like taking the kids a lot more places, going on vacations, getting some new furniture. That kind of stuff that we, with our budget and our family size, we just can't justify right now.

Linda is a full-time mom to eight children, and on a number of occasions during the interview one or the other of them would interrupt to ask her a question. During one such interruption, her son excitedly told her that he had found two quarters in the backyard. Her response to his discovery was "Awesome. Well, take those two quarters back out in the grass and plant them and maybe they'll grow into two dollars." She noted that as soon as the words left her mouth, she wanted to retract them, and so she said, "No, they won't do that. Come here. I'm just kidding!" Her son was already on his way out of the room. Linda told the interviewer, "I knew it would get him out of here. I feel worse than I thought. Because I knew he would leave, but now he's probably like 'Really? I'm going to go get some money from upstairs.'" She then yells, "Honey, Mommy was teasing. That can't really happen! But if you put that in your piggy bank and save it or let Daddy deposit it in your savings account it could grow with interest." Her son was already out of earshot, so she got up to go after him, telling the interviewer, "He went upstairs. I hope he's not getting more money. Let me just check. Yeah, sorry." Later in the interview she reflected, "I just wish there was a money tree in the backyard!"

During the interview Linda discussed her mother's influence on her Acquisition Seeking orientation: "I would actually say that maybe some of my mom's bad financial behavior has rubbed off on me. I just, I'll give freely or spend freely even if it's not necessarily there, so that rubbed off on me, in a way." She explains:

> I like to shop. I'm not in love with shopping. I think if I had, if we had more money I could very easily be sucked in to that "Oh, I love to shop, 'shop till I drop' [mentality]." . . . But I don't know, I think buying more than you need is stupid. Or if you have something that's in very good condition, going to replace it just because the newest model's out, I think that's just a little ridiculous, when there's so many people who have nothing.

We see from this conversation that Linda has a desire to acquire possessions, but she also recognizes how much more she has than others. This, combined with her Prosperity Outlook and Collective Conscious orientations, appear to moderate her Acquisition Seeking orientation.

Prosperity Outlook (Moderate)

Despite Linda's desire for a higher standard of living, she appreciates that her family has what they need: "Having a roof over my head and clothes on my back and a car to get from point A to point B, I mean that's a necessity, and I couldn't imagine living without those things." When we asked Linda if her general orientation is more about scarcity or more about abundance in the world, she replied:

> Probably right in the middle, based on situations. I'm very content with my home life and stuff. I think there's an abundance of love and just, I'm very content with home. . . . I know that I'm comfortable. And I also know that there's people in this world who don't even have clean drinking water. It's sad.

We asked Linda if she feels she is losing or gaining something when she gives, and she said:

> Maybe a little bit of both. You're losing that money, I mean it's—I can't believe he [my husband] just did that [donated money]. But I feel like maybe I'm gaining appreciation, because if people were to ask, or it's, if they didn't really truly need it, or really couldn't still use it, so I'm sure that these organizations, and even the church, they appreciate it. But I think sometimes they also take it for granted. I would like to see that they don't take it for granted.

Linda explains further, "I'm pretty appreciative and grateful for what I have and try not to take things for granted." However, she confesses, "sometimes I also feel like maybe I might take my family or friends for granted." She wants to increase her Prosperity Outlook, especially the characteristic related to the relational generosity of others.

We asked if she thought that financial giving is a moral duty. Her answers shows why she scores in the middle range on a relativist morality:

> I don't think it's a moral obligation, but I think it's fine if you can do it and want to do it. But I don't think that, like I said, that it's going to secure you a place in heaven if you do it, and it's going to make sure you go to hell if you don't. . . . I think you need to do [it] for yourself and your own family first. And if you want to, and you can, help out a friend or a neighbor in need, I mean you shouldn't turn your back on anyone, you should help if you can. But I feel like it's not a moral obligation, like you're obligated to.

Social Responsibility (Moderate)

Linda's primary responsibility is to take care of her family as her full-time job. When asked what the most important things are in her life she said, "Family, friends, that's, those are [the] top two importants in my life anyway. I can't speak for other people." She continued, "Well, I feel like I was given the responsibility to take care of them, so I have to value them and ultimately be semiresponsible for them. And it just, it's a priority of mine over just about anything. My family is [the] number one priority in my life." She describes this family responsibility as moderating her responsibility to general society by describing her care of "my family, but not other people outside my family, no." Later she reiterates, "I mean ultimately my family is my responsibility and my most important responsibility, but yet I don't like to see other people going without or other people doing wrong. So just a mixture of both, I would say."

Social Trust (Moderate)

Linda also scores in the moderate range on Social Trust. She says, "For the most part, people, I think, are good and trustworthy." But then she adds, "I mean maybe I watch too much TV too. You hear on the news about all the violence . . . and always hearing about something awful. . . . It's scary, and it makes me sad that we live in a world like we do, where there's just violence for no reason at times." Interpersonally she describes a somewhat skeptical orientation: "I'd say probably more cautious. And a lot of it's in my head, and I know it is. But I feel like people are always judging me. Just maybe, just comments I've heard or looks I'll get, maybe it's all in my head, but I feel more cautious." She continued:

> So I feel like I have to be cautious even amongst neighbors and other parents at school, not that I have any big secrets, but I wouldn't want to say something that might be embarrassing to one of my kids and they run and tell their kids, "Oh so-and-so's mom said this," and it gets back. I don't know. I just feel like people are judgmental.

Yet when we asked if she was ever concerned about being taken advantage of in her giving, she said, "No, I don't feel as if I've been in on any of those, you know, the scams where they target people. . . . No, no, because you can always say no." And when we asked, "Do you ever have concerns that the resources you donate are not being used responsibly?," she answered, "Not really, no. I'm not very skeptical." We see from this conversation that Linda scores high on some aspects and low on other aspects of Social Trust, so she ends up with a middle-range score.

Collective Conscious (Moderate)

Linda has a fairly moderate level of Collective Conscious. She mentions politics in her thoughts on collective conscious, saying about US political issues, "I try not to engage in too much of that, because it's just, it's sad to me. That there is poverty in this country." She continued, "I pull myself away from that [politics] because it just disgusts me." Later she explained:

> I think as parents we want our kids to do right, and we just think that other people's children should do right also. I mean it's just, you know the difference between right and wrong. Do what's right; don't do what's wrong. And even here in our neighborhood I've seen some kids that went to elementary school with my daughter who's now 17, who were just like the sweetest, good, little kids, and now they're always in trouble with the law, and I think that's, I think that a lot of that's bad parenting. And I think if I were to spend too much time thinking about everybody else's problems then I'd be a mess, so I'm more inclined to go with the aspect that my family is important, and what else is going around me is just stuff that's going on around me.

Social Solidarity (Moderate)

Linda also expresses a moderate degree of Social Solidarity. She does describe herself as high on the emotional attachment characteristic:

> I'm pretty comfortable sharing information with people that I meet.... I think relationships should have an emotional connection, because if ... I just feel like when there's emotional connection, it's a better connection. You really get one another, and you can depend on those people, rely on those people or trust those people more than you can have from just somebody that you aren't very emotionally connected to.

She continues by describing her high, almost debilitating degree of empathy:

> I wear my heart on my sleeve. So I'm always, when something happens to one of my friends or they lose a parent or a child gets sick, I really feel for them. Sometimes where it kind of semiparalyzes me for that moment, like "That's so terrible, that's horrible." And I try to be there for them, but sometimes I feel like I'm too much of a mess, that maybe I should pull myself back a little bit, so that they can try to get stronger rather than have somebody who's just as upset as they are.

Linda further emphasizes, "I'm naturally empathetic. I sympathize with people all the time, and sometimes I think it's to my detriment. I can't separate myself." In this way her high level of empathy seems to prevent her from developing a stronger sense of Social Solidarity with others because of its emotional intensity.

Linda describes how she reacts to the problems of others: "I genuinely feel bad or sympathetic when people lose a loved one, or lose their job, or you know." However, she also explains:

> But then there's times, too, that I have friends who it seems like they complain nonstop about everything. And I try not to, and [try to] be sympathetic, but it's like, "You're the one who continues to put up with the deadbeat dad," or whatever the situation that they're always complaining about. So I feel like we reap what we sow. And we do have some power over where our lives go, and what direction it goes in. And if they continue to put themselves in that situation, not that they deserve it, but that's what they're gonna get.

We see from this that Linda strongly empathizes with suffering but also finds herself seeing others as responsible for their recurring suffering. This situation makes it difficult for her to feel a high sense of Social Solidarity despite her strong empathy.

Life Purpose (Low)

As is typical of people who donate smaller amounts, Linda does not see a great deal of purpose in her life: "Yeah, I, sometimes I feel like I'm just living, and what purpose I'm here for, maybe to be a mom, but I don't [know]. I don't know that that was carved out like that as your purpose in life." When we asked how much control she feels she has in her life, she replied, "Moderate amount of control. I sometimes let my emotions run me and, not a good thing, because then if I'm upset by something I feel like nothing gets done." She indicates that there are some moments when she feels out of control: "But I mean that's very rare that I feel like that, but there's times I'm just overwhelmed, period."

When we asked if she ever felt paralyzed by a sense of inability to control her life, she said, "Not paralyzed, slightly overwhelmed by it at times, but for the most part I would say that I do feel in control. And then when I feel out of control it's not like earth-shattering or anything." As for what kind of impact she thinks she could have on the world, she said, "I think I would be kind of helpless to make a difference, just because I'm very shy. So if I, if it were out of my comfort zone, I would certainly feel like there was nothing I could do about it. . . . I try to stay clear of the unfamiliar." In short, she is not exactly clear on her purpose in life, has a moderate locus of control, sometimes feels mildly helpless or overwhelmed, and does not feel socially efficacious.

Linda is fairly exemplary of a low giver. She has a low life purpose, which makes it difficult to integrate behaviors to give abundantly to others. Her marital commitment and her husband's dedication to giving boost her participation over what it would otherwise be. Linda has the orientation levels of a typical Selective giver, as represented in Figure 4.3: moderate Social Trust, Social Solidarity, Social Responsibility, and Collective Conscious. She has a lower Prosperity Outlook level and higher Acquisition Seeking than most Selective givers, and these would likely inhibit her giving if it were not for her husband. Nevertheless her own personal involvement with giving remains fairly low, and she exemplifies that low Life Purpose usually goes hand-in-hand with small giving amounts.

Tanika Sandaval: Single Los Angeles Mom Fights for Her Children's Future

Tanika Sandaval, the single mom in L.A., is an Impulsive giver and demonstrates many of the social psychological orientations associated with that approach. She marks a transition in the case studies to our interviewees who have considerably lower personal and social orientations than those previously described. Tanika ranks high on Social Solidarity and moderate on Collective Conscious, but otherwise her orientations are low. Although her financial donations are low, Tanika volunteers at a moderately high rate at her children's school. She seems to have begun volunteering entirely as a result of having been asked by a personal connection, a point we revisit in chapter 5.

Social Solidarity (High)

Tanika describes her high sense of Social Solidarity:

> I mean, you never know where at your time or what your life is gonna be. So it's hard to just turn your back on people. . . . When

you're helping someone, you never know if you're gonna need that same predicament at one time in your life. And when it's there at that time, you wanna be able to have someone help you out, that's all.

In this way Tanika evinces a mentality of "we're all in this together." She feels this way even more strongly when she focuses specifically on the solidarity she feels with her immediate neighbors: "I feel connected cause I've been around here for so long, so I know there's people who knows me. I know them; I feel connected to it, I do, yeah. . . . We're very watchful."

Collective Conscious (Moderate)

Tanika does not have a great deal of the Collective Conscious orientation at a larger, broader, national level, but the more locally she thinks, the more she feels aware of and engaged with the needs of others. She describes feeling connected in this way:

> It's one person at a time, hmm [pause]. I guess locally, cause I don't really know nationally, but I, my heart feels for those people. Even though I'm not there, I can feel for them, and that's part of being human, I guess. But I feel like I have more of a local [orientation] cause I'm here within the neighborhood. . . . I put myself in someone else's shoes.

When it comes to her volunteer work with the other parents at her children's school, Tanika has a higher Collective Conscious: "We're together, exactly. We have to, and then again it comes back to the community, even the neighborhood. Your child, my child, go to the same school, I may see you, [maybe] the grocery person who works during the day, and [at school] I'm the community rep, so we are together." Tanika's Collective Conscious orientation is limited to the local level.

Social Trust (Low)

Despite feeling a high Social Solidarity and moderate degree of Collective Conscious, Tanika does not generally expect others to reciprocate the care and concern she gives. She has a low sense of Social Trust and describes other people by saying, "A lot of people now, everyone is so selfish, so me, me, me, me, me, me, me. You know, and that goes for a lot of people, you know, within families, without families." Trusting others is not feasible when they are in it for "me, me."

Social Responsibility (Low)

Tanika also scored low on Social Responsibility on the survey, and in her interview did not talk much about having an obligation to take care of strangers. Her sense of responsibility is directed not toward others, in general, but toward particular people in her life. Her volunteering in her children's school exhibits this:

> Now I kinda feel like it's a must, to be there, [that] you should try to volunteer sometime. It's important nowadays. Things are not the same. I think back in the days when my mom's still going to school and we went, when I went to school, kinda your parents, when you went to school, and that's like the safe haven. And that was parents just working. But nowadays, you need to be truly involved. We have to take back the schools, I mean bring it back to them [the children].

Tanika describes her volunteering activity as her responsibility as a mother, not as a wider responsibility to help others. To some degree it is her low trust (in this case, in the school) that propels her to volunteer: it is a mother's intervention to ensure the educational success of her children.

Life Purpose (Low)

When we asked about her life purpose, Tanika said, "I'm living, of course, but I know I have to have a purpose. I may not know everything, you know, but I know that there is a purpose, I definitely know there is a purpose." She does not feel aimless or helpless, but characteristics of control and goal direction are absent from her purpose orientation. She says:

> Sometimes I can get a little stressed with things, but then I just try to chill out and just take [a] day at a time. That's really what I have to do, cause you're [older], you get overwhelmed just thinking about all the things. You're gonna have stress. Stress is gonna be there. That's not gonna change. Just try to minimize it, that's all.

She shows the "trying to stay afloat" mentality that lacks a sense of control. Many of our low-income interviewees have this outlook. She says, "Just keep doing what you're doing." She says she likes to be in control of things, but when asked how much control she felt she had in her life situation, she said, "I feel helpless to my situation and that's something that I could not have had control over, so again, so that goes, now that's what makes me feel [vulnerable], that gives me my vulnerability cause I need to ask people to do things sometimes."

Prosperity Outlook (Low)

Though generally a grateful person, Tanika does feel somewhat deprived of abundance in life: "Sometimes you can't, people's gonna, sometimes people can disappoint you. And that's the thing you have to realize, people do disappoint you, so you can't always leave the responsibility on another person." However, she goes on to say she has "always had a place, always had a roof over my head, always had food." And she thinks things could have been worse: "It wasn't like, we never lived in no extra, extra bad neighborhoods. There was times when we had, you know, circumstances, but mostly we was good for the most part." Yet overall she still ranks low on having a Prosperity Outlook, which is understandable, given her restricted resources and the stress of trying to make ends meet for three children on a modest disability check.

Acquisition Seeking (Low)

When we asked Tanika about her overall approach to shopping and buying things, she showed that the impulsive tendencies evident in her giving also affect her spending habits. She describes the factors going into her decisions when making a purchase: "I will say a good price, definitely a good price. But at the same token, how I'm getting treated as a good person, whatever I'm purchasing, cause it's in that, type of that relationship with [a] client, you know?" It seems that sometimes she gets swept up by a good interpersonal exchange, coupled with a sale, and feels compelled to purchase something that she otherwise did not need. She continued:

> I love shopping, don't get me wrong—that is the thing, but I learned you can't just keep shopping, shopping, shopping. It is, you know, comes to a time, where it be like, okay, I learned, so I'm moderate now to where I do go shopping. I'm not gonna go and buy no $400 purse, nothing like that, no. [I'll buy one] for $25. That's me [laughs]. She may have the one expensive, but I'm gonna be less.

With shopping she has learned she needs to try to restrain her impulsive urges. And she is not nearly as focused on acquisition as some of our other interviewees, describing the "good life" as "Just bein' happy. When you can say that you're happy. For whatever it is that you may have, don't have, when you can feel content and just say that I'm just truly happy, whatever you may have, you know."

Together these personal and social orientations, especially the lack of a clear Life Purpose, correlate with trends that predict Tanika will be a fairly low monetary giver but a moderately high time giver. True to her Impulsive giver approach, her volunteering appears to be entirely the result of having been asked by someone to get involved rather than the result of a decision considered and planned in advance. It is likely that she responded positively to the request to volunteer due in part to her orientations of high Social Solidarity, Social Trust in her immediate community and lack of trust in her children's education, and a sufficient Prosperity Outlook. As our models would predict, this combination of factors can turn someone into a Selective giver.

Deon Williams: Retiree Living It Up in Detroit in Residual Poverty

Deon Williams represents how having limited resources plays an ongoing role in shaping personal and social orientations. Deon is our one Atypical giver case. As we have discussed, he has a residual poverty mentality: his childhood experience has left him with the perception that his resources are limited, even though he has actually achieved a comfortable, middle-class adult lifestyle. Deon's mix of orientations matches the mixed approach to giving that makes him an Atypical giver.

Social Trust (High)

Though Deon rated himself on our survey as very high in Social Trust, he described himself during our interview as "cautious, careful, not necessarily trusting of other people, for sure." When we asked, "Why's that?," he said:

Oh man, because—you read the paper? This world is crazy, man. This world is crazy. There's just so many con games and crooks out here. Makes it hard to trust anybody, especially somebody you don't know, shoot. I wouldn't trust them no further than I could throw a piano.... But like I said, I don't trust, I don't trust a whole lot.... There's so many con games, so many untrustworthy individuals out here.

Just as he does not approach giving in a consistent way, Deon exhibits inconsistency in his responses. It seemed that his responses varied dramatically based on whether he had been drinking that day. Rather than calling his giving style Atypical, we could easily label it Inconsistent. This may be the case with other Atypical givers as well.

Social Solidarity and Collective Conscious (Moderate)

Deon is not very focused on the well-being of others, he admits:

> I'm the type of person that I, the only world that I'm really concerned about is my own world. Because I see the way people act when you try to change their world, when you try to do something to influence their world. Only world that's important to me is mine. Seriously.... I'm just concerned with my own life, my own thing. God gave me one ass to carry, and that's the only one I'm concerned with.

However, Deon expressed a different outlook when we asked him our Social Solidarity question. The interviewer said:

> Some people tend to see the whole human race as one common family of people, and believe everyone is responsible to help take care of others. Then other people tend more to believe that each individual and/or family is only responsible for themselves. How would you describe yourself on this issue?

Deon replied:

> That's kind of a side question right there, because a lot of people do think that they're supposed to take care of their own as far as families go and everything there. But you didn't mention do they put down other families and stuff like that. Are they racist, or what? But I believe the whole world is like a melting pot. The whole world, we all bleed red. We all should be brothers, and work together, and stand together, and help each other, period. Unless you're a racist. Only the racists put other families down, talk about other people, make up all the insulting names and that stuff. But as far as them, we all should be together. Everybody should be together and help each other. Stand together.

We hear mostly from Deon that he considers himself to be rather selfish and not focused on the collective good or a broader sense of social solidarity, yet this last excerpt shows that he also has a sense of brotherhood, especially when it comes to potential racial divides, and expresses disgust at the lack of solidarity in others.

Prosperity Outlook (Moderate)

Deon has had a modest, blue-collar lifestyle, yet he describes himself as grateful that he has managed to keep his head above water in deprived circumstances. He focuses on the little things, like waking up in the morning:

> I've got a lot of gratitude for what happened in my life, a lot of it. I'm grateful for everything. When these eyes pop open in the morning, I'm grateful for that. I'm thankful. So I'm not one of them people that got a problem with it or whatever. I'm loving it. And I'm grateful for it, and I thank God every day for it. . . . Waking up in the morning, having my own place, having a car outside, got a good income, a lot of friends, associates and stuff, health is pretty decent, mother's still living, family's still doing good, living in a decent neighborhood, got a great landlord.

He explains why he has this perspective given his modest life circumstances: "I was satisfied with just keeping my head above water. I was satisfied with just having something to own. Satisfied with just having something, just satisfied with having nothing." However, perhaps as a result of growing up in poverty, Deon still worries about scarcity: "Some things are threatening and kinda bad, and a lot of things are blissful and blessings, and I kinda see both sides to that." His middle score on Prosperity Outlook aligns with this middle-ground perspective.

Life Purpose (Low)

Deon scored low on questions related to Life Purpose orientation on the survey. However, when we asked him in person about the most important things in life, he replied enthusiastically with an answer that did not seem to align with his lifestyle but instead was a relaying of his religious upbringing. It did not strike us as necessarily aligning with Deon's lifestyle. He said:

> Most important things in life is, first of all, living life the way—see, I'm a religious person—living life the way God said to live your life. Ten

Commandments: "Thou shalt not kill, thou shalt not bear false witness, or sleep with thy neighbor," and all the rest of that. And not only that, but life is helping others. Life is like a bank, you don't put nothing in it, you don't get nothing out of it. When you get things out of life, it's what you do to, it's what you do for other people. It's how you treat other people, it's how you treat your life. That's what life is all about.

He goes on to describe his personal purpose as mainly avoiding jail or getting killed. He continues to explain what a bad life would look like: "If I wasn't educated, if I didn't work, if I didn't support my child, if I didn't respect my mother, and if I didn't worship the Lord. Then I would feel like I had a lousy, that would be account for a lousy life." Deon expresses a strong sense of control, a characteristic of Life Purpose, for the way his life turns out:

I feel like I'm in full control. . . . Because I know what I'm doing, and I know how to do it. I know how to stop it. That's what you call control, ain't it? When you're behind the wheel? You know what you're doing, and you know how to stop it. Or you know how to continue with or change it, or whatever. It's up to you. You're behind the wheel, you've got the control, you've got the keys.

Despite conveying a sense of purpose and self-direction in these statements, Deon's goals were general and not directed. He tended to engage in little reflection on his life's meaning and purpose. Many of his answers seemed to be canned snippets from things he had heard; some seemed to come from television, others sounded like quotes from a pastor or his mother, and few of them seemed truly to fit with the nonchalant and aimless life that he described throughout our conversations.

Acquisition Seeking (Low)

Deon clearly has a taste for certain material possessions, but at the same time he describes himself as satisfied with what he has and not in need of more:

I got everything, I mean I got a lot of stuff. Got a nice PC [computer]. Got a nice cell phone. Got a nice car. Got a decent house. I'm satisfied. I've seen, I'm one of the type of people, I don't buy something until something breaks down, see. Some people might have things that they want to upgrade. I'm not a big upgrade person. I wait till something quits working. Force me to have to replace it. You know. I don't feel like I need anything, I got, shit, everything I want.

He continues, "I'm not a big shopper, period. I am kind of thrifty-wise, so I try to hold onto my money as long as I can. I can be a stingy person." Deon has the possessions he wants and does not focus on acquiring more or upgrading to keep in fashion.

Social Responsibility (Low)

In discussing why he has never been interested in volunteering, Deon points to his low sense of Social Responsibility:

> It's not wanting to be responsible. Not wanting to have anything cut into my time. Cause volunteering for something, that's your time, that's your free time, that's time that you might want to do things that makes you happy, that satisfies you. I guess it's my time, I don't want to be responsible for somebody else on my time.

He is socially "tuned out"; as he says, "I live in a bubble." Caring for others, or taking responsibility for helping them, is simply not something that Deon feels obligated to think about, or do in any systematic way.

In summary, Deon exhibits a fairly unreflexive self-assessment. While all people have some logical inconsistencies, Deon's are above average. His responses to questions about giving approaches did not go together, making him an exemplary Atypical giver. Deon's low Social Responsibility orientation helps make sense of his response patterns, as he may feel little obligation to engage in social survey and interview questions in an engaged and meaningful way.

Anthony Ross: In Between, Regrouping, and Poor in D.C.

Anthony Ross, a prototypical nongiver, exemplifies the "keeping your head above water" mentality about resource scarcity that is common to all our nongivers. His life is fairly chaotic, and he is currently regrouping to figure out his career trajectory. Because his future is unclear, it is understandable that he rates low on every personal and life orientation. Anthony, in fact, has the lowest set of orientations of any of our case studies, and shows how the result of very low orientations is typically giving little to nothing.

Given his circumstances he focuses on taking care of his own welfare as a way to not be a burden to others.

Life Purpose (Low)

When we asked Anthony to describe his main goals in life, he concentrated on pure survival: "[I'm] flat broke, living day-to-day, eating, surviving." He is among our interviewees who are trying to survive the challenges of daily life. Despite these circumstances, he expresses some directed goals: "I would say I'm here to actually learn more. To actually learn how things work. Use them in my own life. Avoid procrastination, avoid ignorance." He describes his sense of intrinsic locus of control through adaptation: "A lot of things on my end come from adaptability. So I mean I adapt myself to a situation." He senses where his life is headed and copes with lack of control by developing his ability to adapt to his circumstances.

Social Responsibility (Low)

Anthony's sense of Social Responsibility is also low, primarily because he needs to focus first and foremost on bettering his own lot. He explains, "I've been probably influenced before by my family to believe that probably you should look after your own family, or you should not necessarily look at the world as your own family." The end result, he says, is that he is "probably selfish in some regards." But this is not the same selfishness that we find in those who have resources that they choose not to give away. This is a need-based sense of doing what it takes to survive another day.

Social Trust (Low)

Anthony says that he does not trust other people readily: "I don't usually trust other people. .... I'll accept you as who you are, but not necessarily going to let you in." When we ask, "Do you think most people are good and trustworthy?," he simply says, "Not really." He continues, "I pretty much close myself off. I'm pretty much apathetic." This exhibits how the low care ethos characteristic relates to Social Trust.

Acquisition Seeking (Low)

Possessions are literally a burden for Anthony, given how often he moves residences. "I think if you have too much things, you have too much baggage," he says. Acquiring more would just make his life harder, not happier.

Anthony is a typical nongiver, someone who has such low personal orientations that it is not surprising he is not really able to turn his attention to improving the lives of others. Perhaps at some later point, if Anthony is able to further establish his own set of orientations, he may become able to give more to others. For now, he is focused on keeping his head above water and trying to get by.

Bringing Everyone Together

These case studies show how personal and social orientations are shaped by life experiences and fluctuate according to changes in resources and other life events. Anthony demonstrates that basic needs must be met in order for someone to even modestly participate in giving. Deon shows that even after gaining more affluence those who have lived in poverty can still be shaped by it. The shadow of scarcity experiences lives on in ongoing personal and social orientations. Tanika illustrates how dedication to one's children can start the giving process, and that resources can constrain giving beyond the family circle. Linda shows that more generous giving is possible even with thinly stretched resources and a high-need family circle. The middle-class life trajectory of Jackie and Susan shows that more resourced positions allow personal and social orientations to turn outward in giving to others. Their orientations, life circumstances, and approaches result in varying degrees of giving participation. It is in considering all of these in tandem that light is shed on a more thorough picture of who gives and why.

Generous Self-Identity

Returning to our quantitative analyses, our investigations of social psychological orientations to giving culminate in a final analysis of the role of a self-identity as a generous person. Based on the "looking-glass self" theory of identity,[13] we propose that personal and social orientations dialogue with the perception of self in relation to others. By this we mean that people "try on" various roles and identities and then receive positive or negative feedback from others with whom they interact. From this feedback people reevaluate the extent to which they sustain those identities and roles. We think this process also works in the context of generosity—that people try on and get feedback about their generous identity.

We expect Americans to vary in the extent to which they identify as generous, and the salience of this identity is likely to relate to their personal and social orientations, as well as the extent to which and how they participate in giving behaviors. In short, seeing oneself as generous could be part of the social psychological explanation related to generous outcomes.

Before we explore the relationship of a generous self-identity to orientations, giver types, and giving outcomes, we first examine in greater detail the concept of a generous identity. To assess the extent to which Americans have a generous self-identity, we asked on the survey how much respondents agreed or disagreed with the statement "It is very important to me to be a generous person."[14] For the sake of brevity, we often refer to responses to this generous self-identity measure as "GSID."

The vast majority of Americans take on the identity of a generous self, as Figure 4.4 shows. In all, only 10 percent of Americans disagreed in any way (slightly, mostly, or strongly) that it is very important to them to be a generous person. Twenty-four percent answered as "neutral," meaning they neither agreed nor disagreed with the prompt. The remaining 66 percent agree in some way (slightly, mostly, or strongly) that it is very important to them to be a generous person. As we can see, few Americans outright reject a GSID, indicating that it is a socially desirable characteristic.

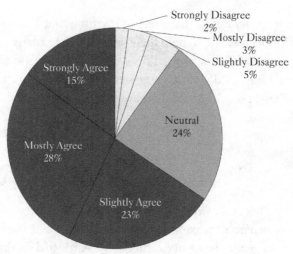

FIGURE 4.4 Generous self-identity (GSID).

Case Study Excursus: Part 2

To show how a generous self-identity looks in the context of real lives, we take a second excursus through our case studies. Our participants who mostly agreed that they have a GSID were Susan Baker, Jackie Sawyer, Cindy Phelps, Tanika Sandaval, and Rosa Perez. Our cases who slightly agreed with a GSID were Ryan Dewey, George Nettleson, Regina Buckner, and Deon Williams. The one case study who was neutral, neither agreeing nor disagreeing with a GSID, was Linda Chesterfield. The only person among our case studies who disagreed in any way with a GSID was Anthony Ross, who slightly disagreed. In the following discussion we highlight a few participants' GSID in relation to their overall giving type.

Mostly Agree GSID

Among our participants who mostly agreed that it is very important to them to be a generous person, we see the influence of place, resources, and social status. As sociologists we refer to this as the power of context: how you perceive yourself is relative to your surroundings. Among our case studies, Susan, Michael, Cindy, and Rosa all mostly agreed that they had a generous self-identity, and we here highlight Michael as an example of this group.

Michael describes his overall identity as a generous person in this way:

> I think I'm generous in the sense of my time that I'm willing to spend with people, and to help them out. In fact in many cases I'd say that I've really done some things above and beyond the [call] of duty, in terms of donating volunteer work or making charitable contributions. I think I could do more than what I do. And I would like to do more.

Slightly Agree GSID

Among our participants who slightly agreed that it is very important to them to be a generous person were Ryan, Regina, and George, whose identification as generous we highlight here. George told us that he "can't stop thinking that maybe I ought to be more generous. So if you're always thinking like that, it makes it hard to be comfortable with where I am." He explains why his desire to identify with this generous trait matters to him: "Wouldn't that matter to everyone? Being generous is a positive and admirable trait. . . . It would certainly matter to me if people thought I was an ungenerous person." This exemplifies that the desire to avoid being perceived as ungenerous by others can serve as a motivating factor of giving.

Neutral GSID

Linda, one of our Selective givers, was among the 24 percent of Americans who answered "neutral" to our question about the importance of being a generous person. When we asked Linda if she considers herself to be a generous person, she answered, "Generally." In person she said that she does give time generously in taking care of her children full time: "I'm generous with my time. I have to be." Thus she feels obligated to live out a parental form of generosity but feels neutral toward helping others outside her immediate family.

Slightly Disagree GSID

Of our 12 cases, only Anthony disagreed to any extent that being a generous person is important to him, and he described himself as "not very generous." He explained this by saying: "You're not gonna give your money to just anyone. You're gonna cherry-pick who you give money to." For Anthony this justifies maintaining a low GSID.

Generous Self-Identities

In summary, our case studies, like most Americans, are likely to agree that they have some degree of a generous self-identity. Those who disagree, and even those who are neutral, tend to have very low participation in any form of giving. Having seen how having a generous self-identity plays a role in giving participation, we investigate it along with the seven key personal and social orientations.

GSID with Orientations, Giver Types, and Giving Behaviors

In the case studies we saw that personal and social orientations provide relative perspective on a generous self-identity. In this final analysis of the chapter, we test quantitatively how personal and social orientations

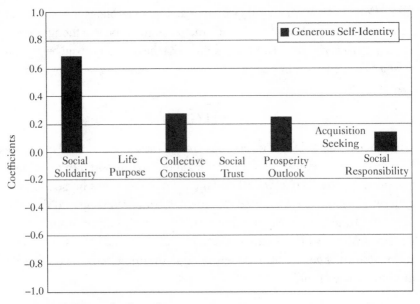

FIGURE 4.5 GSID and orientations.

relate to a GSID. We control for the social status and resource differences between Americans and examine the relationship between GSID and the seven social psychological factors in our analysis. Figure 4.5 illustrates the results. We again present only the statistically significant relationships (see Appendix Table A.4.5 for full details).

Five of the seven orientations relate to a generous self-identity. The results indicate that Acquisition Seeking has the strongest negative association with GSID, and Social Solidarity the strongest positive association. Collective Conscious and Prosperity Outlook have a positive association with GSID at about half of the strength of Social Solidarity's association, and Social Responsibility at about one-fifth as strong. Social Trust and Life Purpose are not significantly related to GSID.[15] This pattern is unlike the others discussed in the chapter, so we think that the generous self-identity rating is indeed distinct from reports of generous actions.

We also modeled the extent to which a generous self-identity differentiates giver types. Employing the same multinomial logistic regression technique discussed in chapter 3, we compare each giver type to Atypical givers with all the social status measures from chapter 2 included. Figure 4.6 shows only the statistically significant relationships discovered in this test. These results indicate no significant difference in GSID between Impulsive

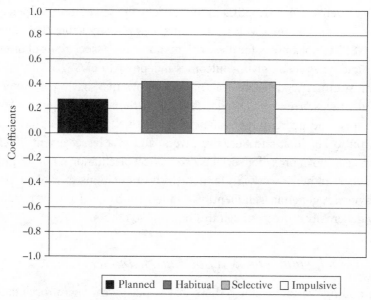

FIGURE 4.6 GSID and giver types.

and Atypical givers. GSID is most strongly related to Selective and Habitual givers. The strength of the relationship between GSID and being a Planned giver is about two-thirds the magnitude of the relationships for Selective and Habitual givers. Considering that Habitual and Selective givers share no common approaches to giving, it seems this GSID is the only commonality between these two types.

These GSID findings may help explain why Planned givers make use of both conscious attention and a regular system to maintain their giving: if there is a lower self-identity with generosity, there may need to be more attention to the details to maintain giving. These results also help us see how Habitual givers are able to run their generosity on autopilot, relying on their higher GSID. Likewise Selective givers may be maintaining their GSID by picking and choosing the causes to which they contribute and the amounts. Impulsive givers, on the other hand, appear to not identify as generous in a way that supports regular involvement. Our case studies describe these situations and the quantitative analysis confirms that they are true more generally.

Finally, we explore how levels of GSID relate to actual giving behaviors. We want to answer this question: When we account for GSID, are there changes to how we understand the role of orientations and types in giving?

In fact when we include GSID in the models, the associations of personal and social orientations with giving outcomes remain stable. This means that GSID is not a proxy for these orientations: the associations of orientations and types act on giving outcomes independent of GSID.

In summary, our statistical models show that having a generous self-identity is primarily related to less Acquisition Seeking, greater Social Solidarity, and giving larger financial donations. GSID is especially significant to Habitual and Selective givers, and to a lesser extent Planned givers. It is not a proxy for social psychological orientations, nor for giving outcomes; rather it works in tandem with orientations to explain giving behaviors. A generous self-identity uniquely contributes to understanding how generosity expresses itself through and to others.

Conclusion: The Why of American Generosity, 1.0

The findings of this chapter show that social psychological orientations help to explain variation in American giving. We began by analyzing more than 100 different measures for personality and well-being dispositions, values and morals, life dispositions, relational styles, "temperature readings" on the social milieu, and orientations specific to giving. From these we identified seven key underlying personal and social orientations: (1) Social Solidarity—"we're all in it together"; (2) Life Purpose—"I am here for a reason"; (3) Collective Conscious—"we are here to help each another"; (4) Social Trust—"people are trustworthy and are not out to get me"; (5) Prosperity Outlook—"the world is abundant, and there is plenty to go around"; (6) Acquisition Seeking—"life is for the taking"; and (7) Social Responsibility—"we are all our brother's (or sister's) keeper." Multiple analyses and robustness checks confirm these seven measures well represent the principal factors identifying different Americans' personal and social orientations.

We evaluated the relationships between these personal and social orientations and giving outcomes. Given our finding in chapter 2 regarding the important role that financial giving plays in the Big 3 generosity forms, our focus was on the relationship between orientations and financial donations. In particular we assessed how the orientations relate to whether Americans give money, how much money they give, and types of giving approaches. The results indicate that having greater Prosperity Outlook and less Acquisition Seeking most differentiate givers from nongivers. Higher Prosperity Outlook, Collective Conscious, and Social

Responsibility most distinguish which givers donate greater amounts of money.

As for the types of giving approaches, we found that all giver types are set apart from Atypical givers by their higher levels of Prosperity Outlook and Social Trust. Within the giver types we found that Planned givers are most characterized by lower levels of Acquisition Seeking and a high degree of all the other personal and social orientations, especially Collective Conscious, Prosperity Outlook, and Social Responsibility. Habitual givers associate with three of the seven orientations and are most differentiated from Atypical givers by high levels of Social Responsibility. Like Planned givers, Selective givers associate with nearly all the orientations, though to a lesser degree. Planned and Selective givers are the only two types to have an association with Collective Conscious. Impulsive givers are moderately related to four of seven orientations, with the largest association being lower Acquisition Seeking.

Recognizing that different types of givers have different orientations driving them to give brings greater nuance to our understanding of why people act generously. On the one hand, the reasons cannot be reduced to a simplistic formula shared by all American givers. On the other hand, the story is not so complicated that we cannot make sense of it. People act in patterned ways, and adequate, nonreductionist explanations of giving outcomes entail combinations of personal orientations and approaches to giving.

Thanks to these analyses, we can see that the identified giver types share some characteristics in common with other types, while also differing from one another. For certain orientations (e.g., Collective Conscious and Prosperity Outlook), Planned and Selective givers are most similar. For others (e.g., Social Responsibility), Planned and Habitual givers are most similar. Still others show a connection between Selective and Planned givers (e.g., Social Solidarity) or between Selective and Impulsive givers (e.g., lower Social Trust than Planned and Habitual givers). Even Impulsive and Planned givers share something in common (lower Acquisition Seeking), though still in distinguishing ways (Planned even lower than Impulsive).

A look into the lives of our case study participants shows how these personal and social orientations exist together in various combinations and how these combinations help to explain giving outcomes. We saw exemplary cases of each type of giver with regard to their personal and social orientations. The case studies also demonstrated that unique circumstances can alter personal and social orientations over time.

The case studies also revealed the "residual poverty" that Deon
Williams described. His story revealed how growing up in an impoverished household left him with the mentality that he does not have enough
resources to help out others. On the surface Deon could be taken as a "live
it up" kind of guy who is fairly selfish, given his relatively high monetary
resources (of which he gives virtually nothing) and his high levels of discretionary time (of which he not only gives nothing but almost takes pride
in not taking time to care for others). However, in the context of his life
history it makes sense that for Deon living a generous life has meant keeping his head above water and successfully making it through adulthood
self-sufficiently. He sees that as enough, and more than the model he grew
up with as a child. He told us that it was all he could do to keep himself
off the streets and out of prison. Giving to others was not an option to him
beyond that. Despite being able to give now, it simply has not been part of
Deon's social psychological makeup to give.

Both of our nongiver cases, along with Deon as an Atypical giver,
showed patterns of low personal and social orientations. Life has been
challenging for them, and they are focused on survival. Much the same
is true for Regina and Tanika, who have been able to reach a bit beyond
taking care of themselves in order to work tirelessly to provide their
children with a better life. We see in these cases how a high degree
of personal and social orientations within the bounds of immediate
family needs calls these mothers to give generously to their children,
but they are otherwise protecting themselves from the broader social
world rather than engaging with it. On the other end of the spectrum,
the cases of Susan, Ryan, Jackie, and George are clear evidence of how
higher levels of personal and social orientations translate into high and
sustained giving practices. After taking an in-depth look at these cases,
it is hard to imagine what set of circumstances could ever shake their
higher levels of giving. They are invested in it as part of their broader
orientation to who they are as people, and giving makes sense within
broader life trajectories that have always been focused on helping others
in some way. We do see that Susan's lower levels of Social Trust mean
her giving behavior requires a greater degree of maintenance, and we
can imagine that a negative giving experience may change her giving
more dramatically than it would for Jackie. These stories combine to

breathe life into the quantitative patterns we find, showing how these social psychological factors work in the case of individual lives.

Another primary finding of this chapter is that having a generous self-identity is part of the picture explaining generous outcomes. We found that a GSID is a highly desirable trait, with most Americans identifying with it to some degree. Our case studies again explained to us how having varying levels of GSID fits within the context of real personal and social lives. Studying GSID alongside the orientations and giver types revealed that higher Social Solidarity and less Acquisition Seeking are strongly associated with identifying the importance of a generous self-identity. There are also relationships between a generous self-identity and giver types: Habitual and Selective givers have the strongest GSID associations, and Planned givers have a more moderate association. A GSID does not appear to be important for differentiating Impulsive from Atypical givers.

Social psychological orientations help answer the why and how questions of Americans giving. Specific combinations of personal and social orientations and different levels of self-identity as a generous person orient Americans toward greater or lesser generosity. Some Americans are more inclined than others to a generous disposition of sorts. This tendency can be more or less actualized through the approach they take to giving, but they are also likely to take particular approaches to giving based on their personal and social orientations.

This chapter showed how *intra*personal orientations relate to giving. We now turn to address to what extent interpersonal, social affiliations are also part of the explanation. The next chapter investigates this second part of the "why" question, which we affectionately call "Why 2.0." Chapter 5 examines how social affiliations and social-contextual norms of generosity complete the full picture of American generosity.

5

Giving Webs of Affiliations

A SOCIORELATIONAL APPROACH

WE TRANSITION IN this chapter to a set of analyses focused on what we affectionately call "Why 2.0." In choosing this name we purposefully invoke the comparison to the dramatic shifts in our online culture in the move from Web 1.0 to Web 2.0. As such Web 1.0 is presented as a unidirectional interaction with Internet-based information, allowing users to access documents and information that were stored inside others' computers, whereas Web 2.0 invites bidirectional interaction with information and others online in dynamic, relational ways. The social psychological factors associated with giving are similar to accessing the information related to someone's self-perception. Granted these intrapersonal perceptions were developed through social experiences and interactions, but they are held in the storage space of the giver, as it were. This chapter moves to the "Why 2.0" of giving: we investigate the role of interpersonal, bidirectional relational interactions that influence giving. This chapter examines the external, interpersonal influences, that is, the importance of social relationships in explaining giving behaviors.

Both internal social factors and external social factors influence individuals' behaviors. We have established that people can be personally more or less oriented to behaviors such as giving, and we now shift the lens to color the picture of generosity with the extra-individual, interpersonal factors of social affiliations that explain whether and how people give. Our social affiliations—the social groups in which we as individuals are embedded—establish a back-and-forth exchange between our internalized orientations and our external relationships to others, creating a dynamic interaction of social influences.

In this chapter we use social affiliations to address the puzzle that we expose regarding the relationship between a generous self-identity and giving outcomes. For ease of presentation, and since we know the predictive role of monetary giving, we again focus these analyses on financial donations.

The Puzzle of Generous Self-Identity

We showed in chapter 4 that a generous self-identity associates with giving in a unique and independent way. However, we find an interesting puzzle when we compare levels of GSID to giver participation: there is not much difference in GSID between givers and nongivers. Figure 5.1 shows the comparison of monetary givers and nongivers by whether the person agrees with, is neutral toward, or disagrees with the statement that a GSID is important to them.

As expected, Americans who agree with a GSID participate in giving more often than not (61 percent participate). But there is a striking lack of difference between nongivers and givers who disagree: 52 percent of Americans who disagree that a GSID is important to them are giving, and approximately the same proportion (48 percent) is not giving. At the

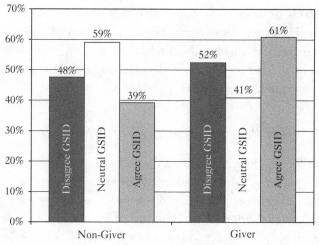

FIGURE 5.1 The puzzle of generous self-identity and giving.

same time, 39 percent who agree with a GSID did not donate to charitable causes, not a single dollar. That means there is only a 9 percent difference between those who agree and those who disagree on a GSID. In addition "neutral" Americans, those who neither agreed nor disagreed with a GSID, have the highest nongiving participation—even higher than Americans who specifically disagree with a GSID. Why does identifying as generous not appear to explain participation in giving? Alternatively why does *not* identifying as generous fail to explain nongiving? Furthermore why does a neutral identification explain nongiving more than explicit disagreement with a generous identity?

When we investigated the relationship of GSID and donation amounts (analysis not shown), we see the same pattern: givers who are neutral on GSID average lower donation amounts than givers who disagree with a GSID. Specifically:

- Forty percent of those who agree with a GSID did not donate anything in the past 12 months.
- Just over 50 percent of those who disagree that a GSID is important to them still donate money.
- Those who are neutral on a GSID give at the lowest rates, even lower than those who disagree.

Having a generous self-identity does increase the likelihood that someone will give, but the relationship is not as strong as we would expect.

What explains this puzzling mismatch between a generous self-identity and actual giving behaviors? We suspect that one possible explanation lies with how social relationships affect behaviors. In particular we investigate the extent to which people are socially affiliated with others who are oriented (or not) toward generosity.

The "Spoke Structure" of Affiliations

According to the "looking-glass self" theories in social psychology discussed in chapter 4,[1] identities develop through ongoing feedback from the interaction between the self and the social world. People's intrinsic, social psychological orientations constantly interact with their social affiliations. Since people interact with others who have different orientations, their identities evolve and develop. As we as individuals are exposed to a wider array of possible identities, roles, and orientations, it only makes sense that we actualize those identities that are most supported among those in our social world. Our personal orientations toward various behaviors can fall away if our relationships do not support them, just as we can forget the meaning of words, especially from a foreign language, if we do not use them regularly. Alternatively our orientations toward various social actions can be supported or enhanced if we are surrounded by people who are also heavily involved in those actions. All of which implies that generous self-identities are not fixed but dynamic, as they reflect people's interactions with others' orientations toward or against giving, which can affect the actualization of generosity.

Based on the ideas of Georg Simmel and similar scholars,[2] we understand that there is a "spoke structure" of social webs of group affiliations that can overlap, reinforce, and at times directly conflict with each other. Figure 5.2 visualizes the spoke-wheel theory of social affiliations, showing an individual as embedded within multiple affiliations. This pluralistic conception of modern social relations views society as historically having changed from concentric circles of affiliations, in which participation in one group necessitated belonging in all others, toward the individual constellation of relationships in the visual. Applying this theory of social relations we continue to fill in the picture of American generosity by investigating the social groups in which an individual is embedded. Just as individuals vary in the degree to which they are oriented toward generosity, so

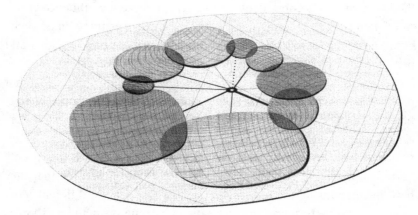

FIGURE 5.2 Simmel's web of group affiliations.

Reprinted from Bernice Pescosolido and Beth A. Rubin, "The Web of Group Affiliations Revisited: Social Life, Postmodernism, and Sociology," *American Sociological Review* 65 (2000): 52–76. Used by permission of the authors and the American Sociological Association. Copyright © 2015.

too do social groups. We propose that we can solve the puzzle of how a generous self-identity gets translated into actual giving behaviors by looking at giving within its sociorelational context.

American Generosity in Sociorelational Context

Applying these theories to American generosity, we expect that a generous self-identity is embedded within this "spoke structure" of affiliations. The people and groups with whom Americans affiliate may themselves be more or less oriented to generosity. The combination of personal identity and group affiliations presents an ongoing dialogue that could reinforce a personal identity as generous, undermine it, or play a neutral role. This means each person has both an internalized, individual degree of personal generosity orientations and an externalized, relational degree of affiliation orientations to generosity. Given the various interests, identities, and roles that pull at each of us in the modern world, we expect that a part of the generosity picture is that people actualize the tendencies for which we have the greatest social support.

Being a part of contemporary society necessitates our understanding of the potential spoke structure of American giving: we no longer exist in premodern configurations in which our social groups are determined by where we live and our family's social status. The spoke structure of contemporary group affiliations highlights the diversity of our affiliations and the idea that this network does not simply reinforce the influence of our "clan" family. Rather contemporary society introduces fragmented social experiences that could lead us to change or abandon the thoughts and behaviors that we learned in the place or family of our birth.

For example, some people may have a desire to win a gold medal, but they will be considerably more likely to do so if they have some interaction with a person who has won a gold medal, and especially so if they are related to that person in such a way that they can, over time, better actualize their gold-medal inclination. Even more complex is that people have inclinations to be gold-medal winners at the same time that they have inclinations to succeed at other things that require different identities and roles. These various inclinations become push-and-pull forces exerting pressures on our time and attention. We are most likely to carry out the inclinations for which we encounter the least resistance, that is, the most support, from those in our social group interactions. Conversely, for instance, if all those around a gold-medal-inclined person continually express disinterest in competitive athletics, there is a steady signal of no support to that person. This discourages the person from pursuing competitive athletics, and therefore he or she will never work to win a gold medal. Over time we would expect the gold-medal-inclined person to be less and less likely to work on winning a gold medal.

We expect a similar sort of process to be the case for generous orientations, people aspiring to live generous lives. However, unlike a goal that is fulfilled by a clear achievement, such as winning a gold medal, achieving a generous life does not have a clear point after which the status has been permanently achieved. Actualizing generosity is one of those pursuits, like parenting, that people need to continually work on, and there is never a clear measure of the extent to which people have "arrived" at their most generous self. In this sociorelational approach to generosity, we argue that people act not as isolated individuals; rather they are connected to people and groups who more or less support their personal orientations. We are, in part, a reflection of our relationships.

Americans today can choose whom they spend time with; they are not limited to their family or neighbors. This is part of the free nature of contemporary social life. This diversity of choice can put us in groups with people who differ significantly on an orientation toward generosity—encouraging or discouraging us from actualizing our personal orientation to generosity. Someone who has a high generous self-identity could actualize generosity more if his or her friends are also volunteering and giving to charitable causes. If the same person is embedded in less generous groups, however, he or she could wind up giving very little. We expect affiliations to reinforce or undermine a person's sense of his or her generous self, and thus to partially explain individual giving behaviors. Thus an understanding of giving affiliations is necessary to complete the picture of American generosity.

A person's web of affiliations can include a host of sociorelational groups. Here we focus on six primary relationships:

- **Parents**: Americans grow up in families with parents who may or may not have modeled and taught generosity.
- **Spouses/partners**: Americans may have romantic partners with their own personal orientations to generosity.
- **Religion**: Americans' religious congregations address giving differently.

- **Friends**: Americans make friends with others who have different degrees of generosity.
- **Local community**: Americans live in communities that they perceive to be more or less generous.
- **National affiliations**: Americans may also generate a sense of group identity with the nation and its giving spirit.

We think the people in these groups with whom members affiliate, in conjunction with the members' own orientations toward generosity, will help explain the "Why 2.0" about why Americans give as they do.

How do webs of affiliations relate to generosity? For example, how do two people give who have the same personal orientation to be generous but are embedded in different webs of affiliations? Perhaps one person grew up with parents who explicitly taught about generosity, has a spouse who is highly aligned toward being generous, has friends who actively give, or regularly attends a religious congregation that frequently calls people to give their time and resources. Another person may have grown up with parents who never talked about giving, has a spouse who is not particularly interested in being generous, has friends who rarely give, or attends religious services that never call the congregants to give (or does not attend religious services). We suspect that these two people would give differently, despite their similar personal orientations toward generosity.

Of course when thinking about these six different affiliations, we would expect a person to encounter varying combinations of "grease" or "friction" toward actualizing generosity. As Simmel explains, contemporary life is about having *multiple* group affiliations that may bolster or conflict with each other to greater or lesser extents. It is easy to assume that people who have social affiliations that are uniformly positively oriented toward generosity would be more likely to give, and that people whose social affiliations are uniformly indifferent to or even antithetical toward generosity would be less likely to give. But predicting behaviors gets complicated when people have myriad configurations, with some giving-supportive affiliations and some non-giving-supportive affiliations.

Webs of Affiliations

Analyzing each of our six affiliations separately allows us to explore how affiliations expose Americans to others who are themselves more or less oriented toward generosity. (Of course not all Americans are married or partnered, nor are all religious. We address these affiliations only if they apply to the participant.) We conclude with an analysis where we account for all the group affiliations in the spoke structure to investigate how the web of affiliations (WoA) relates to generous behaviors.

A graphical representation of the spoke-wheel configuration of the WoA appears in Figure 5.3. The "self" pictured in the middle of the figure is the generous self-identity discussed in chapter 4 (i.e., a person's agreement or disagreement with the statement "It is important to me to be a generous person"). The web encircling the self represents each of these six affiliations. We conceptualize this as representing the idea of the social psychological self as the center that is surrounded by spheres of sociorelational context. Akin to a planet with many moons orbiting around it, this image represents the theoretical lineage of the web of affiliations that undergirds relational sociology and network theory.

We begin by assessing each group's orientation to generosity in relation to a person's own sense of generous self.[3] After discussing each affiliation's relationship to GSID, we will examine the configurations of these

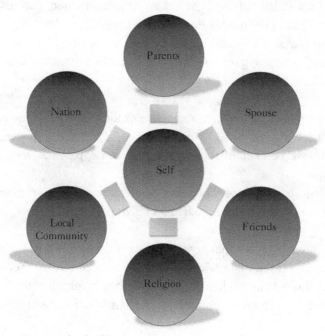

FIGURE 5.3 Giving web of affiliations.

six group affiliations to understand the WoA and its influence on a person's likelihood to be generous as well as a person's donation amounts.

Parental Influence to Give

The first affiliation we explore is the top spoke in Figure 5.3: parental influence to give. Existing literature has well established the influence of parenting on children's outcomes throughout their lives.[4] This parental influence occurs through two primary avenues:

1. Parental teaching: parents influencing their children through direct teaching to give
2. Parental modeling: parents influencing their children through indirect modeling of giving

Children shape their values and actions from the combination of these direct teachings and indirect modeling. We expect these childhood lessons to influence their generosity behaviors in adulthood.

To study this parental influence on giving, we asked survey respondents the degree to which their parents taught them about and modeled generosity. The left side of Figure 5.4 pictures whether "parents taught me it is good to give money to charitable causes,"[5] and the right side of the figure pictures parental modeling with respondents' answers about how often "parents gave money to charitable causes." [6] Our results indicate that:

- Thirty-nine percent of Americans were explicitly taught by their parents to give.
- Seventy-six percent of Americans had some parental modeling of giving.
- Twenty-four percent of Americans were not or could not remember being taught and had no modeling of giving by their parents.[7]

It is interesting to see that fewer than half of Americans were taught about giving yet the vast majority did remember observing their parents giving. Although the explicit teaching was not common practice, it was common for children to remember implicit lessons about giving into adulthood.

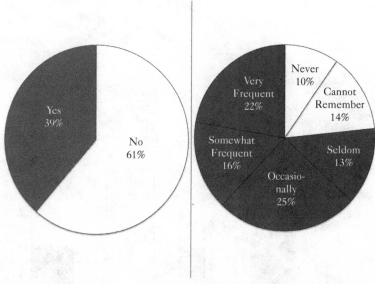

FIGURE 5.4 Parental influence on giving: teaching giving (left), modeling giving frequency (right).

Spousal Alignment on Giving

The second affiliation we examine is spousal alignments around giving, illustrated in Figure 5.3. Connection to a spouse can be one of the most intimate of affiliations and most obviously relates to a person's ability to actualize a generous self-identity through the act of donating. When people are married or living with a romantic partner (subsequently referred to simply as "spouses" or "partnered Americans"), decisions to give usually require negotiation about shared household resources: financial budgets, time resources, and possessions. Any pooling of resources offers potential for disagreement to arise between the spouses and act as friction against acting generously. On the other hand, spouses whose generous self-identities are aligned could together actualize their identity through generous behaviors to a greater extent than if both tried to actualize their inclinations independently.

To measure spousal alignment on giving, we asked married or cohabiting Americans the extent to which they agree or disagree with the statement "My spouse and I agree about financial giving." Figure 5.5 represents the results of four of the web of affiliations. In the upper left we reproduce

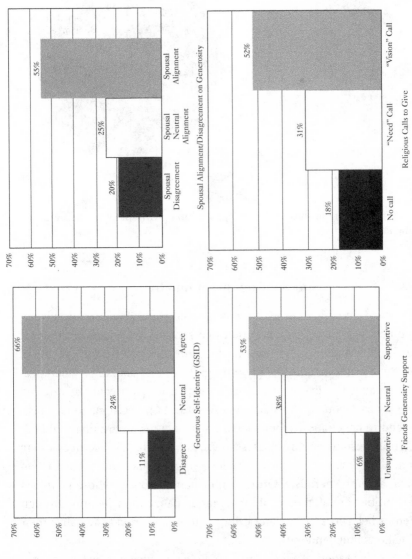

FIGURE 5.5 Generous self-identity (upper left), spousal alignment on generosity (upper right), friends generosity support (bottom left), religious calls to give (bottom right).

the GSID results described in chapter 4.[8] The upper-right quadrant displays the results of this spousal alignment measure. We see that:

- Twenty percent of partnered Americans disagree with their spouse about giving.
- Twenty-five percent of partnered Americans answered the prompt neutrally, which is akin to a "no opinion" or "this does not apply to us" response.
- Fifty-five percent of partnered Americans align with their spouse about giving.

We would expect that spouses who align on giving will be better able to actualize their giving (a positive relationship to giving). For those Americans who disagree with their spouse, we would expect the giving of the giver spouse to be tempered by the nongiver.

Giving-Supportive Friends

Next we examine friend affiliations, the third spoke in Figure 5.3. We know from social network theory that close friends play an important role in social outcomes.[9] For some behaviors friends can even exert greater influence than spouses or family. To rate the impact of friends on generosity, we explore the extent to which Americans find support for giving among their five closest friends. We asked about each friend, "Is this person someone (1) who you know donates money to charitable or religious causes, (2) who has asked you to give money to charitable or religious causes, or (3) who would be *un*supportive of you donating money to charitable or religious causes?"[10] Since we want to think of these close friends as a group, we then calculated a measure of friend affiliation with generosity using the ratio of supportive generous friends in the close friend group.

For example, for those who said that all of the friends they listed were giving-supportive, we calculated 100 percent of their close friends as giving-supportive. If all of their close friends were unsupportive of giving, then we calculated negative 100 percent of their friends as giving-supportive. Those with a mix of supportive and unsupportive friends received a net value equal to the ratio of supportive friends. For example, if they have five close friends and three are supportive but two are unsupportive, they would receive a value of positive 20 percent. People who listed zero friends received a value of zero friend affiliations since they have no friends to be supportive or unsupportive of their financial giving. Likewise if they did not answer any of the friend questions, we assigned a zero affiliation score. We consider both these response scenarios to show a neutral friend influence, that is, the absence of a positive or negative affiliation. Figure 5.5 pictures collapsed results of this measure in the bottom left.

Our results indicate that:
- Only 6 percent of Americans have mostly giving-unsupportive friends.
- Thirty-eight percent have net neutral/absent generosity support among closest friends.
- Fifty-three percent of Americans have giving-supportive friends.

We would expect having giving-supportive friends to enhance giving, while neutral friends would likely exercise little influence over others' giving.

Religious Calls to Give

Next we look at the impact of *current* exposure to religious calls to give, represented as the fourth spoke on the web of group affiliations pictured at the bottom of Figure 5.3. Much of the philanthropic literature on giving focuses on the influence of religion on people's desire to give.[11] The literature shows that religion, like parenting, influences people's behaviors through teaching and modeling. With respect to generosity, people attending religious services are more likely to give due to the influence of leaders in their religious congregations calling them to do so. As was the case for spousal affiliations, this group affiliation does not apply to all Americans. Here we exclude this affiliation as a noninfluence for the nearly half of Americans who did not attend religious services at all or only attended one to two times in the past year.

Before moving further, we feel it necessary to explain in detail how we went about asking Americans about religious calls to give. We did not simply use their religious service attendance as a way to measure this affiliation since we already account for its influence on giving in our earlier models. Instead our formulation of a religious affiliation is informed by previous research by one of the authors and colleagues. In the previous project, that authors investigated how affiliations operate within religious congregations.[12] We concluded that pastors talked about money to the congregation in either a "pay the bills" or a "live the vision" manner. "Pay the bills" appeals ask congregants to give in order to cover the costs of operating the specific church. Pastors employing this approach typically asked parishioners to give in order to replace the carpet, fund a youth group trip, build a new facility, repair the furnace, and so on. This approach focused on teaching the congregants about the specific purposes for which their money was needed. This approach was categorically different from that of pastors who talked about giving as part of "living the vision," which taught congregants that donating money was a means to carry out the mission of their religion. This approach was used on a regular basis as part of the faith tradition, not in requests to fill a material need of the church. There were also some congregations in the study that never explicitly raised the issue of donating money, other than passing around a collection plate or basket.

Based on this research we measure "religious calls to give" using answers to the question "When your religious congregation communicates to its people about money and finances, does the message tend to be (1) more about need and scarcity, (2) more about vision and opportunity, or (3) my religious congregation says nothing about money?"[13] We use this measure to understand the ways in which religious groups affiliate with a generous self-identity. We categorize the religious orientations as "no religious call" when congregations say nothing of giving money, "need to give" when there are calls to give to fulfill a need, and "vision give" when congregations are called to give to fulfill the religious vision. Figure 5.5 shows in the bottom-right corner exposure to the three different "calls to give" among Americans who attend religious services more than a couple times a year.

Our results indicate that:

- Eighteen percent of Americans attending religious services experience no call to give.
- Thirty-one percent of Americans attending religious services experience a "need" call to give.
- Fifty-two percent of Americans attending religious services experience a "vision" call to give.

Combined these figures show that it is more common than not for Americans to have generosity-supportive religious affiliations. Similar to a personal identity as generous, we find a rightward skew toward the majority of Americans having a positive GSID, spousal alignment, giving-supportive friends, and religious vision calls to give. However, this is not the case for significant proportions of Americans who have neutral or less personal or social support for generosity behaviors among their interpersonal affiliations. We expect the "vision call" to more strongly activate the GSID of a giver than a "need" call.

Local Community and National Giving Context

In addition to the more personal affiliations of spouses, parents, friends, and religious calls, we examine two more general spokes of the web of group affiliations: local community and the national contexts of giving. The spokes on the left side of Figure 5.3 represent the local community and national contexts of giving. Based on a long lineage in social theory about the important role of community and national contexts in shaping people's behaviors, we posit that giving behaviors will also relate to the affiliations that individuals have with their local community and nation.

People can perceive their local and national contexts as more or less generous, and we had Americans assess the giving levels of people in the nation and in their local community. For the national context we asked, "If you had to guess, what would you say is the amount of money the typical U.S. household contributed to charitable causes over the last 12 months?" We asked for the local context, "If you had to guess, what would you say is the amount of money the typical household in your neighborhood (or local community) contributed to charitable causes over the last 12 months?" Figure 5.6 illustrates the results of both these measures. National giving perceptions are displayed with the dark, dashed line with diamond markers, and local community giving perceptions are displayed with the light, solid line with x-shaped markers.

For ease of interpretation, we collapse these estimates of donations in Figure 5.6 into three categories: none (for $0), moderate ($1–100), and high amounts (more than $100) for the community and national contexts. The results are similar and indicate that:

- Fewer than 10 percent of Americans think the average American gave nothing to charitable causes in the past year (national context).
- Fewer than 20 percent think typical local community members gave nothing.
- Nearly 20 percent think average Americans gave moderately ($0–$100).
- More than 20 percent think typical local community members gave moderately ($0–$100).

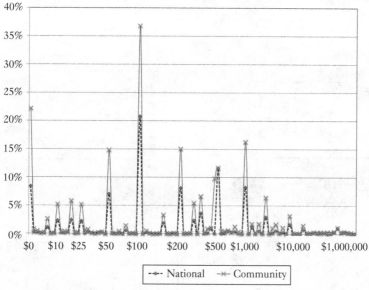

FIGURE 5.6 Community and national giving levels.

- More than 70 percent think average Americans gave a high amount ($100 or more).
- Nearly 70 percent think typical local community members gave a high amount ($100 or more).

Americans perceive their local community as participating in giving more than the nation. However, there is a perception that the national citizen gives larger amounts ($100 or more) than the citizen in their local community.

In summary, when we consider each of the six affiliations separately, Americans are more likely than not to have generosity-supportive affiliations. However, a large minority of Americans have affiliations that are neutral or negative in their generosity support.

Affiliations and Self-Identity

Next we consider each of these affiliations in relation to levels of generous self-identity. What is interesting to investigate here is whether and to what extent personal identity as generous aligns with each affiliation's supportiveness for giving. We illustrate Americans' levels of GSID in tandem with each affiliation's support for giving in Figures 5.7 and 5.8.

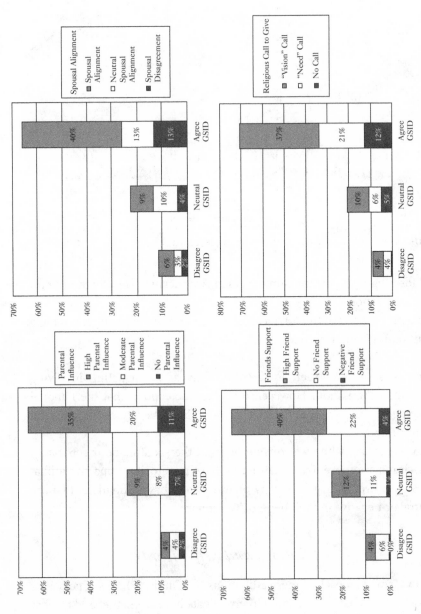

FIGURE 5-7 GSID and parental influence (upper left), GSID and spousal alignment (upper right), GSID and friends support (bottom left), GSID and religious calls (bottom right).

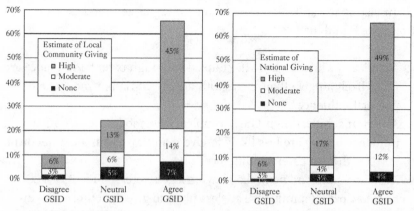

FIGURE 5.8 GSID and local community giving (left), GSID and national giving (right).

Parental Influence and GSID

How does parental influence to give cross-reference with a personal generous identity? To answer this question we combine teaching and modeling into one measure of parental influence to give. In the upper-left graph of Figure 5.7 we visualize a comparison between parental influence to give and a generosity self-identity. We see in the far-right bar that:

- The largest grouping of Americans (35 percent) has a high GSID coupled with high parental influence to give (top).
- Twenty percent of Americans have a high GSID and moderate parental influence (middle).
- Eleven percent of Americans have a high GSID with no parental influence (bottom).

Based on our data we think that Americans at the top essentially had the wheels for giving greased by their parental affiliation and may be more likely to actualize their generous identity as a result, whereas those at the bottom did not have their wheels greased. The gray areas at the top of the middle and far-left bars show an opposite scenario: some people's parental affiliations create friction against their lower generous identity, insofar as their parents promoted a generous life but the current GSID of the child (now an adult) is neutral or low. We think that these Americans may be more likely to give despite their lower personal identity as a result of their parents' influence and their childhood experiences.

In testing the affiliation associations in regression models net of controls;[14] we found that:

- Americans with a high GSID coupled with high parental influence are more likely to give than those with a high GSID but moderate or no parental influence.[15]
- Americans with a high GSID coupled with moderate or no parental influence to give are less likely to give than those with a neutral or no GSID with high parental influence.
- Americans who are neutral on having a generous self-identity and have low parental influence are less likely to give than those who disagree on GSID.

In other words, it appears that the people least likely to give are those who are ambivalent about having a generous self-identity and who have low parental influence. That combination is even less likely to relate to giving than disagreement on having a GSID. When we analyze the donation amount, we again find that Americans who have a high generous self-identity and had no generous parental influence give less money, on average and net of controls, than those who had moderate levels of parental influence. We find that those with high parental influence give more even if their GSID is in friction with their parents' giving orientation.

Spousal Alignment and GSID

When comparing spousal alignment on giving to a generous self-identity, we find a similar pattern but with a more positive, right skew than parental influence (pictured in the upper-right graph of Figure 5.7):

- Most partnered Americans with a high GSID have spouses that align with this generous orientation.
- Twenty-six percent of those with a high GSID have a spouse that is neutral or does not align with this orientation.
- Six percent have a neutral or low GSID with spousal disagreement.

Spousal alignments could grease the wheels for giving, while spousal disagreement could provide friction inhibiting the actualization of a person's generous identity. Interestingly friction can work in both directions, in that spousal disagreement for someone with a low GSID causes friction from the spouse for the person to give, while spousal disagreement for someone with a high GSID causes friction from the spouse for the person not to give. In either case this could help to explain part of the generosity self-identity puzzle of giving.

When we modeled the association of spousal alignment on financial giving net of controls, we found that:

- Partnered Americans with a high GSID are more likely to give if their spouse agrees with them about giving.
- Partnered Americans with a high GSID and neutral spousal alignment are less likely to give than those who are neutral or disagree on having a GSID.

When we model giving amounts,[16] Americans with a high GSID and a neutral spouse donate lower amounts, on average and net of controls, than those who are neutral or disagree on having a GSID. This means that a neutral spouse has a greater negative pull on Americans' giving than lacking a generous self-identity. The bottom line is that there appears to be a frictional influence on giving for Americans who have neutral or negative spousal alignment. We see this as a drag force on ability to enact a personal orientation to be generous. To actualize their generous self-identity, some Americans have to overcome spousal resistance.

Giving-Supportive Friends and GSID

Patterns of generous self-identity and giving-supportive friends resemble patterns for GSID and spousal affiliations, as the bottom-left graph in Figure 5.7 shows:

- Forty percent of Americans have a high GSID and have giving-supportive friends.
- Twenty-six percent have a high GSID and neutral or non-giving-supportive friends.
- No Americans in our survey disagree with a GSID and have friends unsupportive of giving.

When we modeled the association of giving-supportive friends with financial giving net of controls we find that:

- Having giving-supportive friends relates to higher donation amounts.
- Donation amounts increase with greater proportions of giving-supportive friends.

Americans who are the least likely to be givers are those who have a high GSID with neutral friend alignment, and giving amounts are highest among those who have a high GSID coupled with high friend alignment. Thus it appears Americans are more likely to donate and donate greater amounts when they have more generous friends.

Religious Calls and GSID

In comparing religious calls to give with having a generous self-identity, a comparison displayed in the bottom-right graph of Figure 5.7, we again find a similar relationship to the other group affiliation patterns:

- Thirty-seven percent of Americans who attend religious services more than a couple times a year have high GSID and hear "vision" calls to give in their congregation.
- Twenty-one percent of religious Americans have a high GSID and receive "need" calls.
- Twelve percent of Americans with high GSID hear no calls to give at their religious congregations.

When we modeled the association between religious calls to give and financial giving net of controls we find that:

- Religious Americans who hear "need" calls to give are more likely to donate than those who hear no call to give in their religious congregation.
- Those who attend religious services and hear "vision" calls to give have an even greater likelihood of donating than "need" call attendees.

When we model giving amounts, we encounter the same pattern: hearing a "vision" call to give is associated with higher donation amounts than hearing "need" calls, but "need" calls still associate with higher donations than hearing no call to give.[17] Among Americans who attend religious services, the least likely to be givers are those who express a high GSID but have no exposure to religious calls to give; their likelihood of being a giver is even lower than those with neutral or negative GSID. Higher donation amounts are found among religious Americans who have a higher GSID and exposure to religious vision calls.

Thus Americans who attend religious services are most likely to be generous and give the highest amounts if they hear "vision" calls to give in their congregation. Those who hear "need" calls to give are more likely to be generous and give more than those who do not hear calls to give at all. As a result we conclude that religious attendance can grease the wheels for giving, especially within congregational contexts that call people to give as part of living out a religious mission.

Local and National Contexts and GSID

When we investigate connections between GSID and perceptions of local community giving and national giving (portrayed in Figure 5.8 with community on the left and national context on the right), we once more see a pattern very similar to other kinds of affiliations:

- Forty-five percent of Americans express a high GSID and perceive high community giving.
- Forty-nine percent of Americans have a high GSID and also see national giving as high.
- Thirty percent of Americans have a neutral or low GSID, and even they perceive high national and community giving more often than not.

There is a potential drag effect acting on 11 percent of Americans within the high GSID category (here we are only looking at the far-right bars). These Americans believe the average American household donated nothing to charitable causes in the past year; a similar perception is nearly twice as common for high-GSID Americans when it comes to their local communities.

In modeling these national and local giving contexts in regression models, we do not find that perceptions of national or local generosity have any significant influence on whether Americans give, no matter the perceived household donation amount with the GSID (with or without control measures). However, the amount of money donated does relate to perceptions of local community giving, net of all social status control measures.

Summarizing Affiliations and GSID

Across all six affiliations we see most Americans have support for their generosity identity. On the other hand, every type of affiliation we assessed does present some Americans with no support for, or even opposition to, generosity, which potentially exerts a drag effect on the expression of their generous identity. It is not likely that many Americans experience support for giving across every kind of affiliation in their social web, and thus we need to understand how the various influences of different affiliations act in conjunction with, neutralize, or counteract one another. Thus we turn to an analysis of the overall configuration of American webs of affiliations.

Webs of Affiliations and Being a Giver

Now that we have discussed the individual contributions of these group affiliations, we configure them into webs of affiliations and explore their combinations. The "grease the wheels" and "downward drag" influences would be expected to compound across affiliations. For example, what does giving look like for people who agree that being generous is important to their self-identity, but who have an unaligned spouse, parents who did not model giving, and friends that are supportive of giving and attend a religious congregation that talks about "vision" giving? Various possible mixes of affiliations could inhibit or bolster actualizing that person's high GSID. Alternatively, what would happen for someone with a neutral to low GSID with this same configuration of affiliations? In this case spousal misalignment would signal a high-GSID spouse. Does the degree of influence of the affiliations remain the same or does it change because the GSID is different?

Methodologically we model simultaneously held affiliations by employing fsQCA, the method described in chapter 3 on the outcome of whether or not someone gives. This method allows us to test our ideas regarding the influence of configurations, that is, combinations of affiliations, which is distinct from the role of each affiliation in isolation that we just explained. We here test the theory that people may be more likely to give to charitable causes if most of their affiliations are oriented toward generosity, whereas people with more affiliations unsupportive of generosity may be less likely to be givers. In addition to testing this theory, we will explore whether particular kinds of affiliations have greater influence than others when they are assessed together as the web of affiliation.

With these ideas in mind, we here model the complex social reality of how personal generous identity is situated within multiple sociorelational groups that have different levels of support for generosity. The results for modeling whether or not someone gives reveals only one significant affiliation configuration: a person is more likely to give if he or she has a high GSID and higher than average generosity support from all affiliations, except nation. Figure 5.9 pictures this giver configuration, which entails having a high personal generous self-identity in combination with a web of affiliation that supports generosity: spousal alignment, parental modeling to give, friend support for giving, religious calls to give, and perceiving local community giving to be high.[18] This combination applies to 12 percent of American givers.

When we examine the web of affiliation using traditional regression techniques,[19] we find that only two of the six affiliations remain independently influential: parental modeling of giving and giving-supportive friends. When we include the control measures described in chapter 2, only the parental affiliation remains a key differentiator of whether or not someone gives. In other words, the association of friend support affiliation appears to be attributable to demographic factors. We do find a significant

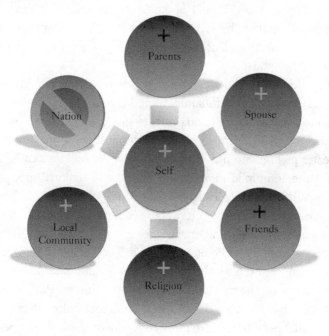

FIGURE 5.9 Web of affiliations and being a giver.

negative relationship between giving and perceptions of greater national generosity once control measures are included. This indicates that people who believe the average American household gives generously are *less* likely to be givers once the differences in demographic compositions of givers are accounted.

In summary, participation in giving relates to having a higher generous self-identity in tandem with support for giving from affiliations across the web: spousal, parental, friendship, religious, and communal. These affiliations can grease the wheels for actualizing a giving orientation, but their impact can be overshadowed by people's social status characteristics.

Webs of Affiliations and Higher Giving

When we investigate the amounts donated (logged) by givers, using this same fsQCA method to examine the configuration "recipes" of webs of affiliations, we find five statistically significant recipes, represented in Figure 5.10.[20] Path 1 shows how parental modeling, friend support, religious calls, and local and national giving contexts create a WoA explaining greater amounts of donations.[21] Of all the recipes this is the only one that holds without the ingredient of a generous personal identity. That is, people donate more if just about everyone around them supports generosity—no matter the level of importance they assign to their own generous self-identity and no matter their giving alignment or disagreement with their spouse.

Path 2 shows how the presence of a generous personal identity substitutes for the national affiliation ingredient in the recipe of Path 1.[22] Path 3 shows that when religious calls to give are absent, all other affiliations, including GSID, must be giving-supportive in order to associate with greater giving amounts.[23] Path 4 shows that religious calls can substitute for the combined ingredients of local and national groups in the recipe of Path 3.[24] Finally Path 5 shows a recipe involving a low generous self-identity; coupled with low spousal alignment (where the spouse provides positive friction that encourages giving), along with the ingredients of friend support, religious calls, and perceptions of high local and national giving, and the result is a recipe for greater amounts of giving.[25] Path 5 confirms our theory that if most of one's primary relational contexts (with spouse, friends, church, and local and national contexts) support generosity, that person will give more *even if* he or she does not personally

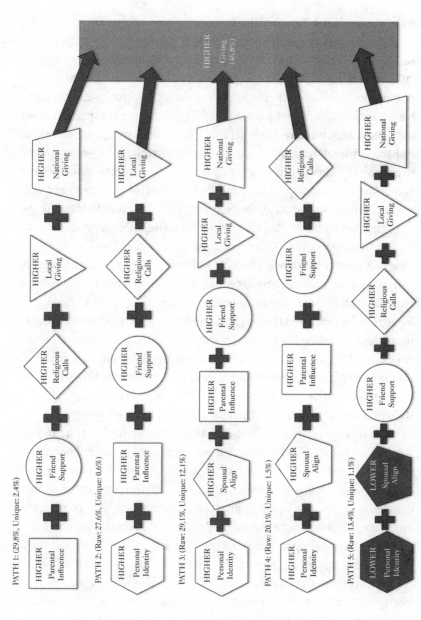

PATH 1: (29.8%, Unique: 2.4%)
HIGHER Parental Influence + HIGHER Friend Support + HIGHER Religious Calls + HIGHER Local Giving + HIGHER National Giving

PATH 2: (Raw: 27.6%, Unique: 0.6%)
HIGHER Personal Identity + HIGHER Parental Influence + HIGHER Friend Support + HIGHER Religious Calls + HIGHER Local Giving

PATH 3: (Raw: 29.1%, Unique: 12.1%)
HIGHER Personal Identity + HIGHER Spousal Align + HIGHER Parental Influence + HIGHER Friend Support + HIGHER Local Giving + HIGHER National Giving

PATH 4: (Raw: 20.1%, Unique: 1.5%)
HIGHER Personal Identity + HIGHER Spousal Align + HIGHER Parental Influence + HIGHER Friend Support + HIGHER Religious Calls

PATH 5: (Raw: 13.4%, Unique: 1.1%)
LOWER Personal Identity + LOWER Spousal Align + HIGHER Friend Support + HIGHER Religious Calls + HIGHER Local Giving + HIGHER National Giving

HIGHER Giving (46.8%)

FIGURE 5.10 Web combinations most closely associated with higher giving.

identify with the importance of being generous. We next explain the place of each affiliation in the five recipes.

1. **Role of Generous Personal Identity.** Only one of the five recipes for greater amounts of giving, Path 1, does not involve having a generous self-identity. This means that in every recipe except this one, group affiliations cannot grease the wheels of generosity and lead to greater donation amounts unless a person first considers generosity important to his or her identity. When a positive GSID is missing, compensating for its absence requires a recipe wherein all affiliations except spouse—that is, parent, friend, religious, local, and national affiliations—are oriented to generosity. Alternatively Path 5 shows that for a person who does not agree that a generous personal identity is important, disagreement with his or her generous spouse, coupled with friends, a religious congregation, and perceptions of local and national giving that orient to generosity, can overcome a low GSID and cause greater donations.

2. **Role of Parental Influence.** Parental influence is an ingredient in every recipe for greater donations except Path 5. In the other four pathways parental influence to give is a necessary ingredient. Path 5 shows that a positive-friction affiliation with a spouse can substitute for the parent ingredient in the recipe toward greater donations. Thus parental influence does differentiate between WoA configurations, but this influence seems to be a key ingredient for greater giving amounts, unless there is a spousal affiliation that counters a low personal identity.

3. **Role of Spousal Alignment.** Spousal alignment plays a role in three of the five recipes related to greater giving amounts (Paths 3, 4, and 5). Path 3 shows that alignment with a generous spouse can substitute for the role of religious calls to give when all other affiliations are oriented toward giving. Path 4 indicates that alignment with a generous spouse coupled with religious calls to give can substitute for both community and national giving ingredients. High personal identity, parental influence, and friend support remain important in this path. The most interesting role of spousal alignment is in Path 5, where we see the positive friction process: the combination of low generous self-identity and low spousal alignment means that the spouse identifies as generous. This positive friction that a generous spouse provides to an ungenerous person—coupled with religious calls and giving-supportive friends, local community, and national context—creates a recipe of more giving from otherwise ungenerous people.

4. **Role of Friend Support.** Affiliating with a group of close friends who are supportive of generosity is the key part of the pathways to greater giving. Giving-supportive friends appear to be a necessary ingredient in all five recipes for greater donation amounts. We acknowledge that we cannot separate the chicken from the egg here: those who give could be choosing to be friends only with other people who are giving, or close friends may allow only other generous people into their friend groups. But in the "grease the wheels" theory, who opted to be friends with whom is beside the point: the established affiliation generates this outcome where the amount of the donation is expected to increase. In a group that is supportive of generosity, we would expect every friend to donate larger amounts than each would give if his or her close friends were not supportive of generosity.

5. **Role of Religious Calls.** Religious calls to give are a key ingredient for four of the five recipes for greater giving amounts. For those without exposure to religious calls to give, all other affiliations are highly oriented toward generosity when greater donations to occur, as Path 3 shows. It is also worth noting the influence of a religious call to give in Path 1 where there is the absence of a personal identity influence.

6. **Role of Local Community Context.** The perception that one's local community is generous plays a role in four of the five recipes for higher giving. Only Path 4 excludes this ingredient (and also excludes the national group context); it appears that for these Americans, alignment across the more personal affiliations is all that is needed in the recipe to greater giving.

7. **Role of National Context.** Perceptions regarding national levels of giving play a less prominent role across the recipes than do perceptions of the local community context. When the national context is relevant, it is always paired with local community. Pathways 2 and 4, in which the national group affiliation is absent, require a substitution of generous personal identity along with giving-supportive parents, friends, and religious calls.

The Big Picture of the WoA Paths

When examining all of these affiliations together in traditional regression models, we see that self-identity, spousal alignment, friends' support, religious calls, and local perceptions of generosity are significantly related to donation amounts. Once we add social status control measures to this model, we find that generous self-identity, giving-supportive friends, and a generous local community context retain independent relationships to higher donation amounts. Spousal alignment and religious calls are compensated by the social status measures.

Webs of Affiliation: Key Points

The complex relationship between generous self-identity and giving behaviors partially explains how people's web of group affiliations can influence their giving despite their GSID. There is little difference between an ambivalent generous identity and an explicit nongenerous identity. It is the generous personal self-identity that stands out as a positive influence. This factor does not appear to have much influence on who gives or not, but it does relate to bolstered giving amounts. A web of affiliation that is supportive of giving appears to play a minor role in explaining *whether* people give and a major role in *how much* givers donate. Greater donation amounts relate to all of the WoA recipes described. Thus webs of affiliations in the sociorelational contexts in which people are embedded helps to explain giving variations.

Case Study Excursus

Before proceeding with our final quantitative analyses, we take an excursus to explore how webs of affiliations look in the context of real lives. People with giving-supportive affiliations are more likely to be givers, to give greater amounts, and to take certain approaches to giving. We find among several case studies examples of the recipes of WoA that we identified in action, and we start our excursus with them. Several participants do not readily fit into one of the five WoA recipes, and we conclude the section with the various ways these individuals stray from the beaten paths.

Case Studies in the Five Pathways

As we have discussed, the quantitative models associate the recipes of WoA with higher giving amounts. It therefore should be no surprise that the six cases that fit into the WoA recipes are also our participants who donate substantial amounts. From their descriptions of their WoA, we can understand how the different affiliations combine to form recipes for greater giving.

Susan Baker: Upper-Middle-Class, "One and Done" Los Angeleno

Susan Baker exemplifies a Path 3 WoA: she has a strong personal identity as a generous giver, has a high degree of alignment with her spouse in giving, had a high degree of parental influence to give, has high friend support for giving, perceives her local community to be generous in giving, and perceives Americans to be giving at high levels. The result, as predicted by the models, is that she gives large amounts of money to charity. She and her husband donate $2,310 per year to charitable causes. She also volunteers 67 hours per month, spends two hours per month taking political action, is an organ donor, lends possessions to friends and neighbors even if she thinks they will not be returned, takes measures to improve the environment and live sustainably, and is relationally generous in effort-heavy ways. Thus Susan is a Planned giver who epitomizes what it means to generously give away her resources of money, time, and attention. She demonstrates that her web of affiliation is a major part of why she is generous.

SPOUSAL ALIGNMENT (HIGH)

Susan and her husband are highly aligned on monetary issues. She describes their overall alignment on household finances more generally:

> We never fight about money. I know that's supposed to be really unusual. I know [my husband] has better money sense than I do. And neither of us are big spenders. We don't have to fight, because I don't go out and buy a new pair of shoes every week. So I'm not blowing the budget; he's not blowing the budget. And if there's something we need, if there's something that I think I need that costs more than a buck or two, I run it by him. And if there's something he needs, he runs it by me. It's really more courtesy than anything else, because neither of us is really gonna say no because we know each other is very reasonable. If it's a big [purchase], like when we get to the point where we have to buy a new car, I mean, we talk about our needs, and then decide what we can afford and get.

When we asked her what would happen if she decided she wanted to give away more money, Susan replied, "I think it would go over fine. We would sit and talk about it. I would explain why I thought we were at a point where we could give more, and we would either agree or disagree. But it would be rational." In this way Susan shows how spousal alignment can work.

PARENTAL INFLUENCE (HIGH)

Susan's parents modeled volunteering, and they also regularly gave money to their church, albeit in small amounts. At the same time, she describes her family of origin as low-income since she received free lunches at school and had her registration fee for the SAT subsidized by a government program. This makes their generous giving even more remarkable. When we ask Susan about the extent to which her parents modeled giving, she answered, "Money? Just to, as far as I know, the only money was to church on Sunday. We each got a dime or a quarter and put it in the basket. I mean they didn't have much money, so I don't think they gave much." Her parents more heavily modeled volunteering: "My dad gave a lot of his time. I don't remember them giving [financially]. I mean, I just don't know that they gave much money. But he did a lot of volunteer work." She continues: "My dad was the kinda person who, and still does, help anybody who needs any kind of help. I mean, he's more than willing to volunteer his physical abilities and his time."

When we asked Susan if she would consider her parents to be generous people, she replied that her dad was very generous and her mom was generous almost to a fault, as she had said of herself early in our interview:

I'd say my dad was very generous. My mom was generous if asked. She's more of a martyr type. Like if a kid needed something, people knew that they could count on her for something like that. . . . She was more than happy to do that sort of stuff, but she wasn't the type that, [if] there's a sign-up list, she'd sign up to do something.

We followed up by asking, "Looking back, how much influence or lack of influence would you say your parents have had on you when it comes to these kinds of issues: giving money, volunteering, generosity, et cetera?" Susan replied, "I'm sure probably a fair amount. It's harder for me to give money than time, and I'm sure that that's because of, probably the way I was raised. I mean that must have something to do with it." Susan's picture of giving looks remarkably similar to her parents'. While she does not consider their financial role-modeling to be influential, it is still more than many Americans ever see and is likely in part responsible for her current financial giving. At the same time, her parents' higher levels of involvement in volunteering probably help explain why Susan gives considerably generously of her time.

FRIEND SUPPORT (HIGH)

Susan also has a considerably high degree of friend support for giving. She exhibits one interesting way this support can work out in the course of typical lives. She claims her sister-in-law participates in giving at a much higher rate than she does, and this appears to raise the bar for Susan to actualize her giving more than if she were acting without that influence:

> My sister-in-law is probably even more clinical than [my husband] when it comes to [giving]. I mean they literally do; they take their income for the year, and they take 10 percent and give it away. They're just very methodical about that, and that's just how they do it. . . . And I'm not quite there yet.

It sounds like her sister-in-law is a Habitual giver, someone who gives very methodically by setting up a system, then allowing it to happen. Susan says this approach results in her sister-in-law giving more than Susan's family does, despite Susan's more concerted planning. Despite the differences in approaches, this friendship affiliation appears to encourage Susan to think about her own giving as she aspires to their model to give more.

RELIGIOUS CALLS (LOW)

Susan does not attend religious services, and therefore has no current influence to give within a religious context. However, she does describe her parents' giving to their church during her childhood as an important way she saw giving modeled. In this sense she has the kind of residual influence of religiosity common to many Americans who had some exposure to religious ideals in their youth that continue to undergird their views on giving. Nevertheless today Susan still gives high amounts as a result of the WoA-Path 3, which is one of the few recipes for high giving that does not require a high level of religious calls to give.[26]

As we recounted in chapter 4, Susan was hesitant to consider herself generous. When we map out the web of her affiliations, we can see why she may have been inclined to downplay her giving. Not only does she perceive her local and national communities as givers, but her friends, especially her sister-in-law, her parents, and her husband, are all actively and freely giving of their money and time to help others. In comparison to the members in her WoA, Susan is a typical giver, and she recognizes she could potentially give more.

Ryan Dewey: High-Achieving, Religious Midwesterner

Ryan Dewey is a fairly typical WoA Path 1. He has a modest personal identity as generous (only slightly agreeing that giving is important to his identity) and does not have a spouse with whom to be aligned. However, he has a high level of parental influence to be generous coupled with high friend support for giving, high exposure to religious giving calls, and high perceptions of local and national giving. Ryan is another Planned giver who donates high amounts of money ($1,850) considering his graduate student salary of approximately $22,500. In addition he devotes 11 hours per month to volunteering for charitable causes. It is clear throughout his interview that his high levels of generosity are situated within a web of affiliation configuration that pushes him to give more than he would by himself.

PARENTAL INFLUENCE (HIGH)

In the course of conversation about the role that his parents played in modeling giving or teaching him to give, Ryan says:

> I'd say they were very generous people, but their generosity was generally in a financial aspect sort of role. They were very generous with their money, but in terms of the other things we talked about, showing hospitality or maybe giving of their time, I'd say less so.

We then asked him how much influence he thought his parents had on his giving. He replied, "I'd say a big influence. They definitely encouraged me not just to think about it, but to take active steps. I sponsor some children through World Vision. I think that is directly related to their example set for me growing up. I'd say they had a big impact on my outlook on most things."

His parents' teaching sent Ryan a clear message that giving was something for him to do himself, to think about, and to be regularly involved in doing:

> I'd say they modeled giving for me, and I saw them giving. Those are the primary ways I saw it in their lives. . . . I think when I was still living at home, my parents encouraged me to give, primarily

through the Samaritan's Purse Christmas catalogue. They would buy cattle or whatever to help people overseas, and they would be like, "Hey, do you want to buy some rabbits?" or something. So they were definitely encouraging in terms of my giving.

We also see evidence in this statement that Ryan learned some of his Planned giving approach from his parents, as they paid close attention to their giving targets.

FRIEND SUPPORT (HIGH)
About friends' giving, and whether he has ever had a conversation with a friend about their giving, Ryan stated:

One of my friends from my high school and college days who still lives [back home], he is very interested in the stock market, very interested in investments, that sort of thing. So I know I have talked to him about giving in terms of what he does in terms of his investments and that sort of thing. So we talked about how he goes about giving and how I go about giving.

This exchange is a considerably more explicit form of influence from a friend than many of our interviewees expressed. Some of Ryan's friends also participate in one of his volunteer activities. We asked, "Does it make a difference to do this activity with this particular group of people?" He replied:

I think it does. I think it is nice to volunteer when you know the other people involved. I think it is nice that you can have kinda a shared experience in doing that. I don't think it would be any less valuable, were it not that way, but I think it makes it a little bit more fun for you anyway.

Thus Ryan has a high proportion of friends who support giving.

RELIGIOUS CALLS (MODERATE)
Ryan is a religious person who attends church every week and sees his religious beliefs at the core of why he gives as much as he does:

I think they [leaders in my congregation] do a pretty good job. I think there is a balance to be struck between encouraging people to give,

and sounding like a broken record, and "guilting" people into giving. And I think they do a good job about being honest about what
the Bible says about it and about encouraging it without constantly
being on that subject.

He proceeds to articulate a "need-based approach" to religious giving
calls: "I think the primary way [they talk about money] is letting people
know about *needs* that there are for giving and highlighting the good that
can come from giving to those causes [emphasis added]." Ryan thus exemplifies exposure to need-based calls for giving, which may contribute to his
Planned giver approach of paying attention to the good that comes from
giving to specific targets.

    Like Susan, Ryan downplays the amounts he gives. He even downplays
the importance of others seeing him as a generous person. He alludes to
his giving as a personal goal, and so others' view of him as generous is
not a priority. Though he lacks a high GSID and spousal influence, his
church, friends, and parents, along with his perception of generous local
and national communities, encourage his giving.

Jackie Sawyer: Thrifty, Type-A, Religious, Midwestern Mom

Jackie Sawyer is a Habitual giver who exemplifies the WoA Path 4 approach
to giving high amounts. She and her husband give $11,850 per year out of
their annual income of approximately $80,000, and they regularly vol-
unteer time as well. She is a prototypical Habitual giver who recounts
the important role of her religious beliefs in her approach to giving; she
believes in giving in principle, sets up a system to give, and then spends
little thought on the subject and lets her giving run on autopilot. She therefore has considerable trust that she has done her part and few feelings of
responsibility to check up on the giving targets or otherwise adjust her system after it is in place. Her giving approach is coupled with a high (mostly
agree) personal identity as generous, alignment with spouse in giving,
high parental modeling to give, high friend support to give, and exposure
to religious calls for giving. Given Jackie's understanding of giving as part
of a unique religious call, it makes sense that there is no need for her local
or national context to be giving-supportive. Her and her husband's giving
exists independent of that broader context; it is their religious affiliation
that provides the norm for giving. This exactly illustrates the typical WoA
Path 4 higher giver.

PARENTAL INFLUENCE (HIGH)

Jackie grew up in a rural family, with a lifestyle that was dependent on the local farming economy. She describes her parents as not terribly well-off and struggling a bit to maintain their lower-middle-class social position:

> I grew up out in the country. My dad was a small business owner. And because he owned a business, he didn't, they didn't make—well, it depended on the farming economy whether or not they were making any money or not making any money. So there were times when making mortgage payments and stuff like that was difficult. Not that we knew a ton about that, but I do, I remember when my parents paid off their mortgage the first time, and then when they remortgaged the house to purchase a bigger portion of my dad's business. But essentially my mom stayed at home most of the time, until I was in later elementary school. And I would say still probably middle class, but on the lower end of middle class.

About her parents' financial giving Jackie said, "They tithed. I don't know what, to what percentage, but there was regular giving to the church, regular giving to the school that we went to." When asked about her parents' involvement in volunteering, she said, "School. School was all-encompassing. ... It required a lot of all the parents to be volunteering and working in the classrooms, cleaning in the summer. That's probably the biggest thing that I remember a lot of volunteerism with." When asked if her parents were politically active she said, "Vague recollections of maybe attending a caucus, but other than that, no. Like once or twice maybe."

Jackie describes her parents' overall level of generosity by saying, "They were fairly generous. Yeah, fairly open and giving. And if you needed help, they'd try to find a way to help." When asked how much influence her parents had on her own generosity, she said, "Probably a fairly large influence. And I think, with my husband and I coming from fairly similar backgrounds, that it probably—having that background together made it easy for that to be our family values." Though she doesn't remember her parents explicitly teaching her to give, Jackie recounts how they modeled giving, "I don't know that I ever sat and had a conversation with my parents about giving. My dad died when I was still in college. I was 19 when he died. I can't say that my mom ever sat down and said, 'You have to give.'

I think it was just an implicit or implied thing." Instead they role-modeled giving:

> They would always, they always had budget envelopes. And they always put the check into the budget envelope. And we saw that happen on a weekly or biweekly basis. And the kids always got a quarter to put into the offering plate. So I think that was not our money. We didn't have our own allowances to give, but we always got a quarter to put in, I think to model it to us, as we were very young.

Jackie's description of how her parents modeled giving money and volunteering looks remarkably similar to the generosity pattern she now has.

SPOUSAL ALIGNMENT (HIGH)

Jackie and her husband have a high degree of alignment on giving, and on money matters more generally: "Generally we don't have money fights at our house, which is a huge blessing because I think that we're probably the exception to that. So [my husband] and I are pretty much on the same page, as far as financial issues and giving." She continues, "It's more of an equal partnership. It's a lot more talking it through." She summarizes their general financial alignment by saying, "We're in agreement 99 percent of the time."

Regarding their alignment for financial giving in particular, Jackie describes their communication process this way:

> Well, usually, it's "Okay, how much is left in that charitable giving fund?" Cause we have that extra—where we just put money to use as needed, or as things come up. . . . We're pretty close together, where we start out. So it's not usually like a huge negotiation that has to take place.

When discussing their household budgeting method, she said, "Well, I think it makes it easier to have a united front." Thus Jackie and her husband are united in their approach to their household budget, which includes their financial giving.

FRIEND SUPPORT (HIGH)

A high proportion of Jackie's friends are involved in generous activities, and her description of this in the interview helps explain why she described her personal identity as generous somewhat ambivalently. She is surrounded by people who volunteer a great deal of their time and energy for charitable causes, so she thinks of herself humbly in comparison. She says, "I see a lot of generous people, in my world.I mean, I have friends who are willing to give time. I think there's a lot of people that I come in contact with that are generous with their time too."

When we asked Jackie if she talks to her friends or coworkers about giving she said, "No, not really. Not that we've not discussed it, but that they've said, 'Ooh, you really should give'? No, not really." She said her own giving activities have occurred as a result of her friends asking her to be involved:

> Usually it's other moms from school. And then, through church, some of the coordinators of some of the children's programs—I've been asked by different people at different times to do different age groups, or whatever, at church. And then with the, at school, it's just another mom who's in charge of something else, volunteering her many hours, that asks for a hand.

When we asked, "Do you talk about these matters of giving, whether money, volunteering, community involvement, or anything like that, with them?," she replied, "No, not really, other than to just say, 'Hey, I'm glad you're here to help.'" Her social network does not explicitly discuss their giving, but there is a general appreciation for each other's involvement, especially when it comes to volunteering.

RELIGIOUS CALLS (HIGH)

Jackie also receives support for giving generously through her church affiliation. She says her church talks about giving "on a fairly regular basis. Probably every couple months or so, there's gotta be a money sermon somewhere." She explains:

> It's not always specifically money, but things, and possessions, and the American good life. . . . Our pastor talks about that the good life is not always having things, that the good life is following God's command, following. And "What would the world look like if everyone was able to stand up to injustices?" And that it wouldn't look like all the things that we have now. The world would be very different if there were not child trafficking, and sweatshops, and some of the other human injustices that happen worldwide. That we just don't realize how blessed we are always here.

In this way Jackie exemplifies exposure to a "living the vision" approach to religious calls to give. This type of religious call has the highest influence of all religious calls.

This vision call coupled with her high exposure to parental modeling, spousal alignment, and friend support produces a Path 4 recipe for greater giving by Jackie. We see this expressed in her generous donations of financial and time resources to help out others.

George Nettleson: Comfortable, Religious Southerner Takes Time

George Nettleson is another example of a classic WoA Path 4. Like Jackie, he is a Habitual giver. George has a somewhat high personal identity as generous, incredibly high spousal alignment on giving (i.e., complete deference to her), parental influence to give, friendship support (among the small number of friends he has), and exposure to vision-based religious calls for giving. This typifies a classic WoA Path 4, wherein the local community and national context of giving are not significant in predicting higher giving levels when this other combination of affiliations support giving. It is not necessarily the case that these local and national perceptions are low; rather they do not surface in the interviews as influencing decisions about how much to give. It is the other affiliations that are considered influential.

SPOUSAL ALIGNMENT (HIGH)

George's nearly perfect spousal alignment is a function of his complete deference to his wife regarding financial matters. He specifically told us in his interview that his own approach to giving prior to marriage was much more of an Impulsive or Selective approach and that his wife has helped him become a Habitual giver. (Interestingly she is a Planned giver, so he can rely on her to put the thought into their giving.) When we asked, "How much agreement is there about money matters between you and your wife?," he said, "Total. She manages it, and I do what she says." We asked, "Do you guys ever have disagreements about voluntary financial giving?" George replied, "It's rare. It has happened, but it's very rare." We followed up, asking, "Have you guys been in agreement on the tithe since the beginning of your marriage?" To which George simply and confidently replied, "Yes." In this way George exemplifies the typical Habitual giver who believes in the tithe and is married to someone who believes in the tithe. She decides more about the targets of their giving, and he trusts her and the church to take care of the giving once the system is in place.

PARENTAL INFLUENCE (MODERATE)

George describes his family of origin as being a generally affluent middle-class family: "We never wanted for food, or clothing, or shelter, or anything like that. And we always had a television. We always had a couple cars. Mom had a car. . . . We always had a maid." He says his parents "tended to stick to themselves" but that his dad still managed to be involved in the church from time to time. With regard to financial giving, George says:

> I think that they [my parents] always tithed. I remember the preacher one time in his sermon he said, "And Mr. [Nettleson] there tithes all the time." Or something like that. I think it embarrassed my father. But really that's the only way I would have known that they did. . . . They didn't talk about it. The [Nettlesons] are—yeah, my father and his brothers and all—they're funny about money. It's like you could talk about sex and politics and all that before you could talk about money.

Thus George learned about his parents' giving not through their explicit teaching but through seeing and hearing about it at church.

Somewhat surprisingly, given that level of parental modeling, George goes on to describe his parents as "kind, and nice, and amiable, and good people. But not the kind of people who are givers." They gave, but their personal identity as generous was not very prominent. During the interview statements like this seem to make him self-aware, and he says, "As I've been answering the questions, it sounds like I've turned out a lot like them. Just in this process, I've kind of felt like, I'll just say I feel like I've turned out a lot like them." He seems to mean he is not giving as much monetarily as he would like and says, "Especially in our conversations in the last couple of days, I've wondered if I shouldn't step it up a little bit and be more giving and generous."

RELIGIOUS CALLS (HIGH)

George experiences a tremendous religious influence to give. Though he says his church leaders do not talk about money often, when they do refer to it, they call it the "tithe and stewardship. And it's always, 'Here's what the Bible says, and we want to obey God. And everything is for a lot of people where the rubber meets the road, so let's talk about that.' They'll do that, but it's never seemed excessive to me." George describes a religious context that is akin to a vision approach to giving. The religious call is not about paying for the needs of the church but described as part of what it means to be a Christian, an obligation of sorts, to give back.

In this way George exhibits an interesting mixture of relational influences to give. On the one hand, his parents modeled tithing, but on the other he does not view them as identifying as terribly high givers. He sees himself as having inherited their model of a generous identity, but his marriage to his Planned giver wife has resulted in his being a high giver by spousal association. George's affiliation with his church is also strong, and it seems to be here that he gets his personal identity as a generous person. This is a classic pattern we see with Habitual givers. Between his high, deference-based spousal alignment on giving, parental influence to give, a high proportion of generous friends, and regular exposure to vision-based religious calls to give, George fits squarely in a WoA Path 4 approach.

Michael Johnson: Hard-Working, Politicking, D.C. Widower Takes Action

Our case study who most exemplifies a WoA Path 2 recipe for being a high giver is Michael Johnson. He is a Selective giver who donates $16,100 per year from his annual income of approximately $200,000, as well as volunteering a couple hours per month and devoting 27 hours per month to political action for charitable causes. Since Michael is a widower, we do not discuss any spousal affiliation, though we gather from his interview that they did align when she was alive. Michael has a high (mostly agree) personal identity as generous, coupled with a high parental influence, friend support, and religious calls to give. He is also one of our few interviewees who explicitly discusses the role of his local community context for giving. Combined these affiliations make Michael a classic Path 2 for his WoA.

SPOUSAL ALIGNMENT (NOT APPLICABLE)
Though Michael was not asked the spousal alignment questions on the survey, due to his widowed status, he reflected on his spousal alignment in the interview:

I would say general agreement. My wife wanted to, would probably like to spend more than I would. I was more of a saver in terms of trying to prepare for the future. . . . But [my wife] never criticized my giving or said that, "You're giving too much." And I never criticized her giving. . . . But again there was no, any disagreement or attempt to limit what the contribution should be.

Thus Michael has residual spousal alignment that provides some background for his giving, though it does not necessarily play a significant role in his affiliations today.

PARENTAL INFLUENCE (HIGH)

Michael scored high on his parental modeling of giving and describes their generosity in this way: "My parents were very generous in what they gave for charities. I mean I would say their primary charity would be the Catholic church that they attended. They gave to many charities." He says that they volunteered for a number of causes, his father primarily to make business contacts. Michael describes his parents' political involvement by saying, "They were not nearly as active as I was. I mean they had political views, but they basically voted." But he goes on to say that his father was involved in the political campaign of a friend and neighbor, likely a definitive moment for his own political campaigning interest.

When we asked Michael, "Overall, when you think back to your parents, in general, how generous or not generous would you say they were as people?," he said:

> I'd say they were very generous in what they gave in terms of charitable cash contributions to organizations, particularly the Church. They were generous in terms of the time that they would assign for doing either charitable or public good–type activities. They were also generous in terms of doing things—in terms of activities that their children were involved in, such as sports.

We followed up by asking, "Looking back, how much influence or lack of influence would you say your parents have had on you when it comes to these kinds of issues? Giving money, volunteering, generosity?" Michael replied:

> Well, they obviously had some impact. I would say my parents are probably more generous than I am in terms of giving. I mean I make charitable contributions, but my parents gave more and I have more income. But it's more because I worked a lot more than

my father did. . . . I mean I give a lot more in terms of political contributions than they did. And in terms of helping people, I think we
have a similar philosophy. But I think we probably went about it in
different ways because of our occupations. I mean, for example, my
involvement in terms of helping people was done to a large degree
through legislation that I work on. . . . My parents were more involved
in terms of maybe giving money and then doing things like working at the church social or things of that nature. And I don't have
that kind of time to do that.

Michael continues by describing how his parents modeled giving in a very
explicit way:

I could see them when I went to church with them. They would give
us the money to drop in the in the basket, so either directly or indirectly I could see that. Did my parents make a concerted attempt to
encourage me to give? I mean it's not as if they sat down with me
and said, "[Michael], I think you should give a certain percent of
your income for charity." I think they did it more by example.

Thus Michael exemplifies having high parental modeling to give to charitable causes. He also demonstrates how their model of giving may still
continue to set the bar high, to the point that he feels his own giving level
does not meet their standard, despite how generously he does give compared to others. This could be one factor that sustains his giving over time,
always calling him to give more than he currently does.

RELIGIOUS CALLS (HIGH)
In terms of his religious influence to give, Michael says:

I mean the Catholic Church is almost always trying to encourage
people to give. And in our church we usually have two donations,
whereas in most other churches that I've attended when I've been
outside the area there's only been one donation. I think the reason
is that the archbishop probably considers this to be a more affluent area, and that people should also give more. And so I always
give twice. I give to the main collection, and the second collection.
I would say that most people in the church probably do not give to
the second collection.

In this way Michael shows how frequent exposure to religious calls to give, through not one but two collections of donations at each Mass, calls him to give even more than he might otherwise contribute.

When asked how his religion inclines him to give, he identified a vision call: "I think religion, at least the Catholic faith, in my view, encourages people to help others who are less fortunate than themselves." When we asked Michael what his primary motivation is for giving, he said, "I guess my feeling about the desire to help people who are less fortunate. I think it's probably influenced by my religion. I think it's also influenced by values that are largely attributable to my upbringing and my family." Thus we see the strong influence of the vision call as Michael's motivator.

COMMUNITY GIVING (HIGH)
Michael is one of our few interviewees who explicitly addressed his perceptions of his local community's level of giving. When reflecting on how he compares to other people in his local community, he said:

> I don't think that what we do is unique. My expectation is that other people would probably think along the same lines that we do, especially those who make donations on a regular basis. I think the type of charities that people contribute to will depend upon maybe some things that are very personal, or the values of the person who gives. But in terms of the overall thrust in the basis for giving, I think many people would probably share my views concerning why I give or why I want to give.

Michael demonstrates how the local context of generosity plays a role in setting the bar for people's giving. Perhaps he actually does live in a high-giving area, especially with regard to the political activism of his D.C. neighbors. Because he thinks about his giving relative to the giving of those around him, he perceives his higher giving as normal, despite the fact that he is actually unusual and gives well above the national norm.

Social norms in his web of affiliations encourage Michael to give time and money and especially to take political action. Often we heard him comparing his donations to others who work for causes for pay, which he did in earlier years. The bar of how much to donate is set not only by other donors but also by full-time workers. Michael's affiliations with politics and his affiliations with the Church (including his parents) make for a dense giving-supportive web.

Linda Chesterfield: Midwestern Soccer Mom Puts Family First

Linda Chesterfield is a Selective giver and marks the last of our case studies exemplifying a straightforward WoA pathway. As a Path 5 giver, she has a low generous self-identity (neutral or disagree), but she is married to someone who gives moderately. Thus the lack of spousal alignment in this case provides positive friction against her inclination not to give. Though Linda is somewhat resentful of their giving amounts, she tries to be supportive of her husband's desire to give. She also has some friends who support giving and moderate exposure to religious calls to give, and she perceives her local and national contexts as generous. As a result of these affiliations she gives more than she otherwise would and follows a WoA Path 5. She and her husband contribute money to their church and some other charitable causes, as well as volunteer regularly.

SPOUSAL ALIGNMENT (DISAGREEMENT)

In a classic Path 5 scenario, Linda gives more than she otherwise would because her spouse wants to give more than she does, and she receives moderate to high levels of support across the rest of her web of affiliations. Though she has a low level of generalized Social Trust, which would likely prevent her from giving as an individual, she does trust in her husband's financial decisions. She says, "I'm horrible at it [taking care of finances]; I trust him." When talking about their household budget, she says, "Yeah, I mean there's things that are priorities, just basic necessities that are [a] priority over something that can wait. . . . We have a family budget that we try to stick to." At the same time she admits, "Not, I'm sometimes not very conscious of what is coming in and what is going out until it's pointed out." When asked about their spousal alignment on financial matters, Linda said:

> We don't really see eye to eye. . . . He's very practical and conservative, and I'm practical but not always conservative. . . . And as far as the kids go, we try to teach that you should save, but I have a hard time making them do it because practice what you preach, and I'm not a big sav[er]. He's the only one who really likes to save. . . . He is the financially responsible one. Like, if there was no

sense of responsibility we'd be screwed because sometimes I don't really take into consideration what we have available to us before I go buy.

Linda says that if it were up to her alone, she would give less: "We typically agree . . . [but the] church [giving] I would rather not. But I just go along with it, just because it is important. You go along with what's important to [your husband]." She continued, "I mean, to some extent maybe the amount will be less to his colleges if I'm a little more uptight some year than others, but for the most part it's primarily what he wants."

When asked about her own enthusiasm for giving she said, "I'm not at all enthused by what we give to the church. . . . I like to give it to people when I can, and it's fun, you know." Later she says:

The college I don't mind, because I know they are using it, and it's, the church is still, I'm bothered by it. It really bothers me. I don't feel as if they take the donations, I think they kind of take them for granted, and they use them just to pay bills and hope that we're financially responsible for their mess.

She is very skeptical when she talks about how the church uses the money, making comments like "Or so that's what they say they were doing with it, but you didn't see any improvement." Thus if it were up to her, their household would give significantly less, maybe even nothing financially, especially to their church. But her husband resists her inclinations, resulting in giving.

PARENTAL INFLUENCE (HIGH)

When we asked her if she remembered her parents giving, Linda said, "Just that my mom went to church every week, would make a donation. She had a favorite charity, St. Jude, that they would give to yearly." She explains that her parents did not agree on this: "My dad hated to do it, but went along with it because it made his wife happy." Linda then recounts a touching story of their eventual agreement: "When my mom passed, he [my dad] made a pretty nice donation to St. Jude in her memory. So, and that surprised me, because I couldn't imagine him ever doing something like that." In summarizing her parents' financial giving, she said, "Yeah, they did. Not a lot." But then she went on to describe their modeling of volunteering by saying, "My mom volunteered for the church quite a bit.

And like I said, being foster parents, they were volunteering there. They weren't paid for that." When we asked how generous or not her parents were overall, she replied:

> They were pretty generous. My mom was very generous with her time, and sometimes generous with money, even if she didn't have it to be generous with. She was just that type of person. My dad was also generous with his time, and he was generous to his family. Like my mother and myself, he didn't want us to go without. And he spoiled us a little bit. So they were generous.

We followed up to ask how much influence she thought her parents had on her generosity, and Linda said, "My mom would sort of, like if the church were looking for volunteers for things, 'Oh [Linda,] why don't you do that, you'd be good at that,' or 'You might have fun,' or 'You might meet people.'" Thus her parents not only modeled but also taught a generous lifestyle.

FRIEND SUPPORT (MODERATELY HIGH)

When we asked, "Do you ever talk to friends or family members about either volunteering or giving money?," Linda said, "A little bit. I mean, not a whole lot. I'll have friends who are doing fundraisers for someone, and they'll ask me to help, or [ask] if I can help, or [ask] if I can just donate some things for the silent auction, or whatever." Thus Linda is surrounded by people who invite her to be generous, especially her husband.

RELIGIOUS CALLS (HIGH)

Linda describes her church as talking about "stewardship a lot." When we asked if it was mainly a vision- or need-based giving approach, she said:

> That's [need-based] what it felt like sometimes, or sometimes they would beat around the bush, they would maybe put out their fiscal plan in the bulletin and then finally, "If you read the bulletin from the week before, you know we're in dire need in this area." But it's being discussed in one way or another.

Linda does not necessarily like the way her church expresses a call to give, but she and her husband are still exposed to its requests. Their religious context appears to exert its influence mostly on her husband's desire to give, which in turn influences her.

Linda exhibits an interesting recipe for high giving that is almost unwilling compliance. It sounds as if her father may have also had this recipe, making it familiar to her. She surrounds herself with a spouse, friends, and a religious congregation that support giving, and she perceives high giving among her local and national communities. When all these connections combine into her web of affiliations, she ends up being a more generous giver than many others and than she would be if left to her own devices.

The Pathless Cases

Our remaining six case studies do not neatly fit on any WoA pathway. We see remnants of some affiliation influences in some of the cases, helping to explain their moderate participation in giving. In others we see how being surrounded by people not interested in or supportive of giving makes it unlikely that these cases would ever get involved in or maintain interest in actualizing their generous impulses.

Cindy Phelps: Young, Professional Texan Tutors in New York City

Cindy Phelps is a "residual" affiliation case who is an Impulsive giver involved in some volunteering. While she does not have a strong enough web of affiliations to push her to give more than she otherwise would, the relational support to give from her parents and friends does link to the WoA that associates with whether or not someone gives (as shown in Figure 5.9).

PARENTAL INFLUENCE (MODERATE)
When we asked Cindy, "To the best of your knowledge or memory, did your parents voluntarily give money to charity, religious organizations, nonprofits, or other people or causes?," she replied, "I think for a while. My mom always would throw away all of my stuff, like give it to Goodwill, and I always freak[ed] out about it." This is one of the more narrow forms of parental modeling for giving that we encountered. However, it is one of the main forms of giving that Cindy herself participates in, demonstrating that parental models for giving play a clear role in shaping generosity in their children as adults.

On the volunteering front, Cindy saw her mom (but not her dad) volunteer: "My mom did a lot of work for the Parent Teacher Association, the PTA. She worked at like the Rape Crisis Center. My mom mostly did all of the volunteering. My dad didn't really volunteer." She summarizes her parents' generosity by saying, "I would say my mom is a very generous person, by spending her time and caring about other people. My dad is not as generous as my mom, but they're both, I think, nice, generous, caring people." However, in the end, Cindy says, "I don't think they were super influential. Yeah, I wouldn't say they were super influential." Thus Cindy has a bit of a mixed bag when it comes to her parental influence to give.

FRIEND SUPPORT (MODERATE)

Cindy has some friend support for the volunteering that she does. She describes doing these activities in a group. When we ask, "Does it make a difference to do this activity with a group of people?," she says, "I think you can get more people to volunteer by doing it in a group, so yeah. . . . I just have become better friends with them." Affiliating with giving friends thus appears to be part of her motivation to volunteer.

Cindy does not have a strong giving-supportive web of affiliations resulting in a defined pathway to higher giving. However, her parental influence to give coupled with some friend support for giving does align with the one significant configuration that makes someone more likely to give. In this case even a moderately giving-supportive WoA results in Cindy's moderate giving behaviors. We could imagine how she could raise her giving levels tremendously were she to marry someone who was a giver, again attend a church with giving calls, or begin to identify herself as a generous person. In the meantime she participates similarly to how her web of affiliations participates: moderately.

Tanika Sandaval: Single Los Angeles Mom Fights for Her Children's Future

Tanika Sandaval is an Impulsive giver who describes a generally low level of support among her web of affiliations for giving. But like Cindy, the modest support she receives helps to explain her participation in giving through her regular volunteering in her children's school.

PARENTAL INFLUENCE (MODERATELY LOW)

Tanika's grandmother served as her primary role model, along with her mom. She describes them by saying, "They were giving, but yet, again like I said, [they were] reserved. My momma always been caring and giving, cause that was her job. She was a nurse, so as being a nurse that was like an automatic." She summarizes her mother and grandmother as "very generous, sometimes too generous." She continued, "Not so much time, I'd say money, if they got it, depending on who was the need, they would, yeah." When asked if her mother or grandmother ever voluntarily gave money she said:

> I mean, definitely to people, but [as] far as organizations, my grandmother, she could have give certain things, cause she had a way of doing things, and her way of giving back. I definitely know with church, so that was already there, yeah.

In discussing her grandmother's involvement in volunteering, Tanika said, "I believe my grandma did, she worked with [an organization helping the blind], she did that. She volunteered. She did something like that, I remember that. My mom volunteered. She did volunteer, but I can't name it right off, cause she also did some volunteer [work]." Thus Tanika had a moderate amount of exposure to giving behaviors in her childhood that has likely influenced her current volunteering behaviors, despite being a distant and now foggy memory.

FRIEND SUPPORT (MODERATE)
Though only a moderate proportion of Tanika's friends are involved in giving, one of these friends played a major role in her current volunteering:

> It was actually a parent, from the school, she was like, "Oh, you gonna come to the meeting?" . . . And that's exactly how it really happened, honestly. I wasn't expecting it . . . cause you don't feel wanted, you don't know what type, so I went and I realized that, on that day, I've been into it all and became the president.

It seems, then, that a great deal of Tanika's support system is made up of the other parents who volunteer at the school. It has become a network of mothers, forming a community of people interested in bettering their children's futures. Tanika's generosity on behalf of her children and the community of parents helps their low-resourced school.

SPOUSAL ALIGNMENT AND RELIGIOUS CALLS (NOT APPLICABLE)
Tankia is not married, and thus the spousal alignment affiliation does not apply. Though Tanika does not regularly attend services at her religious

congregation, she says that she sometimes hears calls for giving when she does attend. About the approach taken, she says, "It varies. ... You learn something each time different."

Tanika does not have enough giving support among her affiliations to be a high giver, yet remnants of giving support from her family and friend affiliations are one reason she does engage in giving. It appears that the paths to greater giving are being paved for her, with her involvement in her children's school, and it could be that she eventually will develop a full recipe for giving.

Regina Buckner: Southern, Rural, Stay-at-Home Mom Takes It Day by Day

Regina Buckner receives a very low degree of support for giving among her affiliations. Based on our quantitative models on the average American giver, we suspect this partially explains the fact that she participates in virtually no giving at all.

SPOUSAL ALIGNMENT (HIGH, INCLUDING NOT GIVING)

Regina says she and her husband are pretty much in agreement on money matters as a whole:

> Well, he makes the money, and he usually hands it over me and says, "Okay, go pay the bills" [laughs]. We're pretty much in agreement. We do have little squabbles once in a while, when there's something he wants, like a new movie or a new game. And I have to remind him, "Well, honey, we've got this and this and this to pay yet, and we've got these coming up, so do you really need it?" [laughs].

She goes on to explain, "Because we live paycheck-to-paycheck, and we struggle paying our bills. A lot of times we have to kinda juggle to keep one from calling and knocking at our door saying, 'Okay, we're gonna turn off your services.'" When it comes to their financial giving they are in agreement on not being able to afford it.

PARENTAL INFLUENCE (MODERATELY LOW)

Regina's parents did not really model giving, certainly not in a financial way. When we asked her, "To the best of your memory, did your parents voluntarily give money away to charity, religious organizations, nonprofits, people or causes?," she replied, "No, not money. My mother, she donated time a lot of times to the church for, like at Christmas time, they'll do the Christmas tree, where they—you pick a name of a needy child or family off a tree." Regina said, "Other than going to church every day and volunteering for things like at Christmas time, no. I mean, she didn't go every day to church. She went every Sunday, but she didn't do, she wasn't on the church council or committees." Regina summarizes her parents' overall generosity by saying, "Probably, on a scale of one to 10, maybe a three. One being not generous [laughs]. I mean, they would help people that really needed it, especially if it was family or somebody they'd already known, a close friend or something. But other than that, no." When we ask how much influence their approach had on her, she says, "Probably quite a bit, cause I'm [laughing] kind of like that with the money too."

Regina describes no other influences on her giving. Her low giving is normative within her web of affiliations and makes sense within that context. She and her affiliations are also embedded within a low-resourced social and physical context that further constricts her giving.

Deon Williams: Retiree Living It Up in Detroit in Residual Poverty

Another of our cases with low relational support for giving is Deon Williams. True to form, Deon gave inconsistent responses on his survey regarding his web of affiliation, for example describing his spousal alignment as neutral despite not having a spouse. These kinds of inconsistencies between survey and interview answers, and even between different survey answers, speak to Deon's generally nonreflective lifestyle. A number of times throughout the interview he commented on how challenging the questions were for him to answer, perhaps a reflection of his low education level (he has a high school degree), along with a lifetime of working in a blue-collar, male-dominant industry where conversations about lifestyle choices were not among coworker conversations.

PARENTAL INFLUENCE (LOW)
Deon describes having grown up in an impoverished household receiving welfare:

> Growing up we were on aid. My mother was on ADC [Aid to Dependent Children]. So it was cool growing up, because I got free bus tickets, free lunches at school. We didn't have a lot of money, so we grew up in that type of a household. We wore hand-me-downs. It was a good loving family. There was no problem with food, cause

food was real cheap back then. You get the highest quality of food. And like about my mother being on aid and everything, I didn't have to worry about any food or anything. Like I said, I didn't have to worry about bus fares, back and forth to school, as a matter of fact, free lunches at school, free books.

Given their meager resources, it is not surprising that Deon reports that his parents did not give away any money: "No, we didn't have any money to give. We didn't have any money, when I was coming up, we didn't have any money to give." He adds that there was not enough time available to volunteer:

They didn't have time to do volunteering work, we had a house full of kids. A house full of kids, the kids had to have—they, they had to be groomed, they had to had clothes, they had to be [fed]. So my parents, too busy. As a matter of fact, I didn't have a father, see. My grandfather was my father. See, I never knew my father, but like I said, there was enough kids in the house where they didn't have no time to do no volunteering work and definitely didn't have no money to give away.

Deon summarizes his parents' generosity overall: "Not generous. I mean, what you talking about, generous as far as financial? Or as far as caregiving, yeah. I mean, they loved they neighbors and cared about people and stuff like that. Fed people and stuff like that. But, as far as financial, ain't no money to give away." Thus his family was relationally generous, but not giving of money or volunteer time. He says of their relational generosity, "They had a lot of influence on me."

RELIGIOUS CALLS (LOW)
Though Deon rarely attends religious services, the religious context of his childhood has had a residual effect on him:

I grew up in a religious household, religion was the whole thing. We lived and breathed religion. What I'm saying, religion tells you, "You treat people the way you want to be treated, and you help people. You love people. You don't hurt people." That's the influence that that had on me. That's why I've never been locked up, or never been in no big trouble or anything like that.

FRIEND SUPPORT (LOW)

Deon describes his friends as not the most generous:

> You know what, the people I choose to be close to are intelligent people you can have a decent conversation with. Are the type of people who have a decent income, so they can buy the beer sometimes. Are the type of people who have a home, a car, and stuff like that, where you can chill at. So, I mean, as far as talking about charitable events and stuff like that, no.

Deon is a low giver who does not have a giving-supportive network of affiliations. Deon's responses indicate that there is no consistent or strong pro-generosity influence around him.

Rosa Perez: Pregnant and Unemployed in Brooklyn

Also among our cases with a weak WoA are our nongivers. When we understand Rosa Perez's life in context, it becomes clear that giving is not well supported among her affiliations.

SPOUSAL ALIGNMENT (SURVEY: NOT APPLICABLE, INTERVIEW: HIGH
IN NOT GIVING)

On the survey Rosa was not asked about spousal alignment, since she is not yet married and did not at the time say she was living with a partner. However, during the interview she did discuss the financial arrangement between her and her fiancé now that they live in the same household: "My money's my money. His is his. But we meet in the middle, and like make a budget. What needs to be paid, how much and stuff, and we put out money together and pay the bills." Although we do not have the survey data to confirm it, we can see from the interview that she and her fiancé align on financial matters, including agreement that they do not have money to give away.

PARENTAL INFLUENCE (MODERATELY LOW)

Rosa had a fairly meager upbringing as a child. She describes their house as crowded with children on these limited resources:

> In the beginning [my mom] was on the welfare system for so many years. And then in the process of being on welfare, she became a foster mother herself and she took in my best friend, her brother.

And then, because we had more room in the house, they gave her two more children. And then, my niece. . . . The two boys we didn't know. We didn't know. And my niece she took in also. So there were five plus myself.

Although Rosa sees her mother as relationally generous in this way, she then recounts that her mom became dissatisfied with her niece's attitude and actually returned her to the foster care system: "And then when she stopped the whole foster thing because, I don't know, she just was tired of the kids, the drama, and stuff."

Rosa describes her mother as having been a sporadic financial giver: "Still to this day, the fire people call her, the police call her, and she gives—they ask for like $20 and she'll be like, 'I don't have $20, but I'll give you $10.'" We asked if her mother ever did any volunteer work that she was aware of, and she said, "No. Not that I know of." In summarizing her mom's generosity, she says, "She was very generous. When she had it, she always gave. Even when she didn't have it, she would figure out something to give." All her examples circle around relational giving, such as helping a relative cover the cost of a funeral. In describing the influence that her mom had on her, Rosa says:

I do basically everything that she's done. Like I'm in the process of becoming a foster mother. I would like to take on, besides my nephew, two other children. If they work out and listen to the rules of my household and go by what I say, I would like to adopt them.

Thus Rosa is following in her mother's footsteps of being relationally generous by taking on a foster child and helping out neighbors. There is a dearth of modeling other forms of generosity besides these examples, however.

FRIEND SUPPORT (LOW)

Rosa's current friend support for giving is low, but she recalls a time during her childhood when it was higher, as her own giving was then: "As of right now, nothing. I don't give. I don't think about it. Growing up was different. . . . I don't know. I just, I haven't found the group or whatever that I'm interested in to give up my time." We asked, "Why do you think that you were doing that more growing up?" To which Rosa replied, *"Cause I had people around me that would do it"* [emphasis added].

Rosa exemplifies how having little support for giving among her current web of affiliations makes maintaining a generous orientation difficult. Her orientation was shaped by her experiences as a child with her
mother and her friends, but her current WoA does not support this orientation. Perhaps the process of fostering a child will provide a new friend
affiliation group that will make active a dialogue about generosity. For now,
her WoA recipe is not one that makes for much giving.

Anthony Ross: In Between, Regrouping, and Poor in D.C.

Anthony Ross does not give, and he too has a web of affiliations that offers
little support for giving. In discussing his web of affiliations, Anthony
seems to be thinking back to an early time in his childhood: "I'm not sure
if my mom did. My grandma did, though. . . . Yeah. Every Sunday she'd give
more . . . to the Catholic Church, yeah." Regarding role models for volunteering, he had this to say: "My grandma. I did some of that when I was 13.
That was when I was baptized, around there. But that's pretty much it. . . .
She volunteered at church. . . . Me, I was, they held bake sales and stuff like
that, so I was helping out with that." Thus Anthony had some exposure
to a generous grandmother and some involvement in church when he
was younger. But today this modeling of generosity seems like a distant
memory.

Summarizing the overall generosity of his family Anthony says, "I
would say they were probably—things changed, so right now they have
the means to do it, so they can donate. Back then they didn't have the
means to do it. So they couldn't spend a dime. Well, my mom couldn't
spend a dime. My grandma, I'm not sure if she could spend a dime."
He discusses their influence on his giving in this way: "Well, yeah, my
grandma said, 'Give.' If someone asks for a dollar, and you really think
they need it. You make a judgment call. You think they need it, it's permis-
sive." It almost sounds as though the norm is not to give, that giving of
your limited resources requires justification, that the recipient has to be
clearly worse off.

Though Anthony regularly attended a Catholic church as a child, that
religious affiliation does not seem to have much of a residual effect on his
giving today because there was no strong call to give when he was in the
church. He recounts:

> I don't know what else they can do, rather than, from what I remem-
> ber, what they were doing. I mean, people who will participate in

stuff will participate. People who give money will give money. I can't say give a certain percentage of money. I don't understand that.

In summary, he says, "Well, it's like you're following how you were taught. You're giving what you were taught to give. Nothing less and nothing more." We could not have said it better.

The Path Taken (and Not)

The six cases with clear WoA pathways to higher giving are surrounded by giving-supportive affiliations. From the six cases with low to no giving, however, we hear about past memories of family or religious affiliations that provided some historical support for giving, but rarely did we hear about giving-supportive affiliations in their current web of social relations. It appears that part of the explanation for these six cases' lower giving is this lack of support. Our case studies also demonstrate that these characteristics and networks are dynamic. We can see how a change in Tanika's friend group seems to have resulted in her increased volunteering, and how Cindy's new membership in a young professionals group supports her after-school tutoring. These examples help show how changes in webs of affiliation can make for greater (or lesser) giving over time.

Putting It All Together

Returning to our quantitative analyses, we now put together the findings of this chapter with those of previous chapters. Chapter 4 found a number of social psychological orientations for giving, and this chapter finds a number of group orientations and affiliations; we want to explain how it all works together. To do so we focus on a picture of giving colored by both the internal and the external social processes. Are the social psychological orientations and webs of group affiliation merely proxies for one another, or do they independently work to encourage giving behaviors? We will assess which measures make a difference in whether or not someone gives and how much they give, then assess how the whole of generosity relates to giver types.

When we model the social psychological and web affiliations measures together, we find that they are not proxies for the other. The internal and external social influences appear mutually exclusive to one another (see

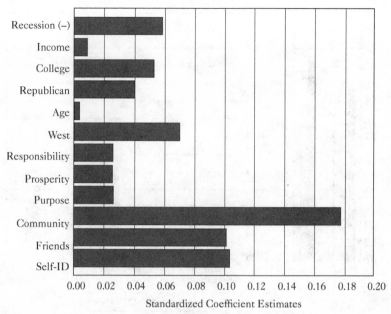

FIGURE 5.11 Higher giving, affiliations, orientations, and GSID.

Appendix Table A.5.11 for details). Figure 5.11 shows only the statistically significant measures associated with greater donation amounts. We see from this figure that the measures with the largest impact are three of the six affiliations. Having a strong self-identity, giving-supportive friends, and the perception that one's local community is generous are all strongly associated with donation amounts. Some social psychological orientations also remain significant influences, net of all the other factors: Prosperity Outlook, Social Responsibility, and Life Purpose. Adding demographic findings from chapter 2, we see that living in the western United States, being older, being Republican, having a college degree, having higher income, and being less impacted by the recession all relate to greater donation amounts. These factors exert significant and independent influences on donation amounts, as they have in our previous models.

Putting It All Together, by Type of Giver

We end with a final set of models examining how all these factors relate to the giver types discussed in chapter 3. When we look at the social psychological and web of affiliations factors together, we see stronger influences from some affiliations and weaker but more frequent influences from

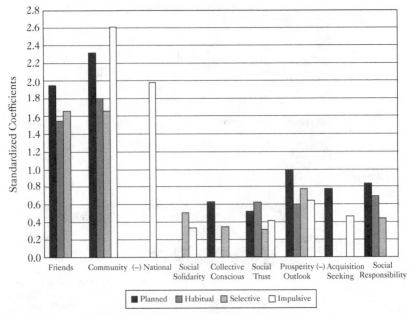

FIGURE 5.12 Giver types, affiliations, orientations, and GSID.

social psychological factors. Figure 5.12 shows the significant correlates for each type of giving approach in comparison to Atypical givers.[27] For simplicity of presentation, we do not show the demographic and social status characteristics related to these types. These characteristics remain the same as those presented in chapter 3, where income, education, age, recession impact, and so on differentiate the types of givers (see Appendix Table A.5.12 for demographic and social status characteristics in these models).

Our results indicate that Impulsive givers are set apart from the other types by their high perception of community giving and low perception of national generosity. The personal orientations of Social Solidarity, Social Trust, Prosperity Outlook, and Acquisition Seeking (negatively) remain influential, net of the inclusion of the web of group affiliations. This seems to imply that Impulsive givers are highly influenced by the normative culture of their immediate local context and assess it in relation to an ungenerous nation.

Net of social status differences, we find that Selective and Habitual givers are similarly influenced by giving-supportive friends and local community giving contexts. This influence is significantly stronger than for Atypical givers. Again we see no changes to the social psychological orientation factors, reinforcing the independence of these internal and external social influences. Selective givers continue to be influenced by social psychological perceptions of Social Solidarity, Collective Conscious, Social Trust, Prosperity Outlook, and Social Responsibility, even after the group affiliations are controlled. Habitual givers are influenced by the same social psychological orientations discussed in chapter 4: Social Trust, Prosperity Outlook, and Social Responsibility. Thus Habitual givers appear mostly driven by a felt responsibility to give back.

Giving-supportive friends and perceiving the local community as generous also significantly differentiate Planned from Atypical givers. Planned givers are the only group for whom the inclusion of the web of group affiliations accounts for some social psychological orientations. The inclusion of group affiliations accounts for the influence of Social Solidarity: the apparent influence of Social Solidarity is an artifact of Planned givers' giving-supportive friend group and generous local community contexts. Coupled with the strong influences of the other personal orientations—Collective Conscious, Social Trust, Prosperity Outlook, Social Responsibility, and less Acquisition Seeking—it seems Planned givers have a "values and expectations" view of generosity. Net of these orientation factors, Planned givers' donations are also very strongly related to giving-supportive networks and community generosity. Thus they seem be conscientious about choosing giving-supportive friendships and local communities as a way of actualizing their giving.

To summarize, we find that when it comes to being a giver, a generous self-identity is a key baseline. Also important are having some personal and social orientations to giving, as well as having enough resources from which to give. Having generosity-supportive relationships, in particular with parents and friends, is also important. When it comes to greater amounts of giving, a generous self-identity is again key, along with affiliating with generous friends and local communities, having personal orientations to give, and having enough socioeconomic resources from which to give. The findings across types of giver approaches indicate that a generous self-identity is again key, as are giving-supportive friends and communities, and that people with different social psychological orientations practice generosity through different giving approaches. In the end all of the factors examined throughout this book are necessary to paint a full, comprehensive, and vibrant picture of American generosity.

Conclusion: The "Why" of American Generosity, 2.0

This chapter presented another angle on the *why* question by focusing on the sociorelational context of giving. Applying the theories of Simmel and others regarding webs of affiliations, we developed a picture of Americans as situated within relationships that are more or less supportive of giving. We posited that relational contexts could grease the wheels for giving or alternatively provide friction that works against giving. Our picture focused on parents' lessons about giving, alignment with spouse in giving, having giving-supportive close friends, exposure to religious calls to give, and perceptions of local community and national giving levels. We found that webs of affiliations do indeed support or constrain personal inclinations to give.

Specifically the combination of giving-supportive affiliation analyses with personal identities as generous showed that having a GSID is key to being a giver, as are generosity-supportive affiliations. In particular, parental influence to give and giving-supportive close friends play a key role in supporting a generous identity. When it comes to giving greater amounts, a GSID and giving-supportive affiliations both remain central. Specifically having giving-supportive close friends and a perception of greater giving in the local community appear to be important in actualizing an inclination to give more. A GSID matters especially for Habitual and Selective givers, as do giving-supportive friends and local community. Based on our analysis, simply having a generous personal identity does not tell the full story of who gives and why; we must also consider giving-supportive relationships.

Typically the more numerous the giving-supportive connections, the more likely Americans are to actualize their giving. However, some pathways to giving still work with less than uniform support. Among the affiliations most consistently associated with greater giving are spousal alignment, parental influence, and exposure to religious calls to give. The exposure to these giving supports appears in some cases to compensate for other, less pro-generosity affiliations. In other words, when Americans have spousal alignment, parental influence, and religious calls to give, they typically give more, even if the rest of their affiliations are less than supportive. Alternatively having close generous friends and perceiving one's local community as generous appear to relate to greater giving with or without support from other affiliations. The direction on this relationship could go either way. Since friends and local community are typically factors over which Americans have the most choice, this finding could reflect greater givers choosing to affiliate with giving-supportive people and contexts, or it could be that having giving-supportive friends or local communities causes greater giving, or both could operate over time, resulting in a "virtuous cycle" of giving. In any case the point is that it is rare to find high giving among Americans who find little to no support for giving in their sociorelational contexts.

Conclusion

Generosity, Philanthropy, and Civil Society in Social Context

DURING THE COURSE of exploring the *who, what, where,* and *why* of American generosity, some overall themes emerged. We use this conclusion to bring into focus these themes and draw out the implications of our findings. These themes and the corresponding theory will warrant more thought and research, but we hope to lay the groundwork here. After considering these themes, we discuss other implications from the research on generosity for some of our primary audiences:

- Educated readers who seek to better understand their own giving patterns, or want to foster giving among their children, spouse, friends, or local community
- Knowledgeable practitioners in nonprofits, foundations, or religious organizations who may be interested in incorporating this research into their fundraising strategies and other participation efforts
- Interdisciplinary scholars who want to elaborate on and apply these findings on generosity to their specific discipline of studies

Circles of Generosity: Targets, Reasons, Identities, and Outcomes

Americans told us many ways that they give to enhance the well-being of others, and we have explored a variety of ways in which economic and social resources contribute to patterns of generosity. Giving is hardly possible for those below a baseline threshold of socioeconomic resources and of the various family, relational, work, and community context resources that also associate with socioeconomic status. Taking this as a whole, we see that concentric circles of generosity exist that encapsulate combinations of constraints and advantages. People are able to give in some way in every circle, but the intensity and impact of their giving appear to ripple outward as their access to resources is greater.

To expound on this ripple pattern, we borrow from Abraham Maslow the idea that self-actualization, the ability to become everything you are capable of being, generally increases with socioeconomic advantage and safety.[1] People with unmet basic needs demanding attention focus mostly on protecting themselves from harm, while people with greater resources, whose survival is less threatened, can focus on abstract ideals beyond their immediate needs. Applying this to generosity, we think the targets, reasons, identities, and outcomes of giving depend in part on availability of both economic and social resources. Different "generosity circles," radiating out to varying distances, represent different degrees of resource availability. It is simply not sustainable for someone struggling to meet their own needs to generously give, just as on an airplane people must put on their own oxygen mask before turning to assist others. Thus people can undertake more abstract giving, that which is focused on the more general good of society, only once their basic needs are fulfilled.

These ideas of concentric circles of resource availability emerged from the empirical findings presented in earlier chapters, and we further investigate them here. We gleaned this theory from reflecting on the data from our nationally representative study in conjunction with the in-depth stories of our interviewees. Interpreting their combined meaning, we propose the existence of (at least) four concentric circles of generosity that ripple outward. Figure C.1 illustrates this theory. In the innermost circle the focus is on meeting one's own needs and reaching self-sufficiency. From the center the ripple extends outward to reach broader, more general social needs, first to relational-parental generosity, then to community-religious generosity, and then to professional-lifestyle generosity.

Self-sufficiency generosity (SSG) is the center of the giving circles and represents givers with:

1. Responsible identity: A striving for socioeconomic self-reliance
2. Resource-based giving: A goal of not receiving the resources of others
3. Personal supporters: Parents or other guardians who benefit from expending fewer resources on these givers (their children)

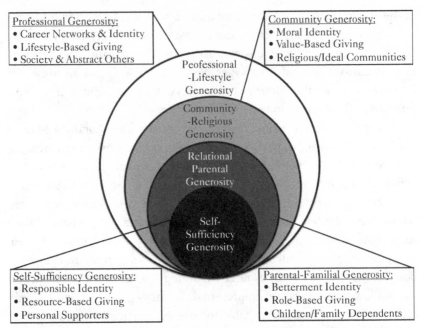

Professional Generosity:
• Career Networks & Identity
• Lifestyle-Based Giving
• Society & Abstract Others

Community Generosity:
• Moral Identity
• Value-Based Giving
• Religious/Ideal Communities

Peofessional
-Lifestyle
Generosity

Community
-Religious
Generosity

Relational
Parental
Generosity

Self-
Sufficiency
Generosity

Self-Sufficiency Generosity:
• Responsible Identity
• Resource-Based Giving
• Personal Supporters

Parental-Familial Generosity:
• Betterment Identity
• Role-Based Giving
• Children/Family Dependents

FIGURE C.I Circles of generosity: targets, reasons, identities, and outcomes.

SSG is far from being selfish. Selfishness is about hoarding resources to benefit oneself, and hoarding is possible only for those with an abundance of resources. At the most basic level of socioeconomic subsistence, extra resources are absent. For cases such as Anthony Ross and Rosa Perez, for example, who live in underresourced and opportunity-deprived contexts, one of the most generous ways to enhance the well-being of others is to be self-sufficient and not rely on others' resources. Not depleting the resources of others benefits those who provide these resources, often parents or other guardians but also frequently the government or other welfare programs. Working to be self-sufficient allows a wider sharing of socioeconomic resources among people in need, including the SSG givers.

In middle-class contexts self-sufficiency is typically a baseline expectation and can therefore be overlooked as a generous behavior. In fact some may scoff at the idea that self-reliance is a form of generosity. However, in the midst of resource-constrained lives, where many members of one's web of affiliations rely on the resources of others, taking care to reach self-sufficiency immediately benefits others, including the givers who might otherwise be sacrificing scarce resources. For example, Anthony talked about times in his life when he more heavily relied on the assistance of his parents to survive, but now he is working hard to support himself and to gain his own resources. Deon Williams grew up in a household that drew welfare to survive, and now he prides himself on not relying on government assistance. Rosa and her fiancé work to support themselves and their growing family, despite her unemployment. Though we are not insinuating there would be something wrong with accepting gifts and assistance during these times of need, we do see in these cases a striving toward becoming or remaining self-sufficient as a way to share those resources with others.

Recognizing self-sufficiency among the circles of generosity is similar to viewing a reduced environmental footprint as a form of giving. They share in common the ideal that lessening resource deprivation is the giver's gift. For example, Anthony and Rosa both talked extensively in their interviews about simply needing to "keep [their] head above water" and "stay alive." Deon still focuses on this SSG center even though he now has access to more resources. His childhood left him with the residual poverty mentality that ensures he will maintain self-sufficiency and not use others' resources.

To limit our understanding of generosity to giving away resources and exclude reserving resources from depletion necessarily makes giving something that can be done only from advantaged positions. Self-sufficiency generosity expands the category of generous people to include those in the most deprived contexts who help others by lessening their socioeconomic demands from those who care for them.

Parental-familial generosity (PFG) moves the focus of generosity outward from self to a second circle of giving and represents givers with:

1. Betterment identity: A striving to better the lives of offspring or other relations
2. Role-based giving: A sense of obligation as parent, child, sibling
3. Children/family dependents: Immediate family who benefits from obtaining a better life

PFG ripples out and enlarges the focus of giving beyond "me" as self-sufficient to "me" as providing for "us." That is, this form of giving typically arises within more resource-constrained lives where, while struggling to survive, people focus on helping immediate family members obtain a better life. Sometimes this includes giving to children or other dependent family members, and sometimes it is because resources are just abundant enough for the giver to allow a wider focus. The working poor, whose statuses and resources often fluctuate, may move in and out of SSG and PFG. Rosa Perez, for example, described a time in the past when she could practice PFG, voluntarily babysitting family members' and neighbors' children, but we see how life circumstances forced her circle of generosity to contract. Since losing her job she has returned to SSG, evidencing how the ebb and flow of socioeconomic resources alter giving.

Working to better the lives of one's own children or other dependent family members is one of the most giving things a person with limited resources can do. We often hear people of limited means finding hope within their situation through their generous efforts to better the lives of their family members, who they believe will have better opportunities as a result of their sacrifice. In some circumstances the giving may be long term, as when parents work overtime their entire lives to afford to pay for college for their children. In other cases it may be a more short-term gift, as in the case of a sick family member with limited health insurance whose family members combine their resources to pay for medical care, with the hopes that the family member will return to health and be able to better his or her own future, and perhaps that of the family if the sick family member is one of the primary providers. Giving in these parental and familial ways may limit the giver's future resources and prospects, but the goal is that the receivers will be able to build upon that sacrifice for a better tomorrow. Parental-familial generosity, in short, supports the American dream.

Our three PFG case studies are Tanika Sandaval, Regina Buckner, and Linda Chesterfield. Linda's sole focus on her eight children—providing them with as many opportunities as possible and ensuring stability in their family—is her sacrifice of giving. For Regina it is finding the appropriate care for her children's ADD and speech needs, even if that means she and her husband must expend their few resources to move homes. Tanika's heavy volunteering as a community liaison for her children's school works to benefit the well-being of her children as well as the neighbors' children. Her role as a parent in a lower-quality school environment and resource-deprived neighborhood prompted her to give to her children through efforts to improve their educational experiences. In more resourced schools, neighborhoods, and families, such heavy school involvement may not be necessary, freeing more resourced parents to focus their giving efforts elsewhere. But in constrained contexts one of the few gifts parents or other family members can give to others is their extra efforts to achieve a better life.

Like SSG, PFG is often overlooked by those who view generosity from more advantaged places. Taking care of children or other immediate family members could again be considered a baseline expectation rather than an act of giving. But this circle of giving is not a baseline, defined as the bare minimum of what everyone can do. Some people are unable to care for their children and immediate family members without relying on the assistance of other family members or societal programs. Working hard to provide for one's loved ones does benefit society more generally, and legislation such as the Family and Medical Leave Act publicly acknowledges the importance of this type of giving for the well-being of society. In resource-strained families, one of the most giving of acts is to invest heavily in the well-being of immediate relations, even if it means sacrificing some personal accomplishments and resources. And this kind of generosity has the potential to ripple farther outward as the receivers of PFG capitalize on their increased opportunity by bettering their own lives and potentially the lives of others. We can imagine how Tanika's children, for instance, could achieve a more comfortable lifestyle than she had and perhaps learn from her giving to them to be generous to others beyond their immediate family.

Community-religious generosity (CRG) is the third circle of generosity, beginning to ripple out beyond immediate relational connections. It represents givers with:

1. Moral identity: A striving to act morally, do good, behave with integrity
2. Value-based giving: A sense of obligation to ethical codes of conduct
3. Religious/ideal communities: Benefiting religious or other ideal-based communities

CRG focuses on living out moral values by helping others. We often see this giving to, through, or on behalf of religious communities, but CRG does not have to be religiously based giving. In fact atheists are as likely to be in this category as are religious devotees, as it includes giving to others to carry out any values and convictions (e.g., LGBT activists, environmentalists, animal lovers). Local activists can be in this generosity circle, as well as church or neighborhood association members, or people who belong to their alma mater's alumni association. The main goal of CRG giving of financial, time, and attention resources is to benefit the religious and other ideals-based communities that support the community members in ways that carry out giving in a particular approach to uphold a morally good life. In short, CRG givers donate to uphold their values in hopes that their giving will improve the well-being of the community to which they belong. They are often passionately engaged in enacting the community vision and consider their religious or community values central to their identity.

Among our case studies, Ryan Dewey, Jackie Sawyer, and George Nettleson are the three who focus on CRG. All give regularly to their church and to organizations such as Compassion International and their alma mater. These three are all driven by their religious values, but there are cases in our broader pool of interviewees who demonstrate the same passionate commitment to other types of communities. Our data on local activists, some of whom are not religious, also fit in CRG. We gathered from these cases and others that CRG becomes possible when one has enough socioeconomic resources to think beyond the survival and betterment needs of oneself and one's immediate family. That is not to say that these cases must be among the highest-resourced people, but that their basic needs are generally met, and they can share with others in their communities.

CRG givers have, in a way, broadened their conception of family to include all the members of their ideals-based community—all people at their church, all members of the neighborhood, all LGBT adults in the community, all animal owners in the city, and so on. CRG givers will often volunteer tirelessly, donate, and otherwise give of their resources so that the community and/or the organization that provides this membership can survive and grow. For example, Jackie's volunteering to teach the church class for toddlers, Ryan's involvement with Campus Crusade for Christ, and George's "no-brainer" tithing to his church show how their CRG upholds a faith community while enabling them to live out their moral belief system.

Professional-lifestyle generosity (PLG) is the fourth and outermost giving circle in Figure C.1 and represents the one with the widest ripple, having givers with:

1. Career identity and networks: Maintenance of a professional, elite social network
2. Lifestyle-based giving: Lifestyle choices supporting diverse organizational ties

3. Focus on society and abstract others: General others benefit through targeted resources

PLG encapsulates the philanthropist, general nonprofit donor, board member, and well-networked community member. Many of these givers express their desire to give as a way to develop, maintain, or promote professional connections—to use professional talents or skills. CRG giving tends to be organizational, and many of these givers' resources go to support an existing nonprofit group or foundation. It is common for these organizations to organize activities in ways that support lifestyles and professional identities. Giving targets tend to extend beyond the local community, with goals to end hunger, cure a disease, preserve natural spaces, and so on. The giving target is more abstract: the donations of money and time are often aimed at a group with no direct contact with givers. For the giver, participating in the organization facilitates relationships with a typically well-resourced group of people, most commonly through attending fundraiser benefits, serving on a board together, or networking through volunteer events. These interactions foster access to social, political, and economic capital.

For example, Cindy Phelps explained that her volunteering with low-income children in New York was a way for her to meet other young professionals. In fact it was her workplace that introduced her to the organization that coordinates her volunteering. Likewise Michael Johnson, the political activist in D.C., explained that his giving of political action time facilitated his professional networks for his accounting business and among his well-resourced neighbors. We also see Susan Baker as a PLG giver. She shared with us that her desire to give came from "academic knowledge" that giving is a good thing to do, and she wanted "in" on that lifestyle. Actualizing a professional identity appears to be part of the PLG giver. It supports the iconic American persona of the respectable, upper-middle-class philanthropist.

Implications of Circles of Generosity

One benefit of painting the entire picture of American generosity is that we gain a broader understanding of giving than individual snapshots would show. With this picture we are able to broaden conceptions of what it means to give in order to more adequately account for the interplay of socioeconomic resource availability and fulfilling the needs of others. The emergent theory of generosity circles helps illustrate the interconnected-ness of generosity, as well as how greater access to social and economic resources enables giving to ripple out and have a wider impact. Yet the giving in each circle would be ineffective without the energy of the other generosity circles adding to its current. The synergy across the generosity circles allows for a variety of giving needs to be met. Too often it seems that the only forms of generosity considered legitimate are the outer two circles, professional-lifestyle generosity and community-religious gener-osity. In part this is because the people defining and reporting on generos-ity typically come from these circles.

In this book, and particularly with this theory, we contest the idea that PLG and CRG are more altruistic than PFG or even SSG. Instead we see all four circles as encompassing both self-beneficial and self-sacrificial aspects. All reinforce a person's identity and all have impacts on others. Indeed each circle potentially impacts all of society. Contrary to popu-lar perceptions, we see SSG and PFG as not selfish or nepotistic but as generous to their intended targets. Conversely we do not see CRG and PLG as purely altruistic and acknowledge the ways they also support the giver. Nevertheless the ripples from each circle of generosity do tend to have broader reach as they spread outward, indicating that having greater access to social and economic resources does facilitate forms of generosity that have a broader impact.

This understanding of generosity highlights how a narrow definition of generosity, as giving to people outside one's immediate family, privileges a better-resourced type of giving and fails to acknowledge the resource abundance that allows for this giving beyond a personal network. People with more limited means often have the same desires to benefit others, but without the resources to achieve a broad impact they give within a more immediate context and their giving is expressed in a greater variety of forms. Generous people like Tanika work hard to better their family's lot in life, and people like Rosa and her fiancé struggle to get through another day supporting themselves in uncertain times. The point of developing this theory on the concentric circles of generosity is in part to challenge the popular notion that conceives only of more abstract, resource-rich forms of giving as generous. Givers across every circle work to be generous in whatever ways they can.

Here, and throughout this book, we compose a picture of generos-ity that is comprehensive in its scope of what counts as generosity, yet nuanced in its explanation of American giving. One of the major benefits of such an approach is a better understanding of the many-colored spectrum of generosity, depending on the circle, social and economic resources, social context, personal orientations, and giving-supportive affiliations. Acknowledging the diversity of American generosity allows for a more complex and yet discernible picture of who gives and why.

Generosity Inequalities

Due to the important diversity among givers, we summarize the main trends we found throughout the book with regard to significantly different social status influences, namely the role of gender, race/ethnicity, age, and education in giving.

Gender

Our analysis in chapter 2 finds men more likely than women to engage in political action, and women more likely than men to donate money. Among volunteers, men claim on average more volunteer hours than do women. The analyses in chapter 3 find that among givers, women are more likely to take Planned, Habitual, or Selective approaches to their giving process, while men are more likely to take Impulsive or Atypical approaches. In chapter 5 we explain the differences in donation amounts by gender as mediated by social psychological and affiliation factors. The personal orientations and social relations that support greater giving are more common in women than men.

In chapter 2 our case studies evidence the male correlation with high levels of political activism and the female correlation with giving money, including one of the male high givers crediting his wife as the reason for their donations. The case studies also express the salient role of gender in expressions of relational generosity (e.g., "As a mom . . ."). Among some of our female respondents, we see relational generosity can go so far as to lose the boundary of self. This was not observed in the male interviews. More women were represented in the second circle of generosity of relational-parental generosity. Given the persistent expectation that women have a more salient role in the daily life of the family, it is not surprising that they would have a greater focus on generosity through familial and immediate relational ties. We propose that one of the ways men and women "do gender" is through their giving behaviors.

Race/Ethnicity

White, non-Hispanic Americans are more likely to donate money than are Americans of other races and ethnicities, and nonwhite Americans are more likely to engage in political action. There were no evident racial or ethnic patterns to differences in giving processes, that is in the giver types analyses.

The chapter 2 case study excursus substantiates that many of the nongivers are nonwhite, while the primary political activist is white. We also observed the salient role of racial/ethnic identity in differentiating the circles of generosity. The two inner circles (self-sufficiency generosity and relational-parental generosity) were more common among nonwhite respondents, while the two outer circles (community-religious generosity and professional-lifestyle generosity) were more common among white respondents. Similar to gender, this appears to be partially a function of privilege. In the case of race and ethnicity, it appears that the socio-economic status of residents' communities, which in the United States is highly correlated with race/ethnicity, contributes to the target of one's giving.

Age

Older Americans are more likely to donate money and in greater sums than are younger Americans. Older Americans are no more or less likely to be volunteers but are likely to volunteer more hours, on average. Age did not correlate with different types of giving processes. The combined models in chapter 5 show that age remains a significant differentiator in explaining greater giving amounts, net of all the social psychological, affiliation, and other social status factors. We wonder if it is age itself or perhaps an untapped factor (e.g., stability, establishment of adult trajectories, or formed identity in dedication to particular causes) that explains this correlation. This book does not fully investigate this, but we think it does make for an interesting future study.

The chapter 2 case study excursus demonstrates that the most generous givers, with one highly religious exception, are older. We hear from the case studies how age influences where and what type of giving occurs. We see patterns where younger and older Americans seem to be more active in their political giving, whereas middle-aged Americans seem to be more active in volunteering. For many of our middle-aged interviewees, age conflates with the role of parent and volunteering to help their children succeed—whether volunteering at school or for extracurricular activities, for example. Age also correlates with income in the United States, so we see the influence of the amount of dollars donated correlating with age as a function of income. We find that age correlates most strongly with the type and target of giving.

Education

Americans with college degrees are more likely to participate in all forms of generosity than Americans with less than a college degree. Among those who donate money, Americans with college degrees give greater amounts of money on average than do Americans with less than a college degree. College graduates are more likely to be Planned, Habitual, Selective, or Impulsive givers, and Americans with less than a college degree are more likely to be Atypical or nongivers. Chapters 3 and 5 highlight the important role of a college degree in predicting giving amounts and in explaining differences in giving processes. Sustained giving of every form is significantly more likely to occur among those with college degrees. As an aside, we may want to consider the implications of this among the current debate in the United States on the importance of supporting higher education funding and whether or not it pays off for American society. Amid reports of growing student loan debt, the findings of our study provide another way of explicating the important intangibles, and even contributions to bottom lines, that higher education contributes to societal welfare.

In the case study excursus in chapter 2 all of the high givers have college degrees and all of our nongivers did not graduate college. Level of educational attainment does not readily stand out in the interviews as having an influence on whether or not someone gives. However, the reasons for giving seemed to differ by educational attainment. For example, the parents who did not complete college voiced investment in a desire to volunteer at their children's school and be a part of the school community. Mothers with a college degree also volunteered at their children's school, but the reason seemed more obligatory, a social expectation. This difference in personal and social norm reasons stood out as differentiated by educational level of the giver.[2]

Thus there are diverse approaches to generosity behaviors. Not all givers are created equal. Understanding American generosity means it is important to take social statuses, regional locations, social orientations, social support, intentions, identity, intended targets of giving, and the ways in which different Americans are able to give with the tremendously varied social and economic resources that they have.

Implications for Readers

Readers of this book mirror the variety of the American givers we studied, representing a range of approaches to and interests in generosity. We focus here on illustrating the implications of these findings for:

1. Individuals: Reader who are interested in being givers, raising children to be givers, supporting friends and spouse in giving, contributing to a generous local community and nation
2. Practitioners: Those interested in improving their nonprofit, foundation, or religious organization's fundraising processes
3. Scholars: Those interested in modifying, revamping, or improving disciplinary practices regarding studying generosity, philanthropy, or civil society with a serious consideration of the social context of giving

We will not cover everything in this section, and there are many more conclusions that can be drawn for these and a variety of other audiences. Instead we highlight the primary, most relevant implications that arise from our findings.

Implications for Individuals

The implications for individuals reflect on the giver in general as well as how the roles of parent, partner, friend, and community member promote giving. We also include a few practical tips to increase giving.

Implications for Givers

We have learned that giving money and time is not as common as readers might have thought: a few Americans give a lot, and many give a little. This means givers cannot rely on others who appear to have more money or time to carry the weight of generosity. In the social sciences the assumption that a few will carry the load of the majority is referred to as a "free rider" problem. In fact if we want the train of generosity to get us to our destination, we cannot expect just a few people to fuel it. These data show the need for all to participate. Clearly some are more able to give than others; however, this book shows that we should question the assumption that someone else is giving, or could give, more than we can. We all need to give for generosity to achieve its goal of the greater societal good.

To younger readers we emphasize that it does not appear to be the case that there is some point later in life when people jump on the giving train, as it were. We do not see evidence that giving suddenly develops when a certain age or lifestyle threshold is crossed. Instead we see minimal changes in giving across age groups. Based on this observation and the information in the interviews and case studies, we extrapolate that people mostly seem to give as much in later life as they had in earlier years. Deon Williams's nongiving habits, formed longed ago, persist in his retirement even though, by his own admission, he is bored and has expendable resources. Michael Johnson, on the other hand, shows us that when circumstances arise to inhibit giving, one can choose to adapt and keep practicing generosity.

Each stage of the life course can have its own pressing needs and demands interfering with giving to others. We face the financial burdens of paying for college, living on the low income of a first job, covering housing expenses, raising children, saving for their college education, and saving for retirement. All along this journey there are also time burdens associated with school, career, and family that require much attention. We highlight this fact for our younger readers to underscore that there is no "tomorrow" after which giving will suddenly be easier, more natural, and more supported. Giving can begin now and appears to be sustained when engrained early.

Generosity can be a lifetime journey. Our data show clearly that giving patterns are not static. While it does not appear to be the case that nongivers often suddenly begin giving, many Americans do recount particular moments after which they became more committed to giving, when the generosity of their parents or other affiliations suddenly clicked. Sometimes people who are generally oriented toward generosity only need an invitation to become a more regular giver. Tanika Sandaval, for example, was not a giver, but when a parent at school asked her to volunteer, it flipped her generosity switch. Like many others she had not led a life completely removed from giving: her grandmother and childhood church provided strong foundations for it. It was common to hear interviewees talk about particular moments when they became aware that they had enough money or time, or that others were in need, and so they began to give. It is never too late to allow a Prosperity Outlook to thrive, to increase a sense of Social Responsibility, or to encounter others in a trying situation and feel the importance of Social Solidarity and Collective Conscious. Our highest givers seemed to remain open to a call to give even more, in whatever ways they were able, never thinking they had "arrived" in their generosity. It sometimes took years for them to achieve the level of giving they aspired to, and many are still aspiring, but they chose to raise the bar, and now more are receiving.

We also observed in American giving patterns the opposite of this process: "behavioral slippage." In generosity, as in many social actions, the gap between our talk and our actions is wide. We sometimes believe we are doing more than we actually are doing. As an example, a good number of people we surveyed said they donated money but then recorded giving $0 in the past 12 months. Given the many factors that play a role in giving, it is not surprising that the stars do not always align for us to carry out giving intentions. Yet there are always obstacles to giving; overcoming them, when possible, simply requires deliberate planning. The highly generous Americans we surveyed and interviewed inspire us to devote thought regularly to our giving portfolio. We do this in other aspects of our lives—holding strategic meetings at work, retreats for organizations, and even family meetings around budgets—so it makes sense to hold ourselves accountable to a regular review of our giving. Such regular attention can help translate generosity intentions into action.

Nearly everyone is busy in some way; there are many things to save for, spend on, and earn. Yet the stories here remind us that there are many who have less, many lives in disarray, many people who might trade in their constraints for the burden of so many opportunities to be busy. The challenge is to give despite our other commitments, to find ways in the course of paying bills and juggling schedules to carve out care for others. Otherwise we will simply never make room after we pay the bills, take the kids to practice, complete our homework, send the kids to college, save for retirement, and finish the shopping. Our lives are full of distractions, many of which are important. However, people who give generously do not have any more discretionary time or extra monetary resources than nongivers. Rather they see what they have as enough and choose to give.

Implications for Parents

Parents play an important role in whether and how much their children give as adults. Giving does not happen in a vacuum, and most people are not able to fully actualize their giving intentions unless they are embedded within giving-supportive relationships. One of the key affiliations for shaping a lifetime of giving is with parents. Many of our givers described how their parents modeled and taught them explicitly about giving during their childhood. As our case studies show, people tended to give as their parents had given, whether generously or sparingly, in the form of money or time, donating clothes as Cindy Phelps did or hoping to foster a child as Rosa Perez did.

Therefore parents who hope to raise generous children must establish a habit of giving early. Children look to parents for how to construct their own lives, and if they see giving, they too will likely give in adulthood. Show kids how to write the check to donate money or bring them along to the volunteer activity. Of course many other factors also influence a child's adult giving, but it is rare to be a giver without some recollection of parental generosity during childhood.

Some parents may feel awkward discussing money matters with children. In fact many Americans feel awkward discussing money with anyone. But this is precisely why children look to their parents for guidance in the unknown world of finances; familial relationships are one of the few, if not the only, sources for people to learn about household budgeting, including monetary donations. Our highest givers had access to information about this from their parents, giving them an example and a baseline for establishing their own giving. Few interviewees said their parents explicitly discussed with them how much money they gave. In most cases parents' guidance took the form of some intentional teaching about the importance of giving money. Just knowing that their parents gave seemed to establish the importance of giving for many of our higher givers.

In other cases no explicit teaching was ever done, but the interviewees saw their parents giving and learned from this modeling. This was easier in the case of volunteering, which involves activity that a child can see and understand. It was a bit less common for people to recall seeing their parents give money and take political action, though some described incidents in which they learned of their parents' giving participation. For example, one day at church Michael heard the pastor mention his father by name as a donor. From that experience he learned that financial giving was something his dad practiced, and that seemed to have been enough to impact some of Michael's reasons for financial giving.

Another tangible way to model financial giving is putting money in the offering plate or basket during religious services. Several interviewees mentioned the offering plate as the way they identified whether their parents gave money. Some parents gave regularly and generously; others threw in a dollar from time to time. Either way, it is a rare visible action in a typically invisible realm of finances. Of course parents do not have to be religious in order to teach their children to give.

It doesn't matter whether parents give financially, volunteer, or offer effort-heavy relational services to their friends and neighbors. Demonstrating the value and importance of the well-being of others is key. Parents who discussed or modeled helping others seemed to make a great deal of difference in whether their children gave as adults.

Implications for Spouses/Partners

Spouses and romantic partners also have an incredible influence on people's giving. Since many financial decisions, as well as decisions about collective family time and priorities, are made within these intimate relationships, spouses can sometimes even compensate for a lacking parental influence on giving. George Nettleson, one of our high givers, came from a family of nongivers but married a very generous woman who influenced his giving. However, the reverse can also occur. Linda Chesterfield resented her spouse's generosity. In these cases, generous spouses might give more if it were not for the spousal friction they experience.

Couples can have conflicts about how much money they give and how to spend their time. But when they are united in their approach to giving, giving becomes simply another household activity to discuss openly and plan together.

Implications for Friends

We found that having giving-supportive friends was consistently important for giving. We were not able to decipher whether people may be more likely to give if their friends give or if giving people are more likely to attract giving-supportive friends. Either way, if one is interested in being a giver or increasing the giving of one's friends, one should surround oneself with giving friends and support those friends' giving. Many things compete for Americans' time, attention, and money, so it is crucial to surround ourselves with giving-oriented people who make it easier to actualize our giving.

Discussions with friends about the value and meaning of giving could make a difference for those who have little exposure to giving. As friends, we can model how to make room for giving in the midst of other obligations.

Implications for Community Members

People use their local community context, as well as their friends, to establish giving norms and practice. If they believe others give little and never encounter anything that challenges this belief, they may not reflect on their own low levels of giving. But if they become aware of the giving activities of their neighbors, their expectations for giving may rise. The implication is that if givers set the bar for giving in their community, their neighbors will be encouraged to be more generous in their own giving.

We do not suggest that people walk around bragging about the giving they do; in fact that would likely result in the opposite of the intended effect. Many of our interviewees who discussed being turned off giving offered "showy giving" as the reason. There is a happy medium between silence and boisterous bragging: simply letting others know about local giving activities may help to raise their awareness about the giving context in which they are embedded. We were surprised to learn that many people aren't aware of the giving opportunities and activities in their local communities. Tanika, for example, was unaware of an opportunity to be involved with her children's school until a friend invited her to participate. As community members, we can spread the word.

How to Be a Giver: Practical Tips

Here we outline a few straightforward ways to implement the changes just discussed. This list is not meant to be comprehensive, nor are these ideas well-researched. They are quite simple but potentially profound tips for increasing one's own giving and enhancing the giving of others.

GIVING JARS

Invitations to give may come all at once, such as during the holiday season when discretionary money may be tight, and then not come at all for a while. To enable givers to donate larger amounts during these pushes, we suggest putting a jar in the house, perhaps in the kitchen, for collecting donations all year round.

A giving jar is one way to increase giving, especially among Impulsive and Selective givers, without requiring the budgeting and planning approaches of Planned and Habitual givers. We know that Selective and

Impulsive givers are generally committed to giving, but they tend to rely on requests from others to provide the opportunity to give.

A giving jar also provides parents with another way to model giving for children. It visually orients the household toward giving and provides teaching opportunities to discuss why giving is important. It could even be set up like a family game to coincide with family events. For example, every time the family takes a vacation, a contribution is made to help other families have fun. Or the family ritual of eating out every Friday night could be donated once a month, the equivalent of the food bill contributed to help others eat. Family members could be invited to think of their own ideas for family events to celebrate through giving. Many possibilities open up when giving money is made visible in a family.

TIME JARS

The model of the giving jar can be applied to giving time. Family members would collect ideas for activities to volunteer time or attention to help others, such as running a race for a cause, offering to watch a neighbor's kids without pay, making meals for an elderly neighbor, helping a needy family rebuild after a storm, or coordinating with neighbors to welcome someone new to the community. The time jar could be made into an ongoing family game in which family members are regularly challenged to think of new ideas to add to the jar, as well as a family ritual around the given activity. These time jars could also be virtually stored and shared with friends, coworkers, and extended family to activate long-distance giving.

SCHEDULE IT IN

We learned from our highest givers the importance of scheduling giving. Whether adding a reminder to a financial budgeting program to give or blocking out time on a personal or family calendar to volunteer, we're more likely to get things done if we schedule them rather than wait for an opening to appear in the schedule. In the middle of busy lives the way we make sure not to forget important events—such as doctor's appointments, school tests, work meetings, paying taxes—is to schedule them and set reminders.

Though not everyone is a Planned or Habitual giver, we do not think a little scheduling will impose on the Impulsive or Selective approach to giving. Scheduling can be as simple as a recurring reminder on the fifteenth of each month, such as "Give today," "Volunteer this Friday," or "Cut the neighbor's grass." The details can be worked out by the Impulsive or Selective giver on that day. Scheduling can ward off the ever-present tendency to let things slip away if they are not on the calendar. Most of us would not rely on our memory to get to a doctor's appointment every year or attend a monthly meeting, so why depend on our faulty memory for something as important as giving? Instead we should schedule it in.

SHARE

A final practical piece of advice that we offer based on the findings of this book is to share giving experiences with others. While no one wants to hear people brag about their giving, the alternative need not be silence. Silence can be misconstrued as the absence of participation, resulting in someone not knowing they have giving-supportive affiliations. Talking about giving does not have to involve a discussion of *how much*; it can instead focus on *how* and *why*. We see this conversation as similar to discussing hobbies. People talk about how they went mountain biking, fishing, or out for a run without being pushy about the details. These conversations often involve people who do not do these activities, and hearing about the hobby may inspire them to give it a try. The same can be true of a conversation about giving. Hearing about what someone else gave may inspire someone to prioritize giving.

Implications for Practitioners

Our findings shed some light on how leaders of religious congregations and nonprofit organizations or foundations can activate Americans' giving spirit. We address these two groups of leaders separately due to their distinct memberships.

Implications for Nonprofit or Foundation Leaders

One of the prominent implications of this book's findings is to avoid treating all givers as a uniform group. The different types of givers warrant and respond to different campaigns for giving. For example, Impulsive and Selective givers often say their giving occurs spontaneously as a result of being asked to give. They tend to engage in volunteering or donate money as a result of particular circumstances: who asked them to give, what the cause is, and whether they have resources available at that moment. These givers would be likely to respond to frequent invitations to give, so solicitations would likely be more effective if they answered for Selective and Impulsive givers the following questions: Why now? Why to this cause?

How they can afford it? Campaigns such as mobile phone messages beginning "Text $10 to . . ." would also seem to appeal to these givers.

These same campaigns may annoy Habitual and Planned givers, for two different reasons. First, Planned and Habitual givers check it off their list once they donate, so repeated and frequent requests will likely be ignored. Second, Habitual givers do not devote continual conscious thought to their giving targets, and so repeated solicitations may bother them, perhaps even to the point of encouraging them to look into a different giving target. Planned givers, on the other hand, will be interested in more details than the Selective and Impulsive givers.

Thus if an organization can figure out their donors' approaches to giving, campaign materials can be prepared and distributed with varying frequencies depending on the giver type. Another possibility is to distribute the same materials with the same frequency to all givers, but prepare them in ways that appeal to the various giver types. For example, flashy pictures that draw on emotional connections to the recipients may appeal to the Impulsive giver. Selective givers would look into the materials a bit further and for the "elevator pitch" of why they need to give to this cause. Habitual givers could be targeted for a brief note on the envelope that says something like "We are glad you are part of our giving community. If your questions are already answered, we appreciate your ongoing support. Otherwise, please read these materials for updates on the results of your giving." The bulk of the brochure, packet, or website could contain more extensive results of research on the giving outcomes, budgets, and so on that would satisfy the Planned givers. As Planned givers typically give the largest donations, their gifts could feasibly compensate for the costs of printing, mailing, or programming such materials.

Another important implication for nonprofit and foundation leaders has to do with the giving portfolio. That is, understanding how donors fit their contributions to each organization within their broader spectrum of giving. In particular, practitioners should reflect on the central role of Big 3 giving, especially monetary donations, in a generosity portfolio. Since most givers are engaged in at least some level of monetary giving, one way of recruiting participants to a program may be to get on their financial giving radar. In other words, the best pool of volunteers may be drawn from the organization's list of financial donors. Considering the higher volunteer participation of Selective givers, elevating volunteering solicitations to the level of a personal phone call or a more intimate form of invitation to give may be more effective than standard approaches. The best pool of new financial donors is the list of volunteers or political activists (as well as participants in the other six forms of generosity), especially if they can be shown how their financial contributions would benefit their existing volunteer efforts.

Leaders of nonprofit groups and foundations should keep in mind that there are millions of Americans who do not give. While their organization's approach can be tailored to those who already give, nongiving Americans represent a great deal of untapped potential. To harness that potential and draw new givers into the world of generosity, leaders should make efforts to activate the social psychological orientations and webs of affiliations that motivate people to give. Campaign events in the community, at house parties, at school—these are all places that offer the opportunity to reach people who have never given and motivate them to give. Once they give, they are likely to begin to identify generosity as personally important and act to support that identity, so leaders should provide continuing opportunities to give.

Implications for Religious Leaders

One of the key implications of our findings for religious leaders is about exposure to giving calls within religious contexts. It appears from our national survey that religious contexts are fertile grounds to recruit givers. Nearly all forms of giving are related to more frequent religious service attendance, and these data show that part of the reason may be exposure to religious calls to give. For some Americans the passing of the offering plate is the only way parents model giving, and the only time children see their parents engage in giving. That is not to say that all religious organizations should therefore have offering plates or baskets; some religious organizations may have good reasons not to solicit donations in that manner. However, religious leaders may want to consider to what extent they could issue a similar religious call to give through some other means, especially in a visible way.

Along those lines, the significance of the physical offering plate raises questions about the potential impact of online giving rather than giving in the house of worship. We are not advising against online giving if it meets other needs of particular congregations. However, the increasing use of online giving programs may mean future generations will lack the most explicit and often the only example of generosity that today's American children see. A technique that some religious organizations employ to make online giving visible is collecting slips of paper in the offering baskets to represent online contributions. Another idea is to devote a time of the year to make giving commitments so that children and others can publicly observe that commitment. There are potentially many ways that congregations can address the possibly negative consequences of online giving based on their particular needs, and they deserve reflection for the future of American giving.

Another primary implication of this book for religious leaders is about the significance of regularly talking about donating money and other forms of giving as part of what it means to lead a religiously based life. Merely presenting the operational needs of the religious organization may underestimate the giving power of the congregation. How much should religious leaders discuss giving from the pulpit? The leaders we talk with from around the country tend to refer to parishioners who attend services most frequently and are heavily involved in the congregation as their main audience. This makes sense, as they are the ones the religious leaders see and interact with the most. However, from a numbers perspective, most people in religious congregations are not those who are heavily involved or regularly attending. This means that while pastors think that all they do is talk about giving, the majority of the congregants may never hear those giving calls. Thus we recommend that religious leaders consider talking about giving more often.

At the same time, nothing annoys regular religious attendees more than getting beat over the head with the financial needs of the congregation. If calls for giving focus solely on those needs, members of the congregation can quickly become annoyed by too frequent reminders of the heating bill, roof repair, or capital campaign. They can start to think they are seen as just a pocketbook. If giving calls focus solely on specific needs, increasing their frequency would likely have negative consequences. Increasing the frequency of calls to give using a diverse array of approaches would be a better method. We have found in this and other research projects that givers are typically more responsive to appeals that help them see giving as part of what it means to be a good person, as a way to enact the vision and theology of the religious congregation, and as part of their identity as a religious person. In this sense calls for giving should focus not on particular needs of the congregation but on other budgetary matters, such as how to handle money as a couple or parent. Rather than merely garnering attendees' support, such an approach may, in the long run, inspire them to give more generously while offering them support for a more financially sound life.

Implications for Generosity-Related Scholars

For scholars who study generosity and its multitude of subtopics we intend these reflections to spark conversations and research that more thoroughly explores the giving character of people.

Generosity as Interdisciplinary and Comprehensive

We consistently see throughout this book how a more narrow definition of generosity can miss much of the broader range of behaviors oriented to the well-being of others. Due to the relationships of generosity forms to social statuses, socioeconomic resources, regional locations, approaches to giving, intrapersonal orientations, and interpersonal relational supports, focusing on just one form of giving may bias generalizations toward particular groups of Americans or regions of the country. Moreover focusing on only one expression of generosity would paint a "glass half-empty" picture. When different forms of generosity were measured separately, giving participation rates were considerably lower than when they were considered together as a portfolio of giving.

In addition understanding the diversity of giving could help to explain the conflicting social science accounts of social capital in the United States as either rapidly declining or merely being reconfigured. A transition to more technologically based expressions, one aspect of such a reconfiguration, would allow for a more fluid interchange of generosity. For example, political action in times past may have revolved primarily around city hall, but it can now occur online in multiple places at once. Volunteering used to entail maintenance of a physical organization that needed considerable overhead resources to reach people through traditional means of communication. Many successful volunteering events today, on the other hand, occur with little overhead cost because they use social media to recruit volunteers. And then of course there is the rapid multiplication of monetary giving opportunities online. This development may make it easier for people to give in multiple forms than in times past, when they may have had to physically visit separate locations to give in different forms. If this is the case, then expressing generosity in multiple forms may be a phenomenon that we can expect to become increasingly common among givers.

Though many of these implications are conjectures based on our findings (and on our broader knowledge of generosity-related trends and our own experiences as givers), they are also possibilities to be investigated further in future studies. Our findings suggest that generosity-related studies will likely not reach new conclusions without employing comprehensive measures of giving. The myriad forms of giving require researchers to broaden the scope of their theories. To form an overarching interdisciplinary theory of generosity in the future, it will be necessary to reflect on all the discipline-specific empirical and theoretical findings of past research on individual expressions of generosity.

Understanding of Generosity as Nonuniform

At the same time, and seemingly paradoxically, one of the major implications of this book is that scholars must stop assessing generosity as operating among a pool of uniform givers. While the expressions of generosity may be becoming increasingly interchangeable for givers, the approaches to and extent of engagement with giving are diversifying. Distinct giver types exist. Impulsive givers will drive national trends since they constitute the largest subset of givers; however, they are not necessarily the most generous or committed donors. Studies that are not nationally representative may be especially vulnerable to selection of predominantly Impulsive givers and may miss Habitual givers (the smallest group of givers) altogether. The particular research question needs to drive the empirical approach. Does the level or commitment of the donor matter? If so, we need to step back from the "population average" findings and instead dig deeper into the characteristics of individual subpopulations of givers.

A key contribution of the giver typology presented in this book is the recognition of a difference between higher numbers of givers, who tend to have lower engagement, and higher amounts of giving, which tend to come from smaller numbers of people. Nationally representative studies without a method to tease apart the subpopulations by giving approaches will underestimate engagement levels and overestimate characteristics related to the largest subpopulation, typically those less involved in giving. Understanding these biases can help reconcile the "glass half-empty" perspective that sees the giving engagement levels of Americans on the decline with the "glass half-full" perspective that the world of philanthropy is thriving. The approach of this book shows how both perspectives may be reached depending on whether one highlights the many Americans who give little to nothing or the few Americans who give large amounts.

Considering Generosity in Social Context

It will come as no surprise to sociologists and other social scientists that generosity behaviors, like all social actions, are embedded in diverse social contexts. We hope scholars from other disciplines, however, gained an appreciation for the important role of social context in explaining behaviors. While economic factors are important, resources do not fully explain the picture of American giving. Likewise psychologists can see how intrinsic states of mind underlie generous behaviors, but they too are only part of why Americans give. Also important are the sociorelational contexts that may be more or less supportive of giving, as well as perceptions of personal giving in comparison to the participation of others. Regional cultural norms and social status norms also shape giving outcomes. Every time we added a new piece to the puzzle of generosity, we explained more variance. Almost never did the inclusion of a new set of factors account for spuriousness: each set of *who*, *where*, and *why* factors stood on its own to produce a 360-degree account of generosity. Thus we see the importance of transcending disciplinary divides to consider how all aspects of individual and social life explain human actions. The result is a more complete understanding of social behaviors.

Theoretically Rich Giving Webs of Affiliation

Based on the ideas of Simmel regarding modern social differentiation into separated webs of affiliation, we found that giving is embedded in sociorelational contexts that support generosity to greater or lesser extents. The primary theoretical contribution of this finding is that the *Homo economicus* understanding of giving misses key insights into the generosity process: purely individualistic understandings of people have serious shortfalls since people are shaped by their ongoing interactions within their web of affiliations. People do not give in a vacuum nor base their decisions to give solely on their available resources. Rather, intra personal orientations embedded within familial, spousal, friendship, communal, and national relationships create the context for giving. With a "looking-glass self" understanding, we separated our individual self from these dialogues.

Theoretically Rich Circles of Generosity

Another major contribution of this book is the introduction of a theoretically rich idea of generosity circles. Incorporating ideas from Maslow's hierarchy of needs, we see generosity as situated within resource and network capacities. The giving targets and giver benefits vary across these giving circles. Giving occurs within a meaningful circle of generosity, each with its own socioeconomically based capacities, targets, reasons, outcomes, and identity affirmations. These generosity circles arise in the context of different childhoods, neighborhoods, and organizational exposures. We discuss how both other-oriented and self-oriented motivations can be at work across all circles of giving. With this idea we highlight important roles of social theory in unveiling hidden aspects of social actions.

We have composed in this book a picture of American generosity that is broad in its scope, nuanced in its detail, stimulating in its generality, and rich in its implications for givers, parents, friends, spouses, community members, practitioners, and scholars. The goal is a deeper understanding of generosity that helps us to fully actualize our giving selves.

Appendix

Table A.I.1 Survey sample descriptive characteristics

	Mean or Proportion	Standard Deviation	Min.	Max.
Age	48.73	15.54	23	102
Female	0.51	0.50	0	1
Married	0.55	0.50	0	1
Youth Household	0.30	0.46	0	1
White, non-Hispanic	0.70	0.46	0	1
Religiously Attending	0.35	0.48	0	1
Republican	0.41	0.49	0	1
College Degree (4 yr)	0.30	0.46	0	1
Employed	0.56	0.50	0	1
Household Income	11.11	4.37	1	19
Recession Impacted	0.33	0.47	0	1
Homeowner	0.74	0.44	0	1
Residential Tenure	12.46	12.23	0	71
Metropolitan Area	0.83	0.37	0	1

Source: Science of Generosity (Herzog and Price 2016).

Table A.I.2 Science of Generosity interviewee survey demographics

Household Characteristics—40 Total Households, 22 Spouses, 62 Total Interviewees*

State	Primary	Spouse*	Total
AZ	3	1	4
CA	5	3	8
GA	3	3	6
IL	3	2	5
IN	2	1	3
MA	2	0	2
MD/DC	4	1	5
MI	3	1	4
NC	5	4	9
NY	3	1	4
OR	1	1	2
TX	3	2	5
WA	3	2	5
	40	22	62

Family Roles	Primary	Spouse*	Total
Married w/children	12	12	24
Single Parent	4	0	4
Married no kids	9	9	18

Income	Primary	Spouse*	Total
Less than $5,000	1	0	1
$7,500 to $9,999	1	0	1
$10,000 to $12,499	1	0	1
$15,000 to $19,999	1	0	1
$20,000 to $24,999	4	2	6
$25,000 to $29,999	1	0	1
$30,000 to $34,999	2	1	3
$35,000 to $39,999	1	1	2
$40,000 to $49,999	2	1	3
$50,000 to $59,999	8	3	11
$60,000 to $74,999	3	2	5
$75,000 to $84,999	1	1	2
$85,000 to $99,999	2	2	4
$100,000 to $124,999	5	5	10
$125,000 to $149,999	4	2	6
$175,000 or more	3	2	5
	40	22	62

Owner/Renter	Primary	Spouse*	Total
Owner	28	19	47

Single, No Kids			
	15	1	16
	40	22	62

Renter			
	12	3	15
	40	22	62

Individual Characteristics—40 Primary Respondents, 22 Spouses**, 62 Total Interviewees

Age*	Primary	Spouse*	Total
25–34	8	5	13
35–44	13	7	20
45–54	8	6	14
55–64	9	4	13
65–74	2	0	2
	40	22	62

Race*	Primary	Spouse*	Total
White	28	17	45
Black	5	1	6
Hispanic	5	4	9
Other	2	0	2
	40	22	62

Gender	Primary	Spouse	Total
Male	16	14	30
Female	24	8	32
	40	22	62

Religion*	Primary	Spouse*	Total
Evangelical Protestant	13	7	20
Black Protestant	6	1	7
Mainline Protestant	2	0	2
Catholic	12	8	20
Jewish	2	1	3
Other Religion	1	1	2
Indeterminate	1	1	2
No Affiliation	3	3	6
	40	22	62

(continued)

Table A.1.2 Continued

Education*	Primary	Spouse*	Total
Less than High School	4	1	5
High School Degree	8	3	11
Some College	9	6	15
Bachelor's Degree	9	6	15
Master's Degree	6	4	10
Professional Degree	4	2	6
	40	22	62

Employment**	Primary	Spouse*	Total
Working—Paid	20	11	31
Working—Self	5	3	8
Retired	2	0	2
Disabled	6	2	8
Not Working—Looking	2	2	4
Not Working—Other	5	4	9
	40	22	62

Source: Science of Generosity (Herzog and Price 2016).

* Survey data represent primary respondent characteristics for household. Spouse repeats characteristic.

** Survey data were not collected on spouses. Data represent primary respondent.

Table A.1.1 Participation in forms of generosity (in percentages)

	No	Yes
Gives Money	44.8	55.2
Gives Time	75.0	25.0
Gives Political Action	87.1	12.9
Gives Blood	88.4	11.6
Gives Organs	57.5	42.5
Gives Estate	95.4	4.6
Lends Possessions	51.5	48.5
Gives Possessions	74.3	25.7
Gives Sustainability	86.5	13.5
Gives Attention—Effort Heavy	54.0	46.0

Source: Science of Generosity (Herzog and Price 2016).

Table A.1.2.a Science of Generosity Survey excerpt of 31 causes to give

	In the past 12 months ...	I Gave Money or Possessions (1)	I Gave Time or Volunteered (2)	I Took Any Political Action (3)	Not Applicable (4)
1	**Family and neighbors,** such as helping a family member or neighbor, working on issues to strengthen families or neighborhoods, crime prevention	❑	❑	❑	❑
2	**Health, physical, mental, and emotional,**	❑	❑	❑	❑
4	**Adult education,** such as tutoring, education, ESL, computer training	❑	❑	❑	❑
5	**Children and youth,** such as tutoring, mentoring, education, afterschool programs, ESL, recreational sports, camps, 4-H	❑	❑	❑	❑

(continued)

Table A.I.2.a Continued

In the past 12 months . . .	I Gave Money or Possessions (1)	I Gave Time or Volunteered (2)	I Took Any Political Action (3)	Not Applicable (4)
6 **Homelessness**	❏	❏	❏	❏
7 **Poverty**, such as low-income housing, welfare programs, job location, microcredit	❏	❏	❏	❏
8 **Alcohol and drug abuse**, such as counseling or education about substance abuse	❏	❏	❏	❏
9 **Prisoners**, such as visiting prisoners, writing letters to inmates, prison ministry	❏	❏	❏	❏
10 **Abused women or children**, such as domestic violence or child neglect	❏	❏	❏	❏
11 **Elderly**	❏	❏	❏	❏
12 **Immigrant, migrant, and refugee populations**	❏	❏	❏	❏
13 **Arts, culture, and humanities**, such as performing arts, cultural or ethnic groups, museums, art exhibits, public television/radio	❏	❏	❏	❏
14 **Animals**, such as promoting animal welfare, ending animal cruelty, protecting endangered species	❏	❏	❏	❏
15 **Environment**, such as recycling, reducing pollution, promoting green living	❏	❏	❏	❏

Table A.I.2.a Continued

In the past 12 months . . .	I Gave Money or Possessions (1)	I Gave Time or Volunteered (2)	I Took Any Political Action (3)	Not Applicable (4)
16 **Food issues**, such as supporting local farmers, community-supported agriculture, sustainable agriculture, co-ops	❏	❏	❏	❏
17 **Community development**, such as community revitalization, park cleaning, community gardens	❏	❏	❏	❏
18 **Civil rights**, such as helping to promote racial, ethnic, or gender equality	❏	❏	❏	❏
19 **Separation of church and state**	❏	❏	❏	❏
20 **Supporting military troops**	❏	❏	❏	❏
21 **Antiwar**	❏	❏	❏	❏
22 **Supporting gay and lesbian rights**	❏	❏	❏	❏
23 **Supporting heterosexual marriage**	❏	❏	❏	❏
24 **Prolife**	❏	❏	❏	❏
25 **Prochoice**	❏	❏	❏	❏
26 **Political campaigns**, such as supporting political candidates, nonpartisan political groups, and community groups	❏	❏	❏	❏
27 **Disaster relief**, such as humanitarian aid, e.g., for the Haitian or Chilean earthquakes	❏	❏	❏	❏

(continued)

Table A.I.2.a Continued

In the past 12 months . . .	I Gave Money or Possessions (1)	I Gave Time or Volunteered (2)	I Took Any Political Action (3)	Not Applicable (4)
28 **Human rights**, such as domestic and international violations, including torture, political imprisonment, religious freedom, death penalty	❏	❏	❏	❏
29 **Labor issues**	❏	❏	❏	❏
30 **Umbrella charities**, such as United Way, community foundations, thrift stores	❏	❏	❏	❏
31 **Religious**, such as activities that are solely religious and not included in the above activities, such as teaching Sunday school, leading Bible studies, or serving as lay leaders for ministries, including as deacons, elders	❏	❏	❏	❏
32 **Other kind of cause or issue** (SPECIFY)	❏	❏	❏	❏
33 Other (SPECIFY)	❏	❏	❏	❏
34 Other (SPECIFY)	❏	❏	❏	❏
35 Other (SPECIFY)	❏	❏	❏	❏
36 Other (SPECIFY)	❏	❏	❏	❏

Table A.1.2.b Charitable causes grid (financial, volunteering, political action, and none)

✓ Family and neighbors	✓ Refugees	✓ Heterosexual marriage
✓ Health (physical/ mental)	✓ Arts, culture, humanities	✓ Pro-life
✓ Adult education	✓ Animals	✓ Pro-choice
✓ Children and youth	✓ Environment	✓ Political campaigns
✓ Health (physical/ mental)	✓ Food issues	✓ Disaster relief
✓ Poverty	✓ Community development	✓ Human rights
✓ Alcohol and drug abuse	✓ Civil rights	✓ Labor issues
✓ Prisoners	✓ Church-state separation	✓ Umbrella charities
✓ Abused women/ children	✓ Military troops	✓ Religious
✓ Elderly	✓ Antiwar	✓ Other kind of cause (five options)
✓ Immigrant/ migrant	✓ Gay/lesbian rights	

Table A.2.3 Logistic regression of Big 3 giving on demographic characteristics

	Gives Money	Gives Time	Gives Action
Age	0.0174***	−0.00146	0.00947
	(0.00548)	(0.00487)	(0.00600)
Female	0.333**	0.130	−0.318**
	(0.138)	(0.125)	(0.155)
Married	0.359**	0.334**	0.0253
	(0.159)	(0.146)	(0.173)
Youth Household	0.179	0.385**	0.0631
	(0.177)	(0.155)	(0.192)
White, Non-Hispanic	0.455***	0.238	0.0932
	(0.168)	(0.160)	(0.199)
Religiously Attending	0.127	0.948***	0.219
	(0.145)	(0.130)	(0.166)
Republican	−0.295**	−0.102	−0.465***
	(0.145)	(0.128)	(0.164)

(continued)

Table A.2.3 Continued

	Gives Money	Gives Time	Gives Action
College Degree (4 yr)	0.485***	0.962***	0.450**
	(0.164)	(0.148)	(0.180)
Employed	0.0379	0.154	−0.0199
	(0.157)	(0.142)	(0.188)
Household Income	0.0705***	0.0188	0.0420*
	(0.0202)	(0.0191)	(0.0234)
Recession Impacted	−0.394***	−0.0813	−0.190
	(0.144)	(0.138)	(0.168)
Homeowner	0.195	0.0131	−0.348*
	(0.178)	(0.163)	(0.202)
Residential Tenure	−0.00540	0.00247	−0.000915
	(0.00642)	(0.00555)	(0.00724)
Metropolitan Area	0.237	−0.111	−0.0474
	(0.186)	(0.163)	(0.212)
Constant	−2.370***	−2.321***	−2.004***
	(0.405)	(0.366)	(0.437)

Robust standard errors in parentheses   *** $p<0.01$,   ** $p<0.05$,   * $p<0.1$.
Source: Science of Generosity (Herzog and Price 2016).

Table A.2.6 Ordinary least squares regression of amount of Big 3 giving on demographic characteristics

	Amount of Money[1]	Amount of Time	Amount of Action
Age	0.021***	0.008*	0.004
	(0.004)	(0.004)	(0.007)
Female	−0.0886	−0.183*	0.0117
	(0.111)	(0.102)	(0.177)
Married	0.0819	−0.0576	0.1000
	(0.126)	(0.125)	(0.212)
Youth Household	0.152	0.165	−0.255
	(0.140)	(0.120)	(0.228)
White, Non-Hispanic	0.0739	−0.0925	−0.710***
	(0.140)	(0.120)	(0.218)
Religiously Attending	0.708***	0.394***	−0.474***
	(0.118)	(0.103)	(0.161)

Table A.2.6 Continued

	Amount of Money[1]	Amount of Time	Amount of Action
Republican	0.285**	−0.0637	0.178
	(0.121)	(0.105)	(0.176)
College Degree (4 yr)	0.524***	−0.0453	0.174
	(0.122)	(0.109)	(0.198)
Employed	0.0276	−0.151	−0.359
	(0.120)	(0.122)	(0.243)
Household Income	0.0798***	−0.0187	−0.0145
	(0.0178)	(0.0170)	(0.0316)
Recession Impacted	−0.360***	0.0720	0.295
	(0.130)	(0.112)	(0.226)
Homeowner	0.0996	−0.122	−0.256
	(0.150)	(0.131)	(0.244)
Residential Tenure	−0.0114**	−0.00240	0.00793
	(0.00555)	(0.00450)	(0.0110)
Metropolitan Area	−0.0987	−0.361***	0.310
	(0.152)	(0.127)	(0.222)
Constant	3.451***	2.991***	2.073***
	(0.360)	(0.292)	(0.466)

Robust standard errors in parentheses   *** $p<0.01$,   ** $p<0.05$,   * $p<0.1$.
[1] Natural log of dollar amount modeled.
Source: Science of Generosity (Herzog and Price 2016).

Table A.3.3 Questions included in full fsQCA analysis

Q#	Question Wording and Answer Categories	Response Codes
1	When it comes to voluntary financial giving, do you follow regular, structured systems or routines that help you be consistent in your giving? Or do you always only give in a spontaneous or situational way?	
	1. Follow systems or routines	1 →System (or not)
	2. More spontaneous or situational	2 →Spontaneous (or not)
	3. I do not give money away	
2	Have you ever in your life made a conscious decision to give away more of your money to charitable, religious, or other good causes? Or has your financial giving mostly happened without a lot of planning and intention?	

(continued)

Table A.3.3 Continued

Q#	Question Wording and Answer Categories	Response Codes
	1. Have made a conscious decision to give more money away.	1 →Conscious (or not)
		2 →Just happened (or not)
	2. Financial giving has just happened.	
	3. I do not give money for charitable, religious, or other causes.	
3	The following are five different methods by which some people decide how much money to contribute to charitable and religious organizations. Which comes closest to your own approach in deciding how much money to give?	
	1. I do not give money away	2,3 →It depends (or not)
	2. I give spontaneously, depending on the situation	4,5 →Predetermined (or not)
	3. I give whatever it seems like I can afford for a period of time	
	4. I decide on a monthly or annual <u>dollar</u> amount that I give per month or year	
	5. I decide on a <u>percent</u> of my annual income	

For questions 4(a–e) and 5(a–d), all response options were:

　　1. Strongly Agree; 2. Mostly Agree; 3. Slightly Agree; 4. Neither Agree nor Disagree;

　　5. Slightly Disagree; 6. Mostly Disagree; or 7. Strongly Disagree

4 a–e	a. When I give money to what seem to be worthy charitable, religious, or other causes it seems that I never end up finding out what my money actually achieved.
	b. I do what I can to find out from the people or organizations I have given money to exactly what my contributions accomplished.
	c. Finding out what my financial contributions have achieved gives me a warm feeling inside.
	d. I have read reports or newsletters, viewed videos, or heard presentations describing the good things that the money I have donated to charitable, religious, or other causes has helped to accomplish.
	e. I have had the opportunity to see firsthand some of the good things that the money I have donated to charitable, religious, or other causes has helped to accomplish.

All five questions were collapsed into one Informational Scale, such that higher scores indicate higher levels of information about the use of donations and lower scores indicate lower levels of information. Scores at the median of 0.5—hypothetical "neither high nor low"—are recoded to fall on the "high" side of the distribution.

Table A.3.3 Continued

Q#	Question Wording and Answer Categories	Response Codes
5 a–d	a. If I decided to give away more money to charitable, religious, or other good causes than I currently give, I really don't know who I would give it to or exactly how to give it. b. I know how to get information about worthy causes, people, and organizations to which I might potentially be interested in donating money. c. It is pretty obvious to me who could really use financial donations and how to get those donations to them. d. There are so many needy causes, people, and organizations asking for money that it's hard to keep them all straight. *All 4 questions were collapsed into one Options Scale, such that the higher scores indicate higher levels of understanding the need for donations and lower scores indicate lower levels of known options. Scores at the median of 0.5—hypothetical "neither high nor low"—are recoded to fall on the "high" side of the distribution.*	

Source: Science of Generosity Survey, 2010.

Table A.3.4 Participation in forms of generosity by type of giver (in percentages)

	Selective	Planned	Habitual	Impulsive	Atypical
Gives Money	81.0	85.2	87.0	84.5	61.2
Gives Time	45.6	59.3	47.8	35.4	28.3
Gives Political Action	30.4	32.8	13.5	24.5	31.9
Gives Blood	12.8	16.2	12.5	12.2	6.9
Gives Organs	43.2	55.9	45.9	51.2	37.1
Gives Estate	9.2	9.9	4.8	3.6	2.5
Lends Possessions	62.9	61.3	53.3	59.1	44.7
Gives Sustainability	18.0	20.5	10.7	15.4	8.7
Gives Attention—Effort Heavy	61.9	53.4	70.1	53.9	55.4

Source: Science of Generosity (Herzog and Price 2016).

Table A.3.8 Multinomial regression of predicted probability estimates by giver type

	Impulsive	Selective	Planned	Habitual
Northeast	0.001	−0.096	0.073	0.310
	(0.203)	(0.243)	(0.276)	(0.378)
Midwest	−0.017	−0.210	0.123	0.256
	(0.190)	(0.242)	(0.244)	(0.337)
West	−0.093	−0.191	0.180	−0.435
	(0.188)	(0.235)	(0.212)	(0.386)
Age	0.012+	0.011	0.026**	0.021*
	(0.006)	(0.008)	(0.009)	(0.011)
Female	0.324*	0.425*	0.592**	0.373
	(0.163)	(0.186)	(0.203)	(0.239)
Married	−0.258	−0.291	0.088	−0.328
	(0.178)	(0.205)	(0.229)	(0.277)
Youth Household	0.162	−0.003	0.022	0.055
	(0.182)	(0.205)	(0.242)	(0.302)
White, non-Hispanic	−0.008	−0.115	0.305	−0.322
	(0.163)	(0.197)	(0.244)	(0.294)
Religiously Attending	0.137	1.066***	2.490***	1.799***
	(0.174)	(0.210)	(0.198)	(0.275)
Republican	0.138	0.457*	0.709***	0.182
	(0.157)	(0.198)	(0.207)	(0.255)
College Degree (4 yr)	0.656**	0.870***	1.200***	0.842**
	(0.204)	(0.257)	(0.242)	(0.317)
Employed	0.290+	0.210	0.171	−0.113
	(0.171)	(0.229)	(0.219)	(0.273)
Household Income	0.060**	0.071**	0.085**	0.123***
	(0.022)	(0.024)	(0.028)	(0.035)
Recession Impacted	−0.229	−0.523**	−1.047***	0.104
	(0.157)	(0.188)	(0.235)	(0.264)
Homeowner	−0.135	−0.274	−0.088	−0.004
	(0.198)	(0.247)	(0.264)	(0.371)
Residential Tenure	−0.005	−0.004	−0.005	−0.003
	(0.007)	(0.009)	(0.010)	(0.010)
Metropolitan Area	−0.130	0.299	−0.096	−0.433
	(0.199)	(0.228)	(0.242)	(0.299)
Constant	−0.441	−1.855***	−4.429***	−3.926***
	(0.419)	(0.524)	(0.621)	(0.732)

Comparison to atypical giver.

Robust standard errors in parentheses   *** $p<0.01$,   ** $p<0.05$,   * $p<0.1$.

Source: Science of Generosity (Herzog and Price 2016).

Table A.4.1 Survey items included in principal components factor analysis

	Variable Name	Survey Item
*	XITALK	EI1= I am talkative.
*	XIRSERVD	EI2= I am reserved.
*	XIENERGY	EI3= I tend to be full of energy.
*	XIENTHUS	EI4= I generate a lot of enthusiasm.
*	XITRUST	EI5= I am generally trusting.
*	XIASSERT	EI6= I have an assertive personality.
*	XISHY	EI7= I am shy.
*	XIOUTGNG	EI8= I am outgoing.
	SSXPLORE	SS1= I like to explore strange places.
	SSFRIGHT	SS2= I like to do frightening or dangerous things.
	SSBREAK	SS3= I like exciting experiences, even if I break the rules.
	SSFRIEND	SS4= I prefer friends who are exciting and unpredictable.
	SSIMPLSV	SS5= I am an impulsive person.
	CTRLNO	NN1= I have little control over the things that happen to me.
	CTRLME	NN2= What happens to me in the future mostly depends on me.
	CTRLPROB	NN3= There is really no way I can solve some of the problems I have.
	CTRLYES	NN4= I can do just about anything I really set my mind to do.
	CTRLPUSH	NN5= Sometimes I feel that I am being pushed around in life.
	CTRLHELP	NN6= I often feel helpless in dealing with the problems of life.
	FEARCRIT	QQ1= Criticism and scolding hurt me quite a bit.
	FEARANGR	QQ2= I feel worried or upset when I think somebody is angry at me.
	FEARWKUP	QQ3= If I think something unpleasant is going to happen, I get "worked up."
	FEARPOOR	QQ4= I feel worried when I think I have done poorly at something important.
	FEARFRND	QQ5= I have very few fears compared to my friends.
	FEARMSTK	QQ6= I worry about making mistakes.
*	HAPPY	HP1= All in all, how happy or unhappy are you?
*	DEPSAD	D1.1= In last 12 months, felt sad or down.
*	DEPHPLSS	D1.2= In last 12 months, felt hopeless about things.

(continued)

Table A.4.1 Continued

	Variable Name	Survey Item
*	DEPSLEEP	D1.3= In last 12 months, trouble falling asleep or sleep too much.
*	DEPNOINT	D1.4= In last 12 months, little interest or pleasure in doing things.
*	DEPEAT	D1.5= In last 12 months, poor appetite or overeating.
*	DEPTIRED	D1.6= In last 12 months, felt tired, could not get going.
*	DEPHURT	D1.7= In last 12 months, thoughts of hurting yourself or ending your life.
*	DEPDIFF	D2= How difficult are these problems for work, home, or with other people?
	GRWHAPPY	JJ1= I often do not feel interested in working on my personal growth.
	PURPACC	MM1= I don't have a good sense of what I'm trying to accomplish in life.
	PURPGOAL	MM2= My life often lacks clear goals or sense of direction.
*	PURPWNDR	MM3= Some people wander aimlessly, but I am not one of them.
	GTDTIME	KK1= Long amounts of time can go by without me feeling grateful.
*	GTDVRTY	KK2= I am grateful to a wide variety of people.
*	GTDTHANK	KK3= I have so much in life to be thankful for.
*	GTDDONT	KK4= When I look at the world, I don't see much to be grateful for.
*	RAEASY	FF1= It is easy for me to become emotionally close to others.
	RAUNCOMF	FF2= I am uncomfortable getting very close to other people.
*	EMPTEND	YY1= I often have tender, concerned feelings for people less fortunate than me.
*	EMPDONT	YY2= Sometimes I don't feel sorry for others when they are having problems.
*	EMPPROT	YY3= When I see someone being taken advantage of, I feel protective toward them.
*	EMPMISF	YY4= Other people's misfortunes do not usually disturb me a great deal.
	STTRUST	PP1= Generally speaking, most people can be trusted.
	STCAREFL	PP2= You cannot be too careful in dealing with people.

Table A.4.1 Continued

	Variable Name	Survey Item
	STTAKE	PP3= Most people would try to take advantage of you if they got the chance.
	STHELP	PP4= Most of the time people try to be helpful to others.
	STSELF	PP5= People mostly just look out for themselves.
	STNOCARE	PP6= Most people do not really care what happens to the next person.
	SELFEFF	W1= Overall, how much impact do you think you can have on community and politics.
	BLFWLTHY	A3= The wealthy are responsible for giving money to charity.
	BLFXTRA	A4= I only feel responsible when I have extra to give.
	SOLHELP	AA1= People owe it to each other to help take care of each other.
	SOLTAKEC	AA4= Taking care of other people beyond one's own family is an important part of being human.
	SOLFAM	AA5= I feel connected to other people because we are all members of one human family.
	SOLOWE	AA6= People are dependent upon societies, so they owe a lot back to societies in return.
	PERUNHPY	D1= I am unhappy about my financial situation/possessions.
*	PERTHANK	D2= I am thankful for my income/possessions.
	PERWANT	D3= I don't have the kind of money/possessions that I want.
*	PERWORLD	D4= I know I enjoy more material abundance than others in the world.
	MVADMIRE	LLL1= I admire people with expensive homes, cars, and clothes.
	MVHAPPY	LLL2= I would be happier if I could afford to buy more things.
	MVSIMPLE	LLL3= I try to keep my life simple as far as possessions are concerned.
	MVSHOP	LLL4= Shopping and buying things gives me a lot of pleasure.
	MVBUY	LLL5= I buy as many things as my income allows.
	MVRESIST	LLL6= I buy less than I can afford to resist consumerism or to help others.

(*continued*)

Table A.4.1 **Continued**

	Variable Name	Survey Item
	MORLREL	RR1= Morality is relative—there are no definite rights and wrongs for all.
	MORLBRK	RR2= It is okay break rules if you can get away with it.
	MORLABS	RR3= Morality should be based on an absolute, unchanging standard.
	MORNO	RR4= There are no absolute truths about what is right and wrong, good and evil.
*	BLFGOOD	A1= It is good for people to give away to the needy or causes.
*	BLFWRONG	A2= Something wrong with those who spend all money on themselves.
*	BLFMORL2	S6= How morally responsible do you feel to help those in need?
	BBMORE	BB1= I believe that it is more blessed to give than to receive.
	BBEQUAL	BB2= Givers benefit just as much as receivers.
	BBLOSE	BB3= Giving money to needy causes or people means they benefit and you lose.
	ENTHUSM	ENT1= Thinking what my donated money could accomplish doesn't excite me.
	SIDGENME	P5= I would be very unhappy about myself if I thought that I was not a generous person.
	SIDMONEY	P1= When it comes to giving away money, what kind of person do you consider yourself?
	SIDVOL	P2= When it comes to volunteering, what kind of person do you consider yourself?
	SIDREL	P3= In relationships, at being open and hospitable, what kind of person do you consider yourself?
	TRUSTNP	TR1= How much trust for nonprofit organizations to handle your money?
	TRUSTYES	TR4= Most leaders of nonprofits are trustworthy about money.
	TRUSTNO	TR5= There is a lot of waste and fraud by leaders of nonprofits.
	TRUSTNO2	TR6= Nonprofits are less careful with money than for-profits.
	SKRWORRY	O1= I often worry about getting a bad deal or being taken advantage of.

Table A.4.1 Continued

	Variable Name	Survey Item
	SKRTAKE	O2= If you don't look like you know what you're doing, people will take advantage.
	SKRTAKE2	O3= The problem with helping people is that they often take advantage of me.
	SKRNICE	O4= Being nice is just asking to get "suckered."
	PROBLEMS	C1= I have problems/objections about giving money that keep me from giving more.
*	AWRNEEDS	SSS1= I know there are a lot of real needs in the world.
	AWRREMVD	SSS2= The problems of the world seem far removed from my everyday life.
	OPTWHO	F1= If I gave more, I don't know who or how to give it.
*	OPTINFO	F2= I know how to get info about who to give to.
*	OPTOBVS	F3= It is obvious who needs money and how to give to them.
	BENYES	BB1= I have benefited a lot from the love and generosity of other people toward me.
	BENNO	BB2= I have had to take care of myself in life, without help from others.
	BENSTNGY	BB3= Growing up, I found most people around me to be stingy/uncaring.
	BENRAISE	BB4= The people who raised me were loving, caring, generous toward me.
	IFFIND	IF2= I try to find out from people or organizations what my contribution accomplished.
	IFWARM	IF3= Finding out what my contributions achieve gives me a warm feeling inside.
	IFREAD	IF4= I read reports describing the good things my money accomplished.
	IFSEE	IF5= I have seen firsthand good things my money has helped accomplish.
*	REINFRCE	N1= I have felt great about the good my donations have has done.

* Reverse coded answers.

Source: Science of Generosity, 2010.

Table A.4.2.a Factor loadings of 25 representative items on seven principal component factors

LABELS	MEASURES	Factor 1 Social Solidarity	Factor 2 Life Purpose	Factor 3 Collective Conscious	Factor 4 Social Trust	Factor 5 Prosperity Outlook	Factor 6 Acquisition Seeking	Factor 7 Social Responsibility	Uniqueness
Personality and Well-Being									
Talkative	I am talkative.	0.3868	0.1084	-0.0634	0.075	0.0892	0.4805	-0.1047	0.5792
Risk-Taker	I like exciting experiences, even if I break the rules.	0.0294	-0.015	-0.102	-0.1007	-0.0337	0.7196	0.0952	0.4504
Intrinsic-Control	What happens to me in the future mostly depends on me.	0.2253	0.3612	-0.0785	-0.2047	0.2173	0.0414	-0.0942	0.7129
Goal-Directed	My life often lacks clear goals or sense of direction.	0.1569	0.7319	0.1483	0.1134	0.006	-0.0182	0.0494	0.4021
Anxious	I feel worried or upset when I think somebody is angry at me.	0.3176	-0.6498	0.0632	0.0658	0.1121	0.0548	-0.0166	0.4527
Depressed	In last 12 months, how often have you felt sad or down.	-0.0104	-0.7357	0.0175	-0.2191	-0.0345	0.0094	-0.0227	0.4085

Social Connectedness

Attachment	It is easy for me to become emotionally close to others.	0.6527	0.0048	0.0744	0.109	-0.0567	0.242	-0.0363	0.4934
Empathy	Other people's misfortunes do not usually disturb me a great deal.	0.694	-0.1101	0.0894	0.0901	0.0398	-0.3063	0.0262	0.394
Connected	I feel connected to other people because we are all members of one human family.	0.5266	-0.0108	0.417	0.0302	0.0357	0.0529	0.0304	0.5429
Hospitality	In relationships, at being open and hospitable, what kind of person do you consider yourself to be?	0.555	0.1587	-0.0881	-0.1092	0.1368	0.0417	-0.0206	0.6262

Values and Morals

Materialism	I admire people with expensive homes, cars, and clothes.	0.1721	0.2134	-0.1914	0.0215	-0.0586	-0.5375	0.2503	0.5328
Consumerism	I buy less than I can afford to resist consumerism or to help others.	-0.0411	-0.0839	-0.3581	0.3402	-0.0271	0.008	-0.445	0.5485

(continued)

Table A.4.2.a Continued

LABELS	MEASURES	Factor 1	Factor 2	Factor 3	Factor 4	Factor 5	Factor 6	Factor 7	Uniqueness
Relativism	Morality is relative—there are no definite rights and wrongs for all.	−0.0811	−0.0733	0.2256	−0.0142	−0.5012	0.3746	−0.3283	0.4377
Outlooks									
Nonselfish	People mostly just look out for themselves.	0.0943	0.1989	0.0487	0.6378	0.0007	−0.123	0.0889	0.5193
Abundance	I know I enjoy more material abundance than others in the world.	0.0049	−0.0437	0.0436	0.1214	0.7925	0.0703	0.0044	0.3485
Care Ethos	Growing up, I found most people around me to be stingy/uncaring.	0.1773	0.1006	−0.0345	0.5814	0.2821	−0.0564	0.1227	0.5214
Grateful	I am grateful to a wide variety of people.	0.4559	0.1648	0.0541	0.0937	0.2152	0.26	0.114	0.6264

Generosity Orientations

Obligation	I only feel responsible when I have extra to give.	-0.0202	0.0636	-0.0357	0.1139	0.0665	-0.0627	0.7543	0.404
Beneficial	Givers benefit just as much as receivers.	0.3649	-0.1088	0.4105	-0.0227	0.4077	-0.1348	0.1174	0.4878
Trustworthy	Most leaders of non-profits are trustworthy about money.	0.0875	-0.0879	0.5164	0.393	0.1176	0.0438	0.0015	0.5478
Unwary	I often worry about getting a bad deal or being taken advantage of.	0.0553	-0.3461	-0.028	-0.546	-0.0062	-0.0378	-0.2026	0.5357
Objectionless	I have problems/objections about giving money that keep me from giving more.	0.0221	-0.0374	0.1614	0.1851	-0.023	0.0773	0.6072	0.5626
Aware	It is obvious who needs money and how to give to them.	0.0978	0.068	0.4536	-0.0975	0.4852	-0.0011	-0.0888	0.5273
Informed	I read reports describing the good things my money accomplished.	0.0556	0.1158	0.7057	-0.0039	-0.0396	-0.034	0.0684	0.478

Source: Science of Generosity (Herzog and Price, 2016).

Table A.4.2.b Regression analyses of social psychological factors on financial giving

	Gives Money[1]	Giving Amount[2]
Social Solidarity	0.322***	0.0923
	(0.0828)	(0.0663)
Life Purpose	0.0810	0.150**
	(0.0850)	(0.0591)
Collective Conscious	0.319***	0.234***
	(0.0825)	(0.0637)
Social Trust	0.0189	-0.0307
	(0.0830)	(0.0561)
Prosperity Outlook	0.731***	0.222***
	(0.0883)	(0.0633)
Acquisition Seeking	-0.352***	-0.0395
	(0.0885)	(0.0608)
Social Responsibility	0.207**	0.227***
	(0.0858)	(0.0467)

[1] Logistic regression.
[2] Ordinary least squares regression.

Robust standard errors in parentheses *** p<0.01, ** p<0.05, * p<0.1.
Source: Science of Generosity (Herzog and Price 2016).
Controlling for age, gender, race/ethnicity, education level, income, employment, marital status, having youth in household, political affiliation, religious attendance, homeownership, residential tenure, metropolitan area, national region, and impact of the recession.

Table A.4.3 Multinomial regression analyses of social psychological factors on financial giving

	Impulsive	Selective	Planned	Habitual
Social Solidarity	0.347***	0.651***	0.428***	0.133
	(0.122)	(0.148)	(0.151)	(0.179)
Life Purpose	-0.0349	0.0689	-0.114	-0.0206
	(0.135)	(0.161)	(0.178)	(0.188)
Collective Conscious	0.179	0.405***	0.751***	0.199
	(0.112)	(0.138)	(0.149)	(0.223)
Social Trust	0.366***	0.312**	0.485***	0.515***
	(0.116)	(0.143)	(0.164)	(0.183)
Prosperity Outlook	0.575***	0.744***	0.811***	0.530***
	(0.131)	(0.159)	(0.175)	(0.185)

Table A.4.3 Continued

	Impulsive	Selective	Planned	Habitual
Acquisition Seeking	−0.331**	−0.141	−0.689***	−0.179
	(0.136)	(0.153)	(0.171)	(0.187)
Social Responsibility	0.144	0.492***	0.844***	0.661***
	(0.133)	(0.146)	(0.160)	(0.175)

Comparison to atypical giver.

Robust standard errors in parentheses *** p<0.01, ** p<0.05, * p<0.1.

Source: Science of Generosity (Herzog and Price 2016).

Controlling for age, gender, race/ethnicity, education level, income, employment, marital status, having youth in household, political affiliation, religious attendance, homeownership, residential tenure, metropolitan area, national region, and impact of the recession.

Table A.4.5 Regression analyses of social psychological factors on generous self-identity

	Generous Self-Identity[1]
Social Solidarity	0.684***
	(0.0369)
Life Purpose	0.017
	(0.041)
Collective Conscious	0.272***
	(0.416)
Social Trust	0.041
	(0.405)
Prosperity Outlook	0.243***
	(0.044)
Acquisition Seeking	0.086
	(0.046)
Social Responsibility	0.129**
	(0.041)

[1] Ordinary least squares regression.

Robust standard errors in parentheses *** p<0.01, ** p<0.05, * p<0.1.

Source: Science of Generosity (Herzog and Price 2016).

Controlling for age, gender, race/ethnicity, education level, income, employment, marital status, having youth in household, political affiliation, religious attendance, homeownership, residential tenure, metropolitan area, national region, and impact of the recession.

Table A.5.11 Donation amounts by generosity self-identity

	Giving Amount[1]
Generous Self-Identity	0.103**
	(0.035)
Friend Givers	0.101**
	(0.034)
Local Community Giving	0.177**
	(0.056)
Life Purpose	0.026**
	(0.010)
Prosperity Outlook	0.025*
	(0.010)
Social Responsibility	0.026**
	(0.008)
West	0.070**
	(0.026)
Age	0.003***
	(0.001)
Republican	0.040*
	(0.0202)
College Degree	0.053*
	(0.021)
Income	0.008**
	(0.003)
Recession	0.059**
	(0.022)

[1] Ordinary least squares regression, natural log of dollar amount modeled.

Robust standard errors in parentheses *** p<0.01, ** p<0.05, * p<0.1.

Source: Science of Generosity (Herzog and Price 2016).

Controlling for other (nonsignificant) web of affiliations and social orientations, age, gender, race/ethnicity, education level, income, employment, marital status, having youth in household, political affiliation, religious attendance, homeownership, residential tenure, metropolitan area, national region, and impact of the recession.

Table A.5.12 Multinomial regression analyses of sociorelational factors and social orientations on financial giving

	Impulsive	Selective	Planned	Habitual
Friend Givers	0.86	0.614	0.424	−0.270
	(0.434)	(0.493)	(0.556)	(0.644)
Local Community Giving	2.609**	1.666	2.323**	1.796*
	(0.798)	(0.885)	(0.960)	(1.039)
National Giving	−1.977*	−0.485	−1.344	-0.581
	(0.720)	(0.850)	(0.885)	(1.023)
Social Solidarity	0.328*	0.498**	0.308	−0.153
	(0.168)	(0.188)	(0.204)	(0.240)
Collective Conscious	0.117	0.345*	0.629***	−0.093
	(0.161)	(0.182)	(0.192)	(0.268)
Social Trust	0.414*	0.316*	0.515**	0.625**
	(0.143)	(0.165)	(0.189)	(0.204)
Prosperity Outlook	0.6415***	0.774***	0.990***	0.596***
	(0.169)	(0.192)	(0.206)	(0.216)
Acquisition Seeking	−0.462**	−0.28	−0.774***	-0.311
	(0.169)	(0.184)	(0.195)	(0.219)
Social Responsibility	0.221	0.435**	0.833***	0.685***
	(0.167)	(0.179)	(0.203)	(0.204)

Comparison to atypical giver.

Robust standard errors in parentheses   *** p<0.01,   ** p<0.05,   * p<0.1.

Source: Science of Generosity (Herzog and Price 2016).

Controlling for other (nonsignificant) web of affiliations and social orientations, age, gender, race/ethnicity, education level, income, employment, marital status, having youth in household, political affiliation, religious attendance, homeownership, residential tenure, metropolitan area, national region, and impact of the recession.

Notes

1. René Bekkers and Pamala Wiepking, "Generosity and Philanthropy: A Literature Review," *Science of Generosity Initiative*, 2007. Retrieved from: http://generosity-research.nd.edu/assets/17632/generosity_and_philanthropy_final.pdf.
2. Ibid., 3.
3. Ibid., 42.
4. Jessica L. Collett and Christopher A. Morrissey, "The Social Psychology of Generosity: The State of Current Interdisciplinary Research," *Science of Generosity Initiative*, 2007: 29. Retrieved from: http://generosityresearch.nd.edu/assets/17634/social_psychology_of_generosity_final.pdf.
5. Ryan Lincoln, Christopher A. Morrissey, and Peter Mundey, "Religious Giving: A Literature Review." *Science of Generosity Initiative*, 2007: 35. Retrieved from: http://generosityresearch.nd.edu/assets/20447/religious_giving_final.pdf.
6. It is worth noting that the Science of Generosity study was conducted in 2010, two years after the financial recession of 2008. This means that, if anything, the results of this study may underrepresent generosity participation during nonrecession years. However, in the nationally representative survey we asked respondents to rate how "hard hit" they were by the recession, and we included this as a control measure throughout all the statistical models in this book. Thus we think the giving patterns here still generally reflect the state of generosity in America, net of the impact of the recession. Likewise during our in-depth interviews we rarely heard accounts of the recession being associated with lower giving participation or changes in giving rates. In some cases we heard that people were *more* involved as a result of seeing others in need. But the majority of interviewees seemed to recount fairly stable giving patterns pre- and postrecession, again indicating the longer term generalizability of this book's findings.

Nevertheless it remains important to replicate the generosity study undertaken here, providing cross-sectional snapshots over time, in order to assess changes during nonrecession years.

7. The 2010 Science of Generosity Survey is a cross-sectional survey of a representative sample of adults aged 23 and older who live in US households. The survey was conducted by Knowledge Networks, Inc. of Menlo Park, California. The survey sample was selected from Knowledge Networks' larger, national KnowledgePanel sample of respondents. Prospective respondents were offered an incentive of $10 per month to complete surveys on the Internet each month for the next 21 months. Households that did not have Internet access were provided a laptop computer and Internet access; in addition survey case managers provided telephone support for all technically challenged households that needed help connecting their computer to the Internet and accessing their email and Internet surveys.

   Before completing the Science of Generosity Survey, respondents completed an online "personal profile" survey consisting primarily of questions about their demographic characteristics, as well as a "financial affairs" survey and a "public affairs" survey containing questions about household financial and budgetary conditions and practices and civic and political behaviors and attitudes. Sampled respondents completed the Science of Generosity Survey over the Internet between May 19, 2010, and June 2, 2010. The final sample size was 1,997 respondents with a completion rate of 65.2 percent.

   For more detailed information on the Science of Generosity Survey procedures, see Christian Smith, Patricia Snell Herzog, and Kraig Beyerlein, "Methods Report and User's Guide for the 2010 Science of Generosity Survey," unpublished paper, University of Notre Dame, 2010. Retrievable from: http://goo.gl/n6ExEX.

8. Random sampling was done with a combination of random-digit dial (RDD) and address-based sampling (ABS). For more detailed information on the Science of Generosity Survey procedures, see Smith et al., "Methods Report and User's Guide."

9. The demographics of survey respondents were compared to national demographics to assess the representativeness of the survey sample. Results are reported in Figure I.1. In addition base and poststratification statistical weights were employed to account for sample design and demographic differences. Statistical weighting was based on a raking procedure on a base weight that accounted for study design and a poststratification weight that accounted for discrepancies in national demographic characteristics, including gender, age, race/ethnicity, education, Internet access (since the survey was conducted online), region, metropolitan area, volunteering level (to account for volunteers' potentially higher likelihood of completing the survey), and nonrespondent status (since we had demographic data on panel participants who did not respond to our request to

complete the survey). For more detailed information on the Science of Generosity Survey procedures, see Smith et al., "Methods Report and User's Guide."

10. All respondent addresses were geocoded and merged with US Census tract-level composition data. The geographic locations of all of the households of residence of the survey respondents were coded with Geographic Information Systems (GIS) geocodes to enable spatial data to be linked to survey responses. Marketing Systems Group was subcontracted by Knowledge Networks to geocode the addresses of all sample members. Linear interpolation is used to maintain confidential security of the exact respondent household location and instead estimate the geocode location for each sampled household. Each household is assigned to a particular location on the street based on the assumed equidistance from the even number on one end of the street and the odd number on the other end. The main advantage of this method and the use of a subcontractor in this situation is that it maintains a very high level of confidentiality around the respondents' exact household location. Using these geocodes, Census Federal Information Processing Standards (FIPS) codes were assigned at the block group and tract levels. All neighborhood data presented in this book draw upon the tract-level census data.

11. In-person interviews were conducted with sampled survey respondents and, if applicable, their spouse or live-in partner. Five hundred twenty-five survey respondents lived in the 12 states selected for interviews. This geographical sample base was used as the pool from which to select potential interviewees based on various survey and contextual measures, in order to ensure a stratified quota sample across different characteristics of interest, described below. A total of 51 survey respondents were selected from this broader sample to complete in-person interviews, of which 40 agreed, for a response rate of 78 percent. Of the 40 survey respondents, 22 had a spouse or live-in partner who was also interviewed, making the overall interview sample of 62 interviewees in 40 households. Because the interview respondents were selected from the broader pool of survey respondents, we have demographic information and survey responses for all those selected for interviews who were not able to complete interviews. To conduct the interviews, interviewers met with respondents in their households to complete two separate halves of the full interview for an average of two hours per half, or an average of four hours of interviewing total per participating household respondent.

The sampling process for selecting potential interviewees consisted of (1) selected geographic locations, (2) household and family characteristics, (3) variation in participation in generous activities and (4) variation in neighborhood contextual characteristics. Interview respondents were selected from different locations around the United States to generally represent the major geographical areas of Northeast/East Coast, Midwest, South/Southeast, Southwest, and West/West Coast. The states selected from the Northeast and East Coast were Massachusetts, Maryland, and Washington, DC. Midwestern states were Illinois, Michigan, and Indiana. The southern and southeastern states were Georgia and North Carolina. Southwestern states were Texas and Arizona. The states from the West and West Coast were California, Washington, and Oregon.

12. All interviewer observations—of interviewees, households, and neighborhoods—were collected upon completion of the interview through an online form that included one structured and one semistructured question on the neighborhoods, as well as spaces for open-ended observations. The one structured question on the neighborhood regarded interviewer rankings of the degree of disorder observed in the neighborhood. The ranking of neighborhood disorder was as follows: no disrepair, very little disrepair, some spotty disrepair, and disrepair. The semistructured neighborhood question asked interviewers to observe what sorts of buildings were in the area, other than homes. Examples include schools, businesses, retail stores, apartment complexes, banks, restaurants, gas stations, churches, doctors' offices, parks. Open-ended spaces for notes requested the interviewees fill out and enter notes on the interviewee (primary and spouse or live-in partner), household (including children present and information about the style of house, belongings, and so on), and neighborhood (including information regarding the level of disrepair, relative socioeconomic status, racial and ethnic composition, types of buildings nearby, and relative safety). The compiled notes from these observations total more than 500 single-spaced typed pages.

13. See, for example, Christian Smith, *What Is a Person? Rethinking Humanity, Social Life, and the Moral Good from the Person Up* (New York: Oxford University Press, 2011); Douglas Porpora, "Sociology's Causal Confusion," in *Revitalizing Causality: Realism about Causality in Philosophy and Social Science*, edited by Ruth Groff (New York: Routledge, 2007); Roy Bhaskar, *A Realist Concept of Science* (New York: Routledge, 2008); Margaret Archer, *Culture and Agency* (New York: Cambridge University Press, 1996).

14. See, for example, Christian Smith and Hilary Davidson, *The Paradox of Generosity: Giving We Receive, Grasping We Lose* (New York: Oxford University Press, 2014); J. A. Zoltan, *Why Philanthropy Matters: How the Wealthy Give, and What It Means for Our Economic Well-Being* (Princeton, NJ: Princeton University Press, 2013); Patricia Illingworth, Thomas Pogge, and Leif Wenar, eds., *Giving Well: The Ethics of Philanthropy* (New York: Oxford University Press, 2010); Robert L. Paton and Michael P. Moody, *Understanding Philanthropy: Its Meaning and Mission* (Bloomington: Indiana University Press, 2008).

15. See, for example, Alexis de Tocqueville, *Democracy in America* (New York: Penguin Classics, 2003); Robert D. Putnam, *Bowling Alone: The Collapse and Revival of American Community* (New York: Simon & Schuster, 2001).

16. See, for example, Joseph D. Lewandowski, "Capitalising Sociability: Rethinking the Theory of Social Capital," in *Assessing Social Capital: Concept, Policy and Practice*, edited by Rosalind Edwards, Jane Franklin, and Janet Holland (Cambridge: Cambridge Scholars Publishing, 2012); Edward J. O'Boyle, "Requiem for Homo Economicus," *Journal of Markets & Morality* 10, no. 2 (2007): 321–337.

17. See, for example, Peter M. Blau, *Structural Contexts of Opportunities* (Chicago: University of Chicago Press, 1994); Peter M. Blau, *Inequality and Heterogeneity* (New York: Free Press, 1977); John B. Cullen, Kenneth S. Anderson, and Douglas D. Baker, "Blau's Theory of Structural Differentiation Revisited: A Theory of Structural Change or Scale?" *Academy of Management Journal* 29, no. 2 (1986): 203–229.

18. See, for example, Patricia Hill Collins, *Distinguishing Features of Black Feminist Thought* (New York: Routledge, 2008); Jörg Rössel and Randall Collins, "Conflict Theory and Interaction Rituals: The Microfoundations of Conflict Theory," in *Handbook of Sociological Theory*, edited by Jonathan H. Turner (New York: Springer, 2002); Mary R. Jackman, *The Velvet Glove: Paternalism and Conflict in Gender, Class, and Race Relations* (Berkeley: University of California Press, 1994).

19. See, for example, Colin Woodward, *American Nations: A History of the Eleven Rival Regional Cultures of North America* (New York: Penguin, 2012); Shalom H. Schwartz and Anat Bardi, "Value Hierarchies across Cultures: Taking a Similarities Perspective," *Journal of Cross Cultural Psychology* 32, no. 3 (2001): 268–290; Robert Morse Crunden, *A Brief History of American Culture* (St. Paul, MN: Paragon House, 1996).

20. See, for example, Jeremy D. Safran, *Psychoanalysis and Psychoanalytic Therapies* (New York: American Psychological Association, 2012); Michelle G. Craske, *Cognitive-Behavioral Therapy* (New York: American Psychological Association, 2010); Stephen K. Reed, *Cognition: Theories and Application* (Boston: Cengage Learning, 2009).

21. See, for example, Pierre Bourdieu, *The Logic of Practice* (Stanford: Stanford University Press, 1992); Pierre Bourdieu, *Outline of a Theory of Practice* (New York: Cambridge University Press, 1977).

22. See, for example, Max Weber and Toby E. Huff, *Max Weber and The Methodology of the Social Science* (Piscataway, NJ: Transaction Publishers, 1983); Tore Lindebeck, "The Weberian Ideal-Type: Development and Continuities," *Acta Sociologica* 35, no. 4 (1992): 285–297.

23. See, for example, Alex Gillespie, *Becoming Other: From Social Interaction to Self-Reflection* (Charlotte, NC: Information Age, 2006); William L. Cook and Emily M. Douglas, "The Looking Glass Self in Family Context: A Social Relations Analysis," *Journal of Family Psychology* 12, no. 3 (1998): 299–309; Herbert Blumer, *Symbolic Interactionism: Perspective and Method* (Berkeley: University of California Press, 1986); George Herbert Mead, "The Objective Reality of Perspectives," in

Proceedings of the Sixth International Congress of Philosophy, edited by Edgar S. Brightman (New York: 1926), 75–85; Charles H. Cooley, *Human Nature and the Social Order* (New York: Charles Scribner's Sons, 1929); Emile Durkheim, *The Division of Labor in Society* (New York: Free Press, 1984); Karl Marx, *Capital, Volume 1* (New York: International, 1987); Max Weber, *Economy and Society* (Berkeley: University of California Press, 1978).

24. See, for example, Bernice Pescosolido and Beth A. Rubin, "The Web of Group Affiliations Revisited: Social Life, Postmodernism, and Sociology," *American Sociological Review* 65 (2000): 52–76; David Frisby and Mike Featherstone, eds., *Simmel on Culture: Selected Writings* (Thousand Oaks, CA: Sage, 1997); Donald, Levine, ed., *Georg Simmel: On Individuality and Social Forms* (Chicago: University of Chicago Press, 1971); Georg Simmel, *Conflict and the Web of Group Affiliations* (New York: Free Press, 1964).

CASE STUDY INTRODUCTIONS

1. All names are pseudonyms to protect the confidentiality of our respondents.

CHAPTER 1

1. See, for example, Science of Generosity Initiative, "What Is Generosity?" Retrieved from: http://generosityresearch.nd.edu/more-about-the-initiative/what-is-generosity/.

2. Spending time taking political action on behalf of a political campaign is included as one of the charitable causes in our survey. However, respondents could perceive their activities with political campaigns more as volunteering than political action. If that is the case, their generosity would have been recorded as volunteering for a political campaign cause, not as a political action. Political action does not include voting since that is not directed toward a charitable cause.

3. All survey respondents were given this prompt: "The following is a list of causes or issues that people sometimes donate money, possessions, time or volunteer work (not for pay), or engage in political activities to support. They may be religious or not religious, faith-based or secular—including held in a religious congregation." They were then asked, "Which, if any, of the following have you supported in the last 12 months through giving money, time, possessions, or by taking political action of any kind? Check all that apply. If the cause or issue is not something that you have been involved in, check 'Not Applicable.'" This text was followed by a grid which asked survey respondents to check whether in the past 12 months they (a) gave money or possessions, (b) gave time or volunteered, (c) took political action, or (d) not applicable for each of the 31 listed charitable

causes. The grid also included five empty spaces for other causes respondents could specify. The 31 charitable causes are listed in Appendix Table A.1.2.b.

4. Since financial contributions are often calculated as a full year for tax-deduction reasons, we asked about financial contributions using a 12-month time frame.

5. Since people do not typically calculate a full year of volunteer and political action hours, we instead asked them to report their time given during the past month.

6. For the purposes of this book, we calculated these measures by summing the columns in the charitable cause grid in Appendix Table A.1.2.a in order to compute the total amount of money or time given to any of the 31 charitable causes, for each of the three forms of generosity. Respondent financial giving represents the combined dollar amounts that they donated to *any* of the charitable causes under the giving money or possessions column in the past year. Volunteering and political action represent the combined amount of time given for causes in the past month. Thus, this aggregation method provides participation total for Big 3 giving across a range of charitable causes.

7. This includes the 39 percent of Americans who specifically entered zero dollars and another 6 percent who said they did not know a dollar amount for their donations. Fewer than 6 percent indicated that they gave time or money to causes for which they then entered in the past year or 0 hours given in the past month. This could be explained by respondents checking activities to which they had given in the past and to which they may still feel committed – despite not having given money to them during the past year. It is also possible that some of these respondents had given some money during the past year but did not keep track of or remember the exact dollar amount. Thus Figure 1.1 shows minor discrepancies between whether or not people gave money to charitable causes and the amount they reported giving to charitable causes in the previous year.

8. Poverty status is defined according to the Department of Health and Human Services poverty thresholds by household size in 2010. About 15 percent of Americans were in poverty in 2010, according to this standard, and about 13 percent of the weighted Science of Generosity sample.

9. Annual household income was asked through a series of questions that assessed income ranges in the following categories: less than $5,000, $5,000 to $7,499, $7,500 to $9,999, $10,000 to $12,499, $12,500 to $14,999, $15,000 to $19,999, $20,000 to $24,999, $25,000 to $29,999, $30,000 to $34,999, $35,000 to $39,999, $40,000 to $49,999, $50,000 to $59,999, $60,000 to $74,999, $75,000 to $84,999, $85,000 to $99,999, $100,000 to $124,999, $125,000 to $149,999, $150,000 to $174,999, and $175,000 or more. In order to estimate giving as a percentage of income, we divided the dollar amounts given per year by the midpoint of these annual household income ranges.

10. Here we analyze responses to the same questions about charitable causes but focus on respondents who recorded that they gave time or volunteered for a charitable cause. We asked those who said they did volunteer to estimate the number of hours they volunteered in the past month. Three percent of respondents said that they volunteered in the past year but recorded no volunteering hours in the past month. For the volunteering and political action measures, this minor discrepancy could be explained by the difference in the initial question asking for activities in the past year and the hour estimate being for time spent during the past month.

A number of respondents reported volunteering hours that exceed the amount of waking hours available in a month. We thus resurveyed the 94 respondents (4.7 percent of our sample) whose hours tallied to more than 500 hours (i.e., those exceeding a reasonable number of hours possibly available to volunteer within a month). In the resurvey we provided respondents with their previously reported total, along with the total number of available waking hours, and then asked them to confirm whether their response was correct or not and why. If not correct, we asked them to update their total and provide an explanation. We kept the initial responses of eight of the cases based on the respondents' explanation of why their previous answer was correct. The responses for the remaining 86 cases were updated. Most of these were due to interpreting the question as asking about number of volunteering hours in the past year rather than past month, so they simply divided their initial response by 12. In other cases respondents had inadvertently counted working hours, despite the question specifying to count only nonworking hours. Thus in 4.3 percent of cases, the revised number of hours was accepted as the correct amount of hours given.

11. Figure 1.5 displays a chart showing the combination between the initial measure of whether or not people volunteered for charitable causes in the past year and the amount of time they reported volunteering for charitable causes in the past month.

12. The estimate of the amount of hours that people have available in a given month is calculated by taking the number of waking hours in a month (i.e., 24 hours per day minus eight hours of sleep or rest for 30 days) and subtracting a rough estimate of the amount of hours spent working by combining working and schooling status into a somewhat crude categorical measure of 480 available hours for nonworking people, 390 available hours for part-time workers and students, and 300 available hours for full-time workers and students. Clearly this ignores the great potential variability across actual number of hours spent working or in school and thus should be taken to be a mere approximation in lieu of a more finely grained measure involving an exact calculation of hours spent on each activity, which this initial analysis indicates the importance of investigating in future studies.

13. The wording for the shopping question was this: "About how many hours per week on average do you spend shopping for non-essential goods (not food or

essential clothes) during an average week?" The leisure time questions inquired how much time respondents had spent doing each activity during the past week, while the volunteering and political action activities were assessed with respondents tallying the amount of time they spent on each cause during the past month. In order to compare the question sets, we multiplied respondents' weekly leisure hours by 4.5 to get their estimated monthly average.

14. These percentages are an approximation and should not be interpreted as precise.

15. Figure 1.9 displays a chart combining the initial measure of whether or not people took political action for charitable causes in the past year and the amount of time they reported taking political action for charitable causes in the past month.

16. In terms of political action, Americans in poverty were slightly less politically involved than others (8 percent of the poor vs. 14 percent of the nonpoor). However, there is not much difference between the two groups since nearly no one was politically active within the past month. When we examine political action hours by time availability status, Americans who are the least able give the least time to political action, and retired, nonelderly Americans give the most. However, only 16 percent of retired, nonelderly people gave any time (even one hour) to political action in the past month. And the amounts of time given are hardly different among full-time or part-time workers and students and the unemployed. Comparing political time donated to leisure hours (time spent on watching TV, surfing the Internet, and shopping), 95 percent of Americans spend at least twice as much time on leisure as on political action in the past month.

17. For additional information on relational giving, or interpersonal generosity, see Christian Smith and Jonathan P. Hill, "Toward the Measurement of Interpersonal Generosity (IG): An IG Scale Conceptualized, Tested, and Validated," 2009. Retrieved from: https://generosityresearch.nd.edu/assets/13798/ig_paper_smith_hill_rev.pdf.

18. The measure of relational giving represents the composite participation in any of these forms of relational giving with a frequency of more than a few times a year.

19. Joel Osteen is a well-known televangelist and pastor of one of the largest Protestant churches in the United States, Lakewood in Houston, Texas.

20. Although many mainstream data sources on volunteering specifically ask respondents to think of their time-giving activities as only those done through an organization (e.g., Volunteering America), the Science of Generosity Survey asked respondents to report their money, time, and action contributions per cause and then followed up to ask whether the contributions were done through an organization. We consider this to be a way of operationalizing structured and unstructured giving that other studies do not often measure. We are therefore able to assess this question directly within the Big 3 giving analyses.

Proportion of *unstructured giving* among the Big 3 forms of giving

- Donating money, not through an organization: 34.9 percent
- Volunteering, not through an organization: 52.7 percent
- Taking political action, not through an organization: 45.7 percent

While it may be surprising to learn that more than half of volunteering efforts are unstructured, it is important to keep in mind that the Science of Generosity Survey asked respondents about giving for such causes as family, neighbors, prisoners, abused women, and the elderly. This allowed respondents to record informal activities in which they give time to people they know, or even those they do not, in times that are not structured by formal organizational participation.

In the next set of analyses we examine the proportion of structured and unstructured giving across different kinds of charitable causes and report findings for each of the Big 3:

Giving money

- Giving money is mostly structured; that is, given through organizations.
- Only cause that is mostly unstructured for giving money is family and neighbors (78 percent unstructured).

Causes that balance 30 to 70 percent of structured and unstructured monetary giving are adult education, children and youth, homelessness, prisoners, elderly, immigration, arts/culture, environmental, food issues, community development, separation of church and state, military troops, antiwar, heterosexual marriage, and religious causes.

Volunteering

- At least 30 percent of all volunteering causes are done in an unstructured manner.
- More than 70 percent of unstructured, nonorganizational volunteering occurs for family and neighbors, prisoners, and elderly causes.

Political action

- In general, political action is balanced between structured and unstructured giving.
- For all causes, except adult education and pro-life causes, at least 30 percent of all political action is unstructured.
- No political action cause is more than 70 percent unstructured.

Though we find that a large proportion of generous activities are unstructured, this does not necessarily mean that they are unplanned or spontaneous. These activities could, for instance, involve a repeated loan to a friend or a regular monthly visit to an elderly home by a family member. Combining the relationship of structured and unstructured giving to the giver types, across all nine forms of generosity, we find that 47.53 percent of respondents participated in a structured form of Little 6 giving, while 90.64 percent participated in an unstructured form. Relating the two to each other for each respondent, we find that only 7.23 percent of respondents perform neither unstructured nor structured forms of Little 6 giving. There are 44.39 percent who perform an unstructured form without performing a structured form and only 2.14 percent who perform a structured form without performing an unstructured one. The most common is for the 46.24 percent who perform both an unstructured and a structured form. Thus the vast majority (90.63 percent combined) either do both structured or unstructured Little 6 giving or only unstructured Little 6 giving. This indicates that unstructured giving is an important aspect of the non–Big 3 giving story, as Americans are extremely unlikely to participate in structured forms of Little 6 giving.

CHAPTER 2

1. Of the 10 percent who do not give through any of these forms, 20 percent have a physical condition that prevents them from giving blood or do not have a will. However, since they could still contribute through one of the other seven forms of generosity, these Americans are still considered part of the 10 percent who do not give through any of these nine forms of generosity.

2. The bars of the chart represent the percentage of Americans participating in each generosity form that hold the social status characteristic represented (e.g., female, white). For instance, women account for nearly 54 percent of financial givers, 52 percent of volunteers, and 45 percent of political activists. The black lines on the chart represent the average among all Americans with that characteristic, such as 51 percent of American adults are women.

3. For the purpose of these analyses, regular religious attendees are considered to be people who attend religious services monthly or more often.

4. Regressions are logistic or ordinary least squares (OLS) models.

5. All models analyze weighted data. Only statistically significant results are displayed as bars on the figure. All coefficients are standardized to compare relative sizes of characteristics. See Appendix Table A.2.3 for full details.

6. This is a continuous measure, meaning income represents a gradient rather than a dichotomous indication of high- compared to low-income earners.

7. See Appendix Table A.2.6 for full details.

8. For modeling purposes, the total of yearly donations is logged.

9. This is a continuous measure, meaning age represents a gradient rather than a dichotomous indication of older compared to younger Americans.

10. This is a continuous measure, meaning income represents a gradient rather than a dichotomous indication of high- compared to low-income earners.

11. We undertake an analysis of regional generosity patterns for two primary reasons. One is that, theoretically, we are interested in the wide-angle view of American generosity and here examine the broad patterns of regional giving rather than the more nitty-gritty state-to-state comparisons. We also think cultural norms and values are more likely to be concentrated in general regions than isolated in certain states. Methodologically, the other reason is that this

data set is not designed for a state-to-state comparison, while regional analysis smoothes state-to-state sample size variations.

State-level analyses are common in media and policy outlets, and thus we add a note here for readers interested in comparing the results of these regional analyses to other geographic-based giving data sources: Justin Myers, Anu Narayanswamy, and Soo Oh, "How America Gives," *Chronicle of Philanthropy*, n.d. Retrieved from: http://philanthropy.com/article/Interactive-Explore-How/149107/#search. Giving USA website: http://givingusareports.org/. "Volunteer Rates," Corporation for National and Community Service, n.d. Retrieved from: http://www.volunteeringinamerica.gov/rankings/States/Volunteer-Rates/2010. The methods for those studies as compared to the Science of Generosity study preclude a direct comparison, for the reasons described below.

The primary issue with comparability between the *Chronicle*'s data and the Science of Generosity data is the data source difference. The *Chronicle*'s data, as reported in the methodological description, is compiled using IRS-reported charitable contributions from individuals who itemize their deductions on their government income tax submissions. This limits data due to differences in income-wealth, political party, state-level income-tax policies, and formal organizational contributions with official nonprofit tax status. The strength of those data is that they are from a complete population within those given parameters. That census-level information therefore allows reliable representation of small geographical units. Readers who are interested in financial data aggregated to smaller geographic units are encouraged to peruse the *Chronicle*'s data, with these important caveats kept in mind as to what the data can be interpreted to represent. In our estimation those data best represent rates of total giving contributions from individuals claiming tax deductions as compared to income data for the full population in the geographic unit of the contributions. Depending on the issues of interest, one dataset may be more suitable to answer questions than the other. Both have strengths and limitations.

Likewise Giving USA and the Corporation for National and Community Service provide excellent summary statistics for charitable giving (the former) and volunteering (the latter) at the national and state levels, with the important caveat that both data sets compile data that best represent *formal* giving. The Giving USA data are also drawn from IRS-obtained data, but in this case from the nonprofit organizations reporting charitable contributions received. Both datasets include organizations that are typically the most formalized and have completed and received an official nonprofit tax status identification number from the US government. The Corporation for National and Community Service specifically measures volunteering through organizations ("We only want you to include volunteer activities that you did through or for an organization, even if you only did them once in a while." "Technical Note," Corporation for National and Community Service, n.d. Retrieved from: http://www.volunteeringinamerica.gov/about/technical.cfm#sthash.kcjim8Ir.dpufFor analysts who are interested in studying formalized charitable contributions, those data work well.

The Science of Generosity data set alternatively provides data on formal and informal forms of giving and allows for a comparison between the two. The data were obtained by asking respondents to check causes to which they contribute, indicate what form of giving they do (money, time, or action), and then a follow-up question on whether or not this giving was through an organization. Interested analysts could parse financial, volunteering, and political data by whether or not contributions were made through an organization. However, given the smaller sample size of the Science of Generosity data set (n = 1,997) compared to the other two, estimates would become unreliable if they were differentiated by formal/informal status of giving in combination with state-level results. Thus our dataset is best for analysts interested in studying one or the other, or differences at the regional level.

12. Maps display the four US Census regions with states grouped as follows. The Northeast region includes (in alphabetical order) Connecticut, Maine, Massachusetts, New Hampshire, New Jersey, New York, Pennsylvania, Rhode Island, and Vermont. The Midwest region includes Illinois, Indiana, Iowa, Kansas, Michigan, Minnesota, Missouri, Nebraska, North Dakota, Ohio, and Wisconsin. The West region includes Alaska, Arizona, California, Colorado, Hawaii, Montana, Nevada, New Mexico, Oregon, Utah, Washington, and Wyoming. The South region includes Alabama, Arkansas, Delaware, Florida, Georgia, Kentucky, Louisiana, Maryland, Mississippi, North Carolina, Oklahoma, South Carolina, Tennessee, Texas, Virginia, Washington, D.C., and West Virginia. Darker colors always reflect a greater amount of the characteristic represented.

13. When we group the Science of Generosity respondents by region, the largest number live in the South (725), followed by the West (460), Midwest (445), and Northeast (365). These proportional differences mirror the regional population dispersion in the 2010 Census. "US Population by Region, 1990–2010," Infoplease, n.d. Retrieved September 16, 2013, from: http://www.infoplease.com/ipa/A0764220.html .

Since the majority of the US population now resides in urban locales, national respondent giving patterns are mostly driven by urban giving. Eighty-three percent of the Science of Generosity respondents live in census metropolitan statistical areas, and 17 percent live in nonmetropolitan, rural areas. Thus the discussion of national-level trends is actually more representative of urban-based patterns of giving than of rural patterns. As we are scholars sensitive to the possible conflation effects of urban-rural context on social behaviors, we included in all analyses a measure to control for metropolitan status in order to exclude the possible conflation of urban effects with other influences on giving.

In addition we performed supplementary analyses selecting only rural respondents to test whether there is another set of social status characteristics at play specifically for rural givers. This allowed us to focus solely on the rural respondents' experiences. The results of those analyses (not displayed) confirm that the control measure in the main models presented in this book does well in controlling for conflation effects. The isolated models on rural respondents identify only minuscule differences between the urban and rural respondents. The small differences occur on standard error changes for a few social status characteristics, indicating a sample size difference rather than substantial ones. The notable exception is that a rural-urban difference accounts for some regional influences on number of hours volunteered.

There are differences in the descriptive statistics regarding each of the nine forms of generosity by urban and rural status. Readers interested in the results of these analyses may contact Patricia Snell Herzog to request more information (www.psherzog.org).

14. A similar example is the fact that in the United States the Jewish population constitutes just 2 percent of the American public, a small statistical size of the overall population. Yet this group remains substantively significant despite their small relative size, and the small statistical size still represents thousands of Americans in an absolute numbers sense. See, for example, Ira M. Sheskin and Arnold Dashefsky, eds., "Jewish Population in the United States, 2012," in *American Jewish Year Book* (New York: Springer, 2012), 143–211.

15. Residents are considered to be adult Americans who are 23 and older and living in US households.

16. Multivariate logistic regression modeling is used for the binary outcome of whether or not someone (1) donates money, (2) volunteers time, or (3) takes political action. Multivariate linear regression modeling is used for the continuous outcome of how much (1) money is donated (logged dollars), (2) time is volunteered (hours), or (3) political action is taken (hours). All models use weighted data.

17. Coefficients are standardized for comparability, and *p* values for each map are indicated as ***>.01, **>.05, *>.1.

18. All models were also run with each of the other three regions as the reference groups, and no nonsouthern regions statistically varied from each other in cases in which they did not also vary from the South. The South is *not* the lowest-ranked region for only two models: the amount of volunteer hours with control measures included and the amount of political action hours with control measures included. In these two cases the lowest-ranked region is the Northeast, which is statistically significantly lower than the South (displayed). There are not statistically significant differences in these two maps with the other two regions.

19. Coefficient for the West is 0.32, both at the p<0.05 level.

20. It is also the case, as it always is the case, that the regional difference could be an artifact of an unobserved characteristic that is not accounted for in this model.

21. Coefficient for the Northeast is 0.45 and for the Midwest is 0.34, both at the $p<0.05$ level.

22. The map of volunteer hours without controls is not displayed because it is the same as Map 2.6.

23. Coefficient for the Northeast is -0.25, at the $p<0.1$ level.

24. Coefficient for the Northeast is 0.44, at the $p<0.05$ level.

25. The map of political action hours without controls is not displayed because it is the same as Map 2.7.

26. Coefficient for the Northeast is -0.64, at the $p<0.01$ level.

CHAPTER 3

1. While previous chapters have examined multiple forms of generosity, in this chapter we focus primarily on approaches to financial giving for two reasons. First, we have shown in previous chapters that financial giving is highly predictive of participation in any of the other forms of generosity, and especially of the Big 3 generosity forms that account for most American giving. Second, it is easy to ask people to reflect on what system they have for their financial giving, while such questions do not translate as easily when applied to other giving behaviors, such as giving blood or volunteering. We suspect, and specifically analyze later in this chapter, that people approach other forms of generosity in a way similar to how they approach financial giving. However, they may be better able to explain that approach when asked about financial donations.

2. See, for example, Charles C. Ragin, *Fuzzy-Set Social Science* (Chicago: University of Chicago Press, 2000).

3. The original fuzzy models included a host of survey items (see Appendix Table A.3.3 for full details), including the two questions related to identifying the system and the cognitive decision making people use to determine their financial giving. In addition to these questions were questions about the methods used to decide where to contribute hypothetical monetary donations, information levels related to the use of monetary donations, and the availability of options of places and needs seeking donations. Responses to the first two questions (about identifying a system and cognitive decision making) continually and consistently identified the types of givers, while answers to the last three questions did not. That is not to say that these other answers are not important, but rather that they might be *determinants* of giving rather than identifiers. The answers to these last three questions will be included later in this book in order to determine how they associate with different patterns of financial giving.

4. Included in this Atypical category are 19 respondents who were categorized by the fsQCA analysis as Impulsive but who replied on a frequency of giving measure

that they gave money on a monthly or annual basis. The question related to this stipulation (M1/ROUTMETH in the Generosity Survey) was found to not be a necessary component in the fuzzy set analysis, but we have manually recoded these 19 out of the Impulsive category and into Atypical due to their exceptional response pattern.

5. The types and the proportional size of the types across other definitions of giving were quite similar when we looked only at volunteers and only at political activists. We ran models to compare our results for the "all givers" model to "all givers, excluding nonmonetary givers," "givers who do not donate money," "givers who volunteers," and "givers who take political action." Ultimately the fsQCA analysis only had sufficient cases to converge upon the models employing all givers or all givers excluding nonmonetary givers, which are similar models since only 16 percent of givers of any type do not give money. As such we proceed using the best-fit model of "all givers" as the generalized process to giving.

These are the other combinations of QCA for subsets of the population. The similar configurations and the similar proportions indicate a stable configuration of four types plus Atypical. For "of those who donate," there is one additional category of r*s*T*O*e (2.6 percent). In all the five types of givers characterizes between 73 and 91 percent of the persons in those subgroups. The distributions into the five types are quite similar across different subgroups by giving form.

6. All the results displayed are statistically significant, except those shown for sustainability and relational giving. The black line across each set of bars represents the national average for participating in each generosity form. See Appendix Table A.3.4 for full details.

7. Readers interested in comparing Figure 3.5 to Figure 3.4 need to keep in mind that the "donate money" bars in Figure 3.4 are based on Americans' yes or no answer about whether they donate money, while Figure 3.5 depicts how many givers donated zero dollars in the past year. The differences between them are because there were respondents who claimed that they donate money but then entered zero dollars when we asked how much they gave.

8. These figures are merely estimates, not exact percentages, because we asked respondents to report their annual household income as a range rather than an exact amount. Income was measured in this way to give respondents more privacy and ensure a high response rate. The annual household income range categories provided to respondents were less than $5,000, $5,000 to $7,499, $7,500 to $9,999, $10,000 to $12,499, $12,500 to $14,999, $15,000 to $19,999, $20,000 to $24,999, $25,000 to $29,999, $30,000 to $34,999, $40,000 to $49,999, $50,000 to $59,999, $60,000 to $74,999, $75,000 to $84,999, $85,000 to $99,999, $100,000 to $124,999, $125,000 to $149,999, $150,000 to $174,999, and $175,000 or more. To compute the median percentage of income donated by each giver type, we divided respondents' total annual giving by the midpoint of their reported income range. While it is not ideal for data accuracy to condense the high range of income

into the bracket of $175,000, other studies have shown that very high-income earners are likely to refuse to provide their exact income, and so this category was used to reduce the potential for missing data among high-income earners. The highest income bracket is capped to a $40,000 range with the upper end of the bracket estimated as $215,000, meaning the midpoint is approximated at $195,000.

9. Dave Ramsey is a well-known speaker on financial matters, especially providing consultation in how to assess household financial matters through a faith perspective.

10. It is worth noting that the national picture of American generosity depicted in chapter 2 can be assumed to be mostly driven by the patterns of Impulsive givers, since they account for the largest proportion (42 percent) of American givers of any giving type.

11. Comparison is to Atypical givers. See Appendix Table A.3.8 for full details.

12. Due to the differences in sample sizes across the giver types, it is important to run multinomial logistic regression models predicting each giver type outcome based upon these social status characteristics. The results of this analysis are not shown but support the patterns displayed in Figure 3.8. Controlling for all social status characteristics and sample size differences, we found that Planned givers are older (0.03), female (0.62), religious attending (2.44), Republican (0.54), have a college degree (1.39), and are less recession-impacted (-1.05).

13. Multinomial logistic regression models were used to produce the predicted probabilities displayed in Figure 3.9. Only statistically significant results are displayed. (a) Planned giver lines are statistically significant at the 0.1 level. (b) Habitual giver lines are statistically significant at the 0.05 level. (c) Selective giver results do not statistically significantly differ from Atypical givers. (d) Impulsive giver lines are statistically significant at the 0.001 level.

14. Multinomial logistic regression models were used to produce the predicted probabilities displayed in Figure 3.10. Only statistically significant results are displayed. (a) Planned giver lines are statistically significant at the 0.1 level. (b) Habitual giver lines are statistically significant at the 0.05 level. (c) Selective giver results do not statistically significantly differ from Atypical givers. (d) Impulsive giver lines are statistically significant at the 0.001 level.

15. On the survey respondents selected from the following options to describe their religious service attendance: never attend, one or two times per year, several times per year, one time per month, two times per month, three times per month, one time per week, or more than one time per week.

16. Multinomial logistic regression models were used to produce the predicted probabilities displayed in Figure 3.11. Only statistically significant results are displayed. (a) Planned giver lines are statistically significant at the 0.1 level. (b) Habitual giver lines are statistically significant at the 0.001 level. (c) Selective giver lines are statistically significant at the 0.001 level. (d) Impulsive giver lines are statistically significant at the 0.001 level.

CHAPTER 4

1. See, for example, Alex Gillespie, *Becoming Other: From Social Interaction to Self-Reflection* (Charlotte, NC: Information Age, 2006); William L. Cook and Emily M. Douglas, "The Looking Glass Self in Family Context: A Social Relations Analysis," *Journal of Family Psychology* 12, no. 3 (1998): 299–309; Herbert Blumer, *Symbolic Interactionism: Perspective and Method* (Berkeley: University of California Press, 1986); George Herbert Mead, "The Objective Reality of Perspectives," in *Proceedings of the Sixth International Congress of Philosophy,* edited by Edgar S. Brightman (1926): 75–85; Charles H. Cooley, *Human Nature and the Social Order* (New York: Charles Scribner's Sons, 1929); Emile Durkheim, *The Division of Labor in Society* (New York: Free Press, 1984); Karl Marx, *Capital, Volume 1: A Critique of Political Economy* (New York: Penguin Classics, 1992); Max Weber, *Economy and Society* (Berkeley: University of California Press, 1978).

2. While we seek an interdisciplinary discussion, we also limit the explanatory factors to the more personal, social, and social psychological orientations of Americans. Factors related to marketing and public relations, such as donation campaigns, are not analyzed in this book, as they are qualitatively distinct from our question about the personal orientations of giving Americans. Excellent work has been and is being done in this area. Economists have been central to analyzing those sorts of factors. See, for example, Dean Karlan, John A. List, and Eldar Shafir, "Small Matches and Charitable Giving: Evidence from a Natural Field Experiment," *Journal of Public Economics* 95 (2011): 344–350; John A. List, "The Market for Charitable Giving," *Journal of Economic Perspectives* 25, no. 2 (2011): 157–180. Though we have a great deal of respect for these scholars' approach and findings, we do not here engage such factors. We focus on the social psychological orientations undergirding Americans' generous behaviors.

3. See, for example, Anton Aluja, Michael Kuhlman, and Marvin Zuckerman, "Development of the Zuckerman-Kuhlman-Aluja Personality Questionnaire (ZKA-PQ): A Factor/Facet Version of the Zuckerman-Kuhlman Personality Questionnaire (ZKPQ)," *Journal of Personality Assessment* 92, no. 5 (2010): 416–431; M. Zuckerman, *Behavioral Expressions and Biosocial Bases of Sensation Seeking* (New York: Cambridge University Press, 1994); L. A. Penner, B. A. Fritzsche, J. P. Craiger, and T. R. Freifeld, "Measuring the Prosocial Personality," in *Advances in Personality Assessment,* edited by J. Butcher and C. D. Spielberger (Hillside, NJ: LEA, 1995); L. A. Penner, J. F. Dovidio, D. A. Schroeder, and J. A. Piliavin, "Prosocial Behavior: Multilevel Perspectives," *Annual Review of Psychology* 56 (2005): 365–392; S. D. Gosling, P. J. Rentfrow, and W. B. Swann, "A Very Brief Measure of the Big-Five Personality Domains," *Journal of Research in Personality* 37, no. 6 (2003): 504–528; A. M. Nezu, C. M. Nezu, K. S. McClure, and M. L. Zwick, "Assessment of Depression," in *Handbook of Depression and Its Treatment,* edited by I. H. Gotlieb and C. L. Hammen (New York: Guilford Press, 2002); Mark

H. Davis, "A Multidimensional Approach to Individual Differences in Empathy," *JSAS Catalog of Selected Documents in Psychology* 10 (1980): 85.

4. See, for example, Penner et al., "Measuring the Prosocial Personality"; Penner et al., "Prosocial Behavior."

5. See, for example, Charles H. Hamilton and Warren F. Illchman, eds., *Cultures of Giving: How Region and Religion Influence Philanthropy* (San Francisco, CA: Jossey-Bass, 1995); James D. Davidson and Ralph E. Pyle, "Passing the Plate in Affluent Churches: Why Some Members Give More than Others," *Review of Religious Research* 36, no. 2 (1994): 181–196; James Andreoni, "Impure Altruism and Donations to Public Goods: A Theory of Warm-Glow Giving," *Economic Journal* 100, no. 401 (1990): 464–477.

6. In technical language this means we use multiple question items to identify latent (hidden, underlying) constructs. For example, we asked eight different questions to measure the underlying characteristic of extroversion-introversion. Using principal component factor analysis and structural equation modeling, we conducted a number of tests to assess and check robustness of the underlying response patterns for these latent constructs.

7. For example, the extroversion-introversion characteristic is predominantly represented by responses to the "talkative" question, which asks "How much do you agree or disagree with the statement: I am talkative." Of all the eight measures used to assess tendencies toward introversion versus extroversion, responses to this question consistently predict responses to the other seven measures (e.g., agree-disagree with "I am reserved"; "I tend to be full of energy"; "I generate a lot of enthusiasm"; "I am generally trusting"; "I have an assertive personality"; "I am shy or inhibited"; and "I am outgoing or sociable").

8. Models are of weighted results for the personality and well-being items. Americans are more inclined to agree than disagree that they are talkative. Being a risk-taker, on the other hand, is skewed toward the "disagree" answers, meaning more Americans disagree than agree that they "like exciting experiences, even if [it] breaks the rules." Americans are highly skewed to agree about intrinsic control, meaning few rate themselves as externally controlled (dependent on others or society) and instead tend to see themselves as independently responsible for what happens to them. Most Americans also see themselves as goal-directed; few (though more so than on the intrinsic control measure) rate themselves as lacking clear goals or direction. Americans answer more ambivalently about the degree to which they worry when they think others are angry at them, meaning that they are unlikely to strongly agree or strongly disagree about feeling anxious about this.

Unlike the other items, we do not measure depression in "agree" or "disagree" language. This is because it is not an opinion but is rather a state that is experienced with more or less regularity. Consistent with previous research, we ask about the frequency of depression in the past 12 months. Most Americans report only "rarely" (32 percent) or "occasionally" (42 percent) feeling sad or down. Thirteen percent report "fairly often" feeling sad or down, and 8 percent report feeling this way "very often." Combined this means that Americans tend to skew to the "left" on this measure, with 79 percent reporting occasional or fewer experiences of sadness and 20 percent reporting more frequent experiences of depression.

We also review frequencies for the values, morals, and life disposition characteristics. Americans slightly skew to the left on the question about materialism, meaning that more Americans disagree than agree that they admire people with expensive cars and homes. We see a similar distribution of answers for the consumerism item that measures an opposite value about people's agreement with buying less than they can afford to resist consumerism or to help others. Nearly 40 percent of people neither agree nor disagree with this value statement. Americans are more skewed to disagree about moral relativism (that there are no moral rights or wrongs), meaning more do think there are absolute rights and wrongs. Combined these three items gauge the social acceptance of these moral characteristics.

On questions related to life dispositions nearly 80 percent of Americans report agreement with being grateful to a wide variety of people. Similarly 25 percent agree that they know they experience more abundance than others in the world. The majority see themselves as being relatively unwary about getting taken advantage of by others. Together these three items show that American life dispositions tend toward the "glass half-full" personal disposition, although they often still retain moderate degrees of skepticism. In reviewing the three social orientations—relational style, social milieu, and charitable giving—we find that most Americans typically agree that they are easily attached to others, disturbed by others' misfortunes, connected to others in the world, and hospitable toward others. These characteristics are far less skewed than the relational style items. This shows that while most Americans think of themselves as relationally connected, they tend to see the role of others in a less positive light. Similarly "temperature readings" on selflessness of others and trustworthiness of nonprofit leaders are negatively skewed. However, items about the extent to which the respondent grew up in a caring environment and belief in the benefit of being a giver are two of the most positively skewed items. Thus Americans are somewhat skeptical of others generally, yet at the same time they tend to think well of themselves and their immediate social environments.

The grouping of charitable giving orientations shows that, in general, Americans tend to disagree about their responsibility regarding charitable giving. That is, they typically do not think that they are personally obligated to give unless they have extra resources available. Most do not have strong objections to giving money away, are very aware of needs for giving, and think that they are moderately informed about what their money accomplishes. Taken together this indicates that the charity industry does not suffer from a problem with public outreach and that the dearth in giving is likely not primarily a result of lack of awareness. It appears that most Americans know there are organizations to which they could contribute to meet others' needs. Their participation, or lack thereof, may thus depend not on their awareness alone but also on their other personal and social orientations.

9. To identify the clustering of these characteristics, we performed principal component factor analyses on these 25 characteristics. Using several types of robustness checks, we found highly consistent results across analyses versions.

10. Since these factors were all created from standardized measures, the distribution of each of them is also near to a mean of zero and a standard deviation of 1. Standardized coefficients are displayed for the OLS regression analyses predicting logged giving amounts.

11. As a refresher, these control measures include age, gender, race/ethnicity, education level, income, employment, marital status, having youth in household, political affiliation, frequency of religious service attendance, homeownership, residential tenure, metropolitan area, national region, and the impact of the recession. Including these measures in the models allows us to avoid mistaking relationships between social psychological factors and demographic traits for relationships between social psychological factors and giving behaviors.

12. Atypical givers, who represent 17 percent of American givers, are a good reference group for the other giver types since they do not fit neatly into one of the four ideal types.

13. See, for example, Cooley, *Human Nature and the Social Order*.

14. It is possible that the use of the word *very* in the prompt may have contributed to a "left-skew," as some may feel being generous is important but not *very* important to them. However, given how socially desirable this quality seems to be, we think the inclusion of the word helped to create more variance on this measure and tease apart Americans who otherwise would have responded the same way.

15. To test the robustness of these findings, we evaluated whether these measures load onto principal factors. We find that Social Solidarity, Collective Conscious, and Prosperity Outlook do load on a single factor with generous self-identity, in that order. It thus appears that these social psychological orientations relate to a generous self-identity.

CHAPTER 5

1. See, for example, Alex Gillespie, *Becoming Other: From Social Interaction to Self-Reflection* (Charlotte, NC: Information Age, 2006); William L. Cook and Emily M. Douglas, "The Looking Glass Self in Family Context: A Social Relations Analysis," *Journal of Family Psychology* 12, no. 3 (1998): 299–309; Herbert Blumer, *Symbolic Interactionism: Perspective and Method* (Berkeley: University of California Press, 1986); George Herbert Mead, "The Objective Reality of Perspectives," in *Proceedings of the Sixth International Congress of Philosophy*, edited by Edgar S.

Brightman (New York: Longmans and Green, 1926), 75–85; Charles H. Cooley, *Human Nature and the Social Order* (New York: Charles Scribner's Sons, 1929); Emile Durkheim, *The Division of Labor in Society* (New York: Free Press, 1984).

2. See, for example, Bernice Pescosolido and Beth A. Rubin, "The Web of Group Affiliations Revisited: Social Life, Postmodernism, and Sociology," *American Sociological Review* 65 (2000): 52–76; David Frisby and Mike Featherstone, eds., *Simmel on Culture: Selected Writings* (Thousand Oaks, CA: Sage, 1997); Donald Levine, ed., *Georg Simmel: On Individuality and Social Forms* (Chicago: University of Chicago Press, 1971); Georg Simmel, *Conflict and the Web of Group Affiliations* (New York: Free Press, 1964).

3. We acknowledge that the measures discussed in this chapter assessing the content of each type of affiliation are not asked in the same way and therefore cannot be used for direct comparisons between each type of affiliation. Purely methodologically speaking, an ideal comparison would be between two questions worded in exactly the same way and varying only in whether the affiliation was with a spouse, parent, friend, and so on. Yet researchers have to adjust methodological ideals to fit the reality of the social world. Clearly an affiliation with a parent is different from one with a spouse, and both are different from the relationship to one's nation. Thus the measure for each type of affiliation must be different to account for such variation. Though this makes direct comparisons problematic, we do not think that this means that nothing can be learned by comparing responses across the different kinds of affiliations. While the influence one receives from a parent is different from that of a spouse, it still means something to have high levels of influence from a parent and high levels from a spouse, or low from each, and all the other possible configurations. We thus here strike a middle ground that allows for the complexity of social affiliations and also toggles a social scientific belief in the ability to make true comparisons between distinct categories. See rich literatures in the philosophy of science, especially on critical realism, for the ontological explanations for this approach. For example, Christian Smith, *What Is a Person? Rethinking Humanity, Social Life, and the Moral Good from the Person Up* (New York: Oxford University Press, 2011); Douglas Porpora, "Sociology's Causal Confusion," in *Revitalizing Causality: Realism about Causality in Philosophy and Social Science*, edited by Ruth Groff (New York: Routledge, 2007); Roy Bhaskar, *A Realist Concept of Science* (New York: Routledge, 2008); Margaret Archer, *Culture and Agency* (New York: Cambridge University Press, 1996).

4. See, for example, Mark O. Wilhelm, Elenor Brown, and Richard Steinberg, "The Intergenerational Transmission of Generosity," *Journal of Public Economics* 92, nos. 10–11 (2008): 2148–2158; Nancy Eisenberg and Richard A. Fabes, "Prosocial Development," in *Handbook of Child Psychology*, 5th ed., edited by Nancy Eisenberg (Hoboken, NJ: Wiley, 1998).

5. We categorize the latter as also representing no for this measure, since we think people need to remember being taught in order for this to be an active influence. Note that 72 percent of Americans who said that their parents did not teach

them that giving money to charitable causes is good or that they cannot remember being taught that attend religious services infrequently (less than weekly), whereas only 56 percent of those who said yes attend religious services at the same frequency. We note this because one way of being explicitly taught that giving is good may is being taught to put money in a collection plate during a religious service. This physical demonstration of giving in many religious settings may provide an opportunity to teach financial giving that other sorts of parent-child interactions do not provide.

6. Note again that 54 percent of Americans who said their parents very frequently modeled giving money to charitable causes attend religious services regularly (weekly or more often), compared with 30 to 33 percent of those whose parents seldom or somewhat frequently modeled giving, and only 24 to 25 percent of those whose parents never gave (or who cannot remember their parents giving). While this measure does not absolutely reflect the level of religious attendance during childhood, one of the major correlates of adult religious attendance is childhood religious attendance. See, for example, Christian Smith with Patricia Snell, *Souls in Transition: The Religious and Spiritual Lives of Emerging Adults* (New York: Oxford University Press, 2008). Thus, as mentioned, an important part of modeling giving may be when children see their parents putting money in a collection plate. It is also interesting to consider how the increasing use of online giving in religious settings may decrease this opportunity to model giving over time.

7. "No parental influence to give" represents the 20 percent of Americans who said they were not taught or could not remember being taught by their parents that it was good to financially give *and* who said their parents did not model giving money. Moderate parental influence represents the 33 percent of Americans who experienced either seldom/occasional modeling of giving by parents (regardless of teaching) *or* received teaching but no modeling. High parental influence represents the nearly 50 percent of Americans who experienced somewhat frequent or more modeling by their parents (regardless of teaching) *or* who were directly taught about giving and had at least occasional instances of modeling.

8. Our subsample includes the 63 percent of partnered Americans (married: 55 percent; living with their romantic partner: 9 percent), and excludes the other 37 percent.

9. See, for example, Mark Granovetter, "The Impact of Social Structure on Economic Outcomes," *Journal of Economic Perspectives* 19, no. 1 (2005): 33–50; Daniel J. Brass, Jenneth D. Butterfield, and Bruce C. Skaggs, "Relationships and Unethical Behavior: A Social Network Perspective," *Academy of Management Review* 23, no. 1 (1998): 14–31; Stanley Wasserman and Katherine Faust, *Social Network Analysis: Methods and Applications* (New York: Cambridge University Press, 1994); Robert M. Kaplan and Sherry L. Hatwell, "Differential Effects of Social Support and Social Network on Physiological and Social Outcomes in Men and Women with Type II Diabetes Mellitus," *Health Psychology* 6, no. 5 (1987): 387–398.

10. We asked Americans to identify the number of people they felt close to: 0, 1, 2, 3, 4, 5, or more. If they identified more than zero, we asked them to name the people so that we could ask them specific questions about each friend. Among all of the questions were three statements that we combined in order to measure the friend group affiliation with generosity. We reverse-coded the last question to create a positive generous affiliation metric for each friend.

11. See, for example, Ryan Lincoln, Christopher A. Morrissey, and Peter Mundey, "Religious Giving: A Literature Review," *Science of Generosity Initiative*, May 2008. Retrieved from: http://generosityresearch.nd.edu/assets/20447/religious_giving_final.pdf. For an updated list of additional literatures on religious giving, see "Religious Giving," Science of Generosity, n.d. Retrieved from: http://generosityresearch.nd.edu/other-resources/publications-2/literature-reviews/religious-giving/.

12. Christian Smith, Michael O. Emerson, and Patricia Snell, *Passing the Plate: Why American Christians Don't Give Away More Money* (New York: Oxford University Press, 2008). Report on in-depth interviews with religious attenders and pastors that were conducted to understand how they teach and model regarding monetary donations.

13. This question came out of a previous study by one of the authors (Smith et al., *Passing the Plate*) that found parishioners tended to hear calls for giving within their religious congregation along this dimension.

14. As described in chapter 2, control measures include age, gender, marital status, youth in household, race/ethnicity, religious attendance, political affiliation, educational status, employment status, annual household income, impact of recession, homeownership status, residential tenure, and metropolitan area status.

15. Logistic regression models of the dichotomous giver/nongiver outcome. Chapter 2 controls included.

16. OLS regression models of the logged amount of money given to charitable causes. Chapter 2 controls included.

17. OLS regression models of the logged amount of money given to charitable causes. Chapter 2 controls included.

18. This model includes single Americans and those who do not attend religious services, assigning them a zero on spousal alignment and exposure to religious calls to give, respectively.

19. Logistic regression of 0 = nongiver in past year and 1 = giver in past year.

20. Combined these five recipes explain higher giving amounts with a 0.85 solution consistency. This means these recipes fail to explain higher donation amounts for 15 percent of the Americans whose web of group affiliations follows one of these recipes.

21. Path 1 covers 29.8 percent of the raw variation, with 2.4 percent unique variation.

22. Path 2 covers 27.6 percent of the raw variation, with 0.6 percent unique variation.

23. Path 3 covers 29.1 percent of the raw variation, with 12.1 percent unique variation.
24. Path 4 covers 20.1 percent of the raw variation, with 1.5 percent unique variation.
25. Path 5 covers 13.4 percent of the raw variation, with 1.1 percent unique variation.
26. Hardly any interviewees explicitly address community and national context, other than answering our survey questions on these. But we think it still influences them by defining for them the norm or expectation of the average person they encounter locally or nationally. There is likely a feedback loop here, where they tend to rate high the giving of others if they are high givers, or low if they are low. However, that in itself is part of the process by which higher giving can be sustained: Americans who think they are simply "measuring up" to the participation levels of the typical person, rather than being simply under or over the average, will likely give more.
27. Multinomial models; Atypical givers are the reference category.

CONCLUSION

1. See, for example, Abraham H. Maslow, "A Theory of Human Motivation," *Psychological Review* 50, no. 4 (1943): 370–396; Abraham H. Maslow, "'Higher' and 'Lower' Needs," *Journal of Psychology: Interdisciplinary and Applied* 25, no. 2 (1948): 433–436.
2. Given the important role of social statuses, we conducted additional qualitative analyses to investigate the idea that action-oriented explanations of social statuses may be important in explaining differences in generous activities. To assess this hypothesis we performed two sets of rhetorical analyses.

   First we conducted an Atlas.ti word cloud search that displayed all words said during the interviews at least 600 times and excludes from the analyses only the words *and, the, that,* and *it.* Through this we found that the word *do* is among the top six of most often stated words, with a total count of 27,828 in the 62 interview transcripts. This provides some initial confirmation of the idea that "doing ____" may be an important part of the generosity story, something to be investigated further in future studies.

   Second, we analyzed the 62 transcript files for a list of keywords that represent various ways in which respondents may talk about the salience of their social status in actions and thought processes. Those phrases are *as a, being a, growing up, having been a, men, women, white, black, Latino, Hispanic, Mexican, older, younger, college, educated,* and *uneducated.* Searching for the combination of these keywords returns 47 instances in which one of these phrases was present in an interview, and a review of these shows some evidence for the role of social status in a nonconfrontational style of personal growth.

   Third, we assessed the idea that social status may be important in differentiating motivations for giving. While we do not necessarily have direct measures for giving motivations, we have the opportunity to indirectly investigate motivations by analyzing social status differences in the 33 causes for which respondents donated, volunteered, or took political action. The following analysis describes the differences in giving causes by gender, race/ethnicity, age, and education level.

Gender

- Men support labor and separation of Church and state causes at twice the rate of women.
- Women support abused women and children causes at twice the rate of men.
- Men support antiwar, political campaigns, and immigration causes at higher rates than women.
- Women support animal, prisoner, disaster, health, alcohol and drug abuse, and elderly causes are higher rates than men.

In general women select causes that support vulnerable persons more than men, while men support government-decision causes more than women.

Race/Ethnicity

- Whites (as compared to nonwhites) have lower support of homelessness and separation of church and state than other causes. Whites have higher support of general umbrella organizations.
- Blacks have lower rates of support for animal causes but higher rates of support for civil rights and religious causes.
- Hispanics have higher support in general as well as higher rates of support for poverty, prisoners, elderly, immigration, and gay marriage rights.
- Other races of non-Hispanic origin have higher rates of support for adult education and the elderly, but lower rates for food issues, military troops, pro-choice, and labor causes.
- People of multiracial backgrounds have higher rates of support for all causes.

In general Hispanic respondents support causes for vulnerable persons at higher rates than other races/ethnicities, white respondents have higher support of general umbrella organizations, and black respondents have higher rates of civil rights and religious causes.

Age

- There is more participation across any cause in middle adult years.
- Adults under 35 have lower rates of support for family and neighbor, adult education, homelessness, civil rights, environmental, food issues, disaster relief, and community development, but higher support for prisoners and pro-choice causes.
- Adults 35–44 years old have higher rates of support for children and youth and animals, but lower support for labor causes.
- Adults 45–64 years old have higher rates of support for health, alcohol and drug abuse, animals, separation of Church and state, and military troops.

- Adults 65–74 years old have lower support for poverty, abused women and children, human rights, and labor causes, but higher rates of support for elderly, military troops, and political campaign causes.
- Adults over 74 have lower support on most causes, but higher rates of support for separation of Church and state and military troop causes.

In general middle adult years have higher support across causes. The causes by age resemble the life course, especially with regard to parenting: young adults without children are about "others" causes; parents of school-age kids are more involved with causes that have to do with kids or can involve kids (e.g., animals); parents of young adults are involved in substance abuse, military, and separation of Church and state; the Baby Boomers and the elderly are still involved with causes related to their young adult years.

Education Level

- Bachelor's degree or higher are generally more involved, and rates are more than twice the average for causes related to adult education, poverty, arts/culture, civil rights, gay rights, political campaigns, and human rights.
- Respondents with less than a high school education are more involved with prisoner and abused women and children causes and less involved with animal, separation of Church and state, and gay rights causes.
- High school graduates are less involved in poverty, immigration, civil rights, gay rights, pro-choice, and human rights.
- Respondents with some college are more involved in children and youth and alcohol and drug abuse causes, but less involved in immigration causes.

In general respondents with at least a bachelor's degree are involved in more systems-level, institution-type causes (more "othering" causes, less personal). Respondents with less than a high school diploma are more involved with causes related to vulnerable persons. Respondents with a high school diploma do not evidence more or less support for any one type of cause. Those with some college, but not a college degree, are involved with causes that are likely tied to family issues: children and youth and substance abuse.

Index